Praise for *Influence Is Your Superpower*

"This book is special. It invites you in with the promise of a truly important topic; charms you with engaging stories and stylings; and treats you to a buffet of beautifully presented, scientifically grounded life-lessons about social influence. By the end, my greatest wish was for even more pages."

—Robert Cialdini, *New York Times* bestselling author of *Influence* and *Pre-Suasion*

"An engaging book on the science of encouraging other people to say yes . . . Zoe Chance's research won't just expand your repertoire of persuasive skills—it might also reduce your anxiety about being rejected."

—Adam Grant, #1 *New York Times* bestselling author of *Think Again* and host of the TED podcast *WorkLife*

"Fun, filled with great stories, and rooted in groundbreaking research, *Influence Is Your Superpower* explains the new rules of persuasion for a better world."

—Charles Duhigg, *New York Times* bestselling author of *The Power of Habit* and *Smarter Faster Better*

"*Influence Is Your Superpower* is so jammed with insight that you'll find useful advice on almost every page. This smart, accessible book will definitely make you a better persuader—and might even make you a better person."

—Daniel H. Pink, #1 *New York Times* bestselling author of *When, Drive,* and *To Sell Is Human*

"This book puts us on the hook. Once you learn the skills of influence, it's on you to do work that matters for people who care, to show up to make things better."

—Seth Godin, *New York Times* bestselling author
of *This Is Marketing and The Practice*

"Essential lessons with the ideal teacher."

—Laszlo Bock, CEO and co-founder of Humu,
and *New York Times* bestselling author of *Work Rules!*

"The secret to leading with humility is here in this smart, lively read."

—Ed Catmull, co-founder of Pixar and
New York Times bestselling author of *Creativity, Inc.*

"Filled with the best science and catchy stories you can't wait to tell your friends, Chance has given us an absolute treasure trove of small (and often surprising!) changes that we can all make each and every day to become more effective influencers. I know I'll be using all these new tips at work, when communicating with family and friends, and beyond!"

—Laurie Santos, Yale professor and host
of *The Happiness Lab* podcast

"Finally, a book about real, everyday influence. Not the salesman-y kind, but the kind of influence we all really care about: how to move coworkers, bosses, friends, and many more."

—Vanessa Bohns, professor of organizational
behavior at Cornell University and author of
You Have More Influence Than You Think

INFLUENCE
IS YOUR
SUPERPOWER

INFLUENCE
IS YOUR
SUPERPOWER

How to Get
What You Want
Without Compromising
Who You Are

———

ZOE CHANCE

RANDOM HOUSE

NEW YORK

2023 Random House Trade Paperback Edition

Copyright © 2022 by Zoe Chance

Published in the United States by Random House, an imprint
and division of Penguin Random House LLC, New York.

RANDOM HOUSE and the HOUSE colophon are registered trademarks
of Penguin Random House LLC.

Originally published in hardcover in the United States by Random House,
an imprint and division of Penguin Random House LLC, in 2022.

Trade Paperback ISBN 978-1-984-85435-3
Ebook ISBN 978-1-984-85434-6

Printed in the United States of America on acid-free paper

randomhousebooks.com

2 4 6 8 9 7 5 3 1

*For Karen Chance, who taught me
the magic of making good things happen*

Contents

INFLUENCE
IS YOUR
SUPERPOWER

CHAPTER ONE

Becoming Someone People Want to Say Yes To

Once upon a time, on an auspicious day in history, you were born—influential. In fact, influence was your only means of survival. You had no sharp teeth or claws to protect you. You couldn't run away or camouflage yourself. You didn't seem that smart yet, but you had an innate ability to express your desires, connect with other human beings, and persuade them to take care of you. Which they did, day and (sleepless) night, for years.

When you learned to speak, you expressed yourself more precisely, using your words to become even more influential. You told people what you wanted and what you absolutely did not want. NO! You learned quickly that life could be negotiable and began asking for later bedtimes, more television, your favorite treats. You were like a tiny carpet merchant in a Moroccan bazaar. Wielding influence was as automatic as breathing. You were growing physically stronger too, but your greatest strength was the power to persuade people to take action on your great ideas.

Interpersonal influence is our human advantage, passed down in our DNA. It is what allowed our species to band together, work together, and span the globe. It will remain our advantage in an increasingly digital world, for as long as people are in charge. It has given you the success you already have, and it's the path to what you're still hoping to do. It's the love you'll share in this life and the legacy you'll leave behind when you die.

But things aren't that simple, are they? Even though you know that all this is true, influence got more complicated as you grew up. While your childhood sphere of influence was expanding, you were also being taught to be obedient and play nice. To comply with norms, rules, parents, and teachers. You were discouraged from being "bossy" or demanding. You were taught to work hard in order to be deserving, wait your turn, not make waves, not take up too much space. Advocating for other people was okay, but doing it for yourself was boastful. The influence you had once enjoyed no longer felt so natural, and you began to have mixed feelings about it.

When people are asked if they'd like to be more influential, they say yes—because influence is power. Being influential gives us the ability to create change, direct resources, and move hearts and minds. It acts like gravity, pulling us together into relationships. It's a path to happiness; to prosperity that's meaningful, durable, and contagious.

But when people are asked about influence strategies and influence tactics, they describe them as "manipulative," "sneaky," and "coercive." The whole idea of influence has been corrupted by tacky, greedy people using tacky, greedy tactics to sell used cars, to promote sponsors' products on social media, and to get us to buy now, while supplies last! Even some of my favorite influence gurus like Robert Cialdini and Chris Voss encourage us to use "weapons of influence" for "beating our opponents." Marketers (I'm one of them) refer to customers as "targets," like a pickup artist or a con artist might. Academic researchers (I'm one of them, too) have called study participants "subjects" and their experiments "manipulations." Transactional influence treats people like objects.

These tactics might be standard for sales and marketing, but they just don't work in most everyday situations. They don't work with your boss, your colleagues, your employees, your friends, or your family. If you want to build a relationship, and maintain one, you can't use the same tricks you'd use to sell a car. Even business success ultimately depends on long-term relationships in the form of referrals, word of mouth, customer loyalty, and employee retention. You want people to be happy to say yes both today and in the future.

When you become someone people want to say yes to, you are heavily rewarded. Money might not be your top priority, but it helps you get other things done, and it can be a benchmark for influence. It's no coincidence that jobs relying on interpersonal influence are well compensated. Top salespeople make more money than their CEOs; lobbyists earn more than the politicians they influence. Becoming more influential pays other tangible dividends too—doctors who communicate better are far less likely to be sued for malpractice regardless of their patients' outcomes, and executives who are trained to communicate get rated as better leaders.

People who shift from transactional, win-lose influence to the personal, mutual influence you'll be rediscovering in this book can reap intangible rewards like becoming a better friend, a more trusted adviser, and a more engaged partner and parent. We can rekindle the childhood spark that had us dreaming, asking, advocating, negotiating, and persisting without second-guessing ourselves. We can see faces light up when we share a great idea or propose something crazy that just might work; we can shake on deals we were embarrassed to even dream of; we can enjoy the comfort and freedom that come from success; and we can sigh in relief as our resistant boss, employee, child, parent, partner, or friend smiles, and says, "Okay, let's do it."

Maybe you already feel influential, say, with customers. But even those of us who are comfortable influencing people in some domains tend to feel helpless in others. I've worked with CEOs who were afraid to ask their teenage daughters to clean up their rooms, Wall Street traders who felt awkward trying to get a busy bartender's attention, rising politicians so uncomfortable "dialing for dollars" that they had to switch careers, and famous activists willing to be jailed for the rights of others who felt their throats close up when trying to advocate for themselves.

I find that kind people are particularly reluctant to try to influence others because they don't want to manipulate anyone. And smart people are more likely to misunderstand the way influence works. So if you're a kind, smart person, you have a double liability that keeps you from being as influential as you could be. But as you shift your perspective and practice some new tools, you'll find some of these obstacles melting away.

Here are ten misperceptions we'll explore.

1. **Pushy = influential.**
   Actually, the opposite is true. Being influential requires being *influenceable*. And making people comfortable saying no makes them inclined to say yes.

2. **If they understand the facts, they'll make the right decision.**

   Because the mind doesn't work the way we think it does, facts are far less persuasive than we think they are. We'll explore how decisions are really made and you'll learn more effective ways to encourage other people to make good choices.

3. **People act on their values and their conscious decisions.**

   We all *want* to act on our values and conscious decisions, but the gap between our intentions and our behavior is a vast abyss. Changing someone's mind doesn't necessarily mean you're influencing their behavior (which is the goal).

4. **Becoming influential involves persuading disbelievers and bending resistant people to your will.**

   No, the success of your great idea depends on enthusiastic allies. Your efforts to find, empower, and motivate them will go much further than your efforts to overcome people's resistance.

5. **A negotiation is a battle.**

   You might assume negotiations are adversarial, but most people are just trying not to be suckers. The more experienced a negotiator is, the more likely they are to be collaborative—which makes them more successful.

6. **Asking for more will make people like you less.**

   How they feel about you depends more on *how* you ask than *how much* you ask for. And when both parties (including you) are happy with how things work out, they're much more likely to follow through.

7. **The most influential people can get anyone to do anything.**

   This isn't how it works, which is a good thing, both for them and for you.

8. **You're a good judge of character and can spot a con a mile away.**

   Unfortunately, we're all terrible at lie detection. But I'll show you some red flags to watch for so you can protect yourself and others from people who would use influence to harm you.

9. **People don't listen to people like you.**

   A voice might be telling you that to get other people's attention, you'd have to be more extroverted, or older, or younger, or more attractive, better-educated, more experienced, the right race, or a native speaker. In this book, you'll learn to speak so other people listen—and listen so they'll speak.

10. **You don't deserve to have power, or money, or love—or whatever you secretly wish for.**

    I won't try to persuade you that you deserve to be influential; I don't even know what that would mean. What I do know is that influence doesn't flow to those who deserve it but to those who understand and practice it. And soon, that will be you.

Being bad at something you care about—and having to study and practice, and work hard at it—might not seem like a gift. But when your skills improve, you'll know exactly how you developed them, and you can replicate the process and even teach it to other people. I know this from personal experience.

————

I didn't sail through childhood and adolescence on my irresistible charm. I grew up in a bohemian-poor family, sharing our apartment's one bedroom with my sister while our mom slept on the couch. Mom was an artist and the most imaginative, fun person I knew. No money for ice cream? We'd search along the bike path for change the Universe had left for us to find. When Mom directed a summer camp, she blindfolded us and dropped us off deep in the woods with only a compass and a topographical map to help us navigate our way back. When my sister or I needed a mental health day, Mom would play hooky from work and make art projects with us: a fortune-telling machine made of food or a life-size dinosaur made of chicken wire and papier-mâché. Mom would bring us to bars where her friends played in punk bands and to parties where they played with Ouija boards.

Home was an adventure, but school was lonely. People talked over me when I spoke. Consistently. The only explanation I could come up with was that the timbre of my voice must be operating at the same frequency as the ambient sounds of the earth's atmosphere. Making friends did not come naturally to me.

My journey to becoming influential began with theater. Realizing that people have to listen to you when you're onstage, I auditioned for a production of *Aladdin* that promised everyone a speaking role. I was cast as Cobbler #3 in a mustache and fez. My line was "Shoes for sale!" I did not shine, but I persisted. Many years later, my acting career ended as awkwardly as it had begun with a starring role in an obscure karate movie so boring that both my parents fell asleep watching it. But years of actor training and practice had taught me something about connection and charisma.

I put those acting skills to work in sales. These weren't fancy gigs either. I knocked on people's doors and called to interrupt their dinners to sell them subscriptions to *Golf Digest*. But I learned how to ask for things and how to survive when people said no. I learned how to get curious about resistance instead of pushing back. After college, I got an MBA from the University of Southern California and went into marketing, first for medical devices, then toys. I learned how to negotiate deals and do market research. I learned how to influence kids— which if you're a parent you know is black-belt level. I ran a two-hundred-million-dollar segment of the Barbie brand, traveling on an expense account and having a lot of fun. But I was frustrated, too.

It was my job to influence customers, but I spent half my time trying to persuade the people I worked with to make smart decisions. I'd work on a toy line for months, running extensive analyses to support the case for bringing it to market, only to have the president make a face and tell us to start over because he had a bad gut feeling about it. How could people running big companies be making such off-the-cuff decisions? And how could they so easily dismiss my attempts to influence those decisions? Seriously, how?

I did what nerds do when they want to understand something—I enrolled in a PhD program. First at MIT, then Harvard. I collaborated with some of the field's most creative behavioral scientists to understand how people *really* make decisions and what *really* influences their behavior. Some of my research has involved nudging people to eat healthier, pay back credit card debt, volunteer, and donate to charity. I've also studied the darker side of psychology that probes why people lie to each other—and to themselves. Google used my behavioral economics framework as the basis for their food guidelines, helping tens of thousands of employees across the world to make healthier choices. I was drawn to behavioral economics because of its underlying moral philosophy: While you're nudging people to influence their behavior, treat them like human beings and respect their freedom of choice.

I joined the faculty at Yale School of Management, and in the MBA course I taught (and still teach there), I brought together everything I knew about influence, the science and the practice: behavioral economics, charisma, negotiating, handling resistance, handling rejection, all of it. People were so eager to develop these powers that we had standing room only from day one, and Mastering Influence and Persuasion soon became the most popular course at the business school, with students joining from across the university. The class has been evolving for a decade as I've tested out new ideas, discovered new science, and learned from the journals in which my students reflect on their successes and failures, as well as discussions with the executives I teach in workshops around the world. My course sparked the idea for this book.

What my students have taught me over the years is that engaging with this material gives you a chance to transform your life—a lot or a little. Whether you're negotiating better deals for yourself and others, generating unexpected favors and opportunities for everyone involved, or creating meaningful change in your family, in your community, or even across the whole world, influence is your superpower.

Rather than try to teach you everything about influence (which would be impossible), I'm going to focus on the low-hanging fruit—surprising insights, small changes, and manageable actions that have an outsize impact. As you practice, it might feel awkward at first, like learning a second language, or a third. In the beginning it takes a lot of conscious effort and isn't graceful. But eventually the new language becomes a habit, firmly rooted in your subconscious. As your skill at influencing others grows, you'll create your own strategies and eventually be able to deploy them without thinking. To get there, you'll need a solid grasp of the psychology of influence, so I'll be sharing some key research in social psychology, behavioral economics, law, public health, marketing, and neuroscience that explains how decisions are really made and what invisible forces truly drive behavior.

I'll give you tools with silly names like "the Magic Question" and "the Kindly Brontosaurus" that have inspired workplace transformations, saved women from sex trafficking, and changed the course of history. I'll show you how to "shine" onstage, comfortably negotiate a job offer or a raise, and spot liars and manipulators trying to influence you before it's too late. I'll teach you how to handle people's petulant inner two-year-olds and introduce you to some incredible business leaders, activists, and students—oh, and also sharks, skydivers, con artists, Jennifer Lawrence, Genghis Khan, a mind reader in a gorilla costume, and the man who saved the world. Along the way you'll encounter time warps, Olympic ring doughnuts, invisible ink, and a revolution.

In each of the whole-number chapters we'll be diving deeply into strategies, science, and stories about a big influence topic like charisma, resistance, or negotiations. By contrast, the half chapters explore a single idea. The chapters can be read in any order, so let your curiosity be your guide. You don't need to get to all of it. Just find the one small thing that could change your life.

Reading this book will make you more knowledgeable about influence, but it's really wisdom and impact we're after. Knowledgeable people win trivia contests. Wise people listen with open minds and healthy skepticism, asking, "How can I improve on that idea?" and "Who else needs to know this?" That's the spirit in which I invite you to engage with this book.

This approach to influence is about connecting to the powers of persuasion you were born with and strengthening them in order to make life better for everyone, starting with you. It isn't rocket science, but it is a science. It's also a love story.

Searching for *Temul*

The practice of influence is fueled by desire. So the first question is: Do you know what you want?

The Mongolian word *temul* describes creative passion and has been poetically translated as "the look in the eye of a horse that is racing where it wants to go, no matter what the rider wants." *Temul* is also the root of the name Temüjin. You know Temüjin as Genghis Khan.

In school, all they taught me about Temüjin was that he was a bloodthirsty warlord. Not that his Mongolian Empire was one of the first large civilizations to practice religious tolerance, or promote universal literacy, or that it established the first international postal system. Not even that it was the second-largest empire in the history of the world, behind only the British Empire. The British took centuries conquering and colonizing. In just one lifetime, Temüjin went from being a homeless child to ruling over a vast expanse including the lands we know as Iran, Pakistan, Afghanistan, Kyrgyzstan, Turkmenistan, Uzbekistan, Azerbaijan, Armenia, Georgia, Northern China, and Southern Russia. I'm glad I never met Temüjin, but whatever else might be said about him, there's no arguing he had *temul* in spades. And *temul* is a creative force.

Kids tend to have plenty of *temul,* too. When my daughter Ripley was seven, I asked her what she'd wish for and she didn't hesitate.

"An everything gun that can shoot anything out of it, whatever I want."

I smiled. "Okay, what would you shoot out of it?"

"First I want the power to heal anything. Then, eternal life and to be able to make other people live forever too. And also a wallet that when you open it, you can say, 'I want twenty dollars,' and it will appear. As much money as you want. If you lose the wallet, it will transport back to your pocket." (She didn't have a wallet, but I was often running around in search of mine.) "Then I want a teleporter to anywhere I want, like even into the book of *Harry Potter.*"

Ripley wouldn't get the everything gun, but like Temüjin, she wanted things and she went for them. She did things like organize her first-grade classmates to write poems and sell them in a fundraiser so they could donate money to the World Wildlife Foundation. In return they got a stuffed scarlet macaw to cuddle and love.

I don't know what you have your heart set on, but if you do, this book can be the rocket fuel hastening you along as you blast off in that direction.

From time to time we don't know where we're going. You might be at a crossroads. Or perhaps you've already accomplished what you once passionately set your sights on. Maybe you find yourself preoccupied with what you don't want, or faced with too many choices. It's okay. You're still in the right place.

And if you do know what you want, the question is: Can you be *sure*?

When I started running behavioral experiments as a doctoral student, my most shocking early discovery was that the majority of my hypotheses were wrong. And not just mine, but those of my classmates, advisers, and everyone else. For our most creative ideas, the failure rate was probably 90 percent. Even now, as a teacher of influence, I watch passionate people getting what they want and only then discovering it wasn't what their heart *really* longed for.

You can't be sure of what you want if you haven't experienced it yet.

To figure that out—and to really be sure—just experiment. And experience. Test your hypotheses. Test other people's hypotheses. Find people who feel the way you want to feel and aim for what they're doing. Or something completely different. I invite you to use this book as an opportunity to experiment and discover what you really want.

One of your inquiries will send you galloping off, your heart aflame with *temul*.

CHAPTER TWO

Influence Doesn't Work
the Way You Think

In Orlando, Florida, at Gatorland, the self-proclaimed "alligator capital of the world," you can hold a baby gator, watch gator wrestling, or take a zipline over the marsh where *Indiana Jones and the Temple of Doom* was filmed with live gators lurking below. If this isn't adventurous enough for you, a gator expert like Peter Gamble will lead you to a restricted area to feed gators on the beach, with no barrier between you and them. As he walked me past the warning signs, Peter was careful to explain, "These gators are trained, but they're not tame."

I could tell they were dangerous even to each other. Predator was missing part of his jaw; a chunk of Blondie's tail was gone. As Peter handed me the bucket of raw meat, I was nervous and excited, anticipating a clash of the titans.

The first bloody morsel I tossed landed a few inches outside Buddy's "bite zone," the sweet spot between a gator's nose and tail. He didn't move. None of them did. My second toss was better. The meat sailed directly toward Buddy's jaws, and he thrashed so fast to snap it up I could hardly see what happened. But the other gators? Not a twitch. I tossed more meat. When my aim was off by even a little, it would land and sit there until a bird flew down to take it.

Gators have evolved for maximum efficiency. Their bodies weigh up to half a ton but require only a tablespoon of brains to operate, and gators need so little food that they can go up to three years without eating at all. They don't waste physical or mental energy. They ignore everything except immediate threats or easy opportunities. And they handle these risks and rewards according to instinctual rules that have helped their species survive for the past thirty-seven million years. The only questions their tiny brains need to ask are simple ones. Will it harm me? Will it help me? Is it going to be easy? The rest is autopilot. This primal cognitive process has much in common with our own mind. Although we have plenty of experiences with irrational behavior (procrastination, impulse purchases, inexplicable passions, and unhealthy obsessions, to name just a few), we prefer to think of ourselves as rational beings making conscious decisions rather than instinctual beings looking for the path of least resistance. In this chapter, we'll take a closer look at how decision-making really happens in daily life. Influence doesn't work the way we think because people don't think the way we think they do. Once you appreciate that most behavior reflects very little "thinking" at all, you can make simple but transformative adjustments to how you're trying to influence other people.

Why We Do the Things We Do

Behavioral economics can help us understand the human decision-making process. Most people in the business world are hard-pressed to define behavioral economics and even researchers don't always agree on what it means. So, at the risk of oversimplification, I'll offer an explanation that may be helpful.

Psychology focuses mainly on mental processes, with only incidental interest in the behaviors they generate. Economics, on the other hand, is interested in social behaviors (trade, labor, consumption, cooperation, marriage, violence, etc.) with almost no regard for the mental processes behind them—rational self-interest is assumed to explain almost everything. Behavioral economics is the love child of psychology and economics. It is the study of the mental processes that give rise to social behaviors. It's not saying rational self-interest doesn't matter, only that it matters less than we think. You fail to follow through with your commitments even though you chose them believing they were in your best interest. You help strangers even though you know they won't reciprocate. Your preferences depend on all kinds of things like your mood, your alternatives, and even the weather. Behavioral economists are curious about all this.

One of the major offerings of behavioral economics is a now-famous dual process theory of cognition, its two processes rather uncreatively named *System 1* and *System 2*. As I explain this idea, I'll focus on what it means for you as an influencer so that even if you're familiar with the general concept you'll get some fresh ideas to ponder.

Most decision-making is habitual and relatively effortless. This is System 1. Like a gator, System 1 mostly lurks below our conscious awareness, monitoring the environment for threats and opportunities. Propelled by instincts and habits, it is always prepared for immediate action. Approach, avoid, fight, bite, tend, and befriend—or, most commonly (as with meat outside the bite zone), ignore. It acts unconsciously and automatically.

System 2, on the other hand, is conscious and rational, like a judge who deliberates on one case at a time, listening to arguments and carefully weighing the evidence. We experience ourselves as rational because System 2 is the mechanism whose workings we're most aware of. Since System 2 demands concentration, we avoid calling on it whenever possible in order to conserve our limited cognitive resources. It's an expert held in reserve for the most difficult and important cases. As philosopher A. N. Whitehead wrote in 1911, "Operations of [conscious] thought are like cavalry charges in a battle—they are strictly limited in number, they require fresh horses, and must only be made in decisive moments."

In Nobel Prize winner Daniel Kahneman's book *Thinking, Fast and Slow,* System 1 is "fast," and System 2 is "slow." But System 1/System 2 isn't the only dual process theory. You've heard of others, like thinking versus feeling, reason versus intuition, and left brain versus right brain. They're all related. In fact, the reason for the generic names "System 1" and "System 2" is that this theory means to encompass all the other dual process theories, emphasizing what they have in common. I've noticed the terms "System 1" and "System 2" can feel a little slippery, so from here on out I'll be calling them the *Gator* and the *Judge* and using the term "Gator brain" interchangeably with "Gator." From an influence perspective, what makes this dual process theory helpful is its focus on how these two processes work and how they interact.

The Gator is responsible for every cognitive process that's quick and requires negligible attention. This includes emotions, snap judgments, pattern recognition, and any behavior that has become easy or habitual through practice, like reading. When you mince garlic, drive home from work, startle at a noise, smile at a friend, notice a typo, multiply three times five, grab your phone when it pings, give a spontaneous hug, or sing along to a favorite song, you're in Gator mode.

The Judge is responsible for every cognitive process requiring concentration and effort. This includes planning, calculating, strategizing, interpreting, preventing errors, following complex instructions, and doing anything you're not adept at yet. When you run a meeting, debate politics, compare insurance plans, navigate rush hour traffic in the rain, or figure out how much tile you need for the bathroom floor, you're in Judge mode. You cannot multitask in Judge mode.

When it's not worthwhile or not possible to carefully deliberate, decisions are relegated to the feelings, habits, preferences, gut instincts, and mental shortcuts of the Gator. When you're making a consequential decision and have the bandwidth to ponder, you integrate feedback from the Gator *and* the Judge, checking in with your gut and also carefully considering your options.

Some behaviors fall into Gator territory for some people and Judge territory for others. An expert skier can hurtle down a treacherous black diamond trail, avoiding cliffs and trees without much conscious effort, enjoying the sunshine and the exhilaration in a state of flow: Gator. A novice skier on the bunny hill will have to focus full attention on trying to keep their skis in a pizza shape and their body facing the direction they want to go: Judge.

To more fully appreciate how all this works, you can experience the Gator and the Judge for yourself. All you need is a couple of minutes and the stopwatch on your phone.

The goal is to time yourself while reading the words in the box below out loud. Say them as fast as you can while still doing this accurately. Just focus on reading the words aloud and ignore the typeface. Stopwatch ready?

Begin.

GREY	BLACK	WHITE	**WHITE**	BLACK
GREY	**BLACK**	**GREY**	BLACK	**WHITE**
BLACK	**GREY**	BLACK	**BLACK**	GREY
WHITE	WHITE	GREY	**WHITE**	**GREY**
GREY	**BLACK**	**WHITE**	WHITE	BLACK

Nicely done. Make a note of how much time elapsed. Now time yourself again, but this time when you go back to the box, say the *color* of the type for each printed word, not the word itself. The color, not the word. Once again, use your stopwatch and do this as fast as you can while still doing it accurately.

Great.

What did you notice this time? Did the second task take longer? Did you feel an inner struggle slowing you down? For most people, naming the colors takes about twice as long as reading the words even though the task itself is no more complex. You might think it took longer because after reading the words it was hard to shift gears and focus on the colors. You're not wrong, but there's more going on.

Because you've had so much practice reading, this function has been turned over to the Gator. You're a lifelong, expert reader, so this behavior has become automatic, like skiing for the Olympic athlete. Naming colors is a simple task too, but you haven't been practicing it daily—especially in a case like this, when the word itself names a different color—so that task requires the Judge's concentration. The Gator, however, never stops giving input. That's not its nature. What's more, it's so fast that it always responds first. Identifying the color regardless of what the word says requires the Judge to override the Gator's input, which takes effort and time.

Cognitive scientist John Ridley Stroop investigated this phenomenon of cognitive systems clashing in the 1930s, when he noticed that people could read the word "red" faster than they could identify the color. The task you just completed was named after him. Did you notice that toward the end of the second round, you were getting faster? If you were to practice the Stroop Test, you would soon become an expert at naming colors, and you would no longer experience that mental lag. The Gator would have taken over the job.

What you just experienced with the Stroop Test is that the Gator (System 1) is the first responder. *Always.* The Judge (System 2) is the second-guesser, but only *sometimes*, when the task is sufficiently important and demanding—and you have the mental bandwidth. The Gator can make decisions without input from the Judge, but the Judge can't make decisions without input from the Gator. This asymmetry is one of the keys to influence.

The Mother of All Misunderstandings

Because so much Gator activity takes place below the level of conscious awareness, most of us have concluded that our rational mind is in charge. One of the big things that distinguishes us from every other species on the planet is our ability to reason, and we make too much of that. We assume that if you want to change behavior—your own or someone else's—you'll need to build a persuasive case. Win over the mind and the behavior will follow. This seems obvious, but it's completely off target. Perfectly understandable and utterly mistaken.

Some researchers have estimated that the Gator may be *solely* responsible for up to 95 percent of our decisions and behavior. The specific amount is unquantifiable, but we know that the Gator is driving the vast majority of our decisions and behavior. When you consider the number of decisions you're making *all the time*—all your physical movements, all your food choices, all the temptations you resist (or don't), all the words you say—it would be impossible to consciously deliberate on each one. Yet it's not easy to accept that the Gator plays such an outsize role in how we respond to the world, and to each other.

As social psychologists John Bargh and Tanya Chartrand write, "Given one's understandable desire to believe in free will and self-determination, it may be hard to bear that most of daily life is driven by automatic, nonconscious mental processes—but it appears impossible . . . that conscious control could be up to the job. As Sherlock Holmes was fond of telling Dr. Watson, when one eliminates the impossible, whatever remains—however improbable—must be the truth."

When I teach people about the primacy of the Gator, some stoutly resist the idea: "Okay, maybe the average person is swayed by the Gator, but aren't some of us Judges?" or "But I'm a numbers person, seriously." You might want people to use logic and data when trying to influence you, and you might use spreadsheets or calculators when you make a big decision. So do I. But that doesn't mean we're not being influenced by the Gator; it just means we don't *want* to be too influenced by it.

This isn't an intelligence thing. Doctors, lawyers, and professors are as biased as anyone else—and so are actual judges.

In a study of parole decisions in Israeli courts, researchers Shai Danziger, Jonathan Levav, and Liora Avnaim-Pesso noticed a weird pattern. If you were a prisoner who went before the judges toward the beginning of one of the day's three sessions, you'd have a 65 percent chance of being released on parole. But by the end of that session, your chance at freedom would have plummeted to almost zero. Then, after a break, it would shoot up again to 65 percent. The judges had no control over the order of the cases; that depended on when a prisoner's attorney arrived. The severity of the crime, the prisoner's time served, a history of previous incarcerations or lack thereof—none of these explained the pattern either. Nor did the nationality or sex of the prisoner.

The researchers concluded that as the judges tired, they were leaning toward the easier, default option. At the beginning of a session, when they were feeling fresh, judges were able to concentrate on the details of each case, providing their full, conscious attention and carefully weighing the evidence as judges are supposed to do. As time went on, however, decision fatigue and hunger took their toll, and the Gator, with its reliance on shortcuts and instinct, stepped in to take up the slack.

Our gut reaction to prisoners? They're dangerous. That's why they've been locked up. Once the Gator took over, the gut reaction determined the default choice. Parole denied. Parole denied. Parole denied. If you've ever graded a large pile of papers or gone through a big stack of résumés, you know how fatiguing it gets and how hard it is to be as fair at the end as you were at the beginning.

The mother of all misunderstandings is that we imagine ourselves to be rational beings, but it's the Gator who's in the driver's seat. It always shows up first, and it's also the default when the Judge gets tired. The Gator is far more influential than you think.

The Gator's Thin Slices

Our instantaneous emotional reactions—gut responses—exert a powerful tug on our judgments, and this is especially true when we're making judgments about other people. The large body of research on this effect was pioneered by the late social psychologist Nalini Ambady and her colleague Robert Rosenthal. They used the term *thin slices* to describe the surprisingly narrow windows of experience we use to form personal impressions—sometimes just fractions of a second.

The first thing that's striking about the research on thin slices is how accurately these rapid Gator impressions can predict social judgments and the meaningful outcomes that result from them. When college students were asked to evaluate a professor's competence based on a silent six-second clip of the professor teaching, those results strongly predicted how professors fared in end-of-year evaluations. Undergraduate students were able to identify the most highly rated salespeople from a sample of regional sales managers using three twenty-second clips of just their voices. When Ambady gave participants incomprehensibly garbled ten-second audio clips of surgeons conversing with their patients, they were able to predict from merely the sound of the surgeons' voices which ones had been sued for malpractice. Whether the thin slices were of body language, tone of voice, or faces, they all conveyed valuable information and yielded remarkable predictive accuracy.

Neuroscientist Alexander Todorov sliced the exposure even thinner. He showed study participants pairs of unfamiliar faces for only a second, then asked them to pick out the more competent person in the pair. Participants didn't know it, but these were the faces of candidates who had run for Congress, and their snap judgments predicted with astonishing 70 percent accuracy which candidates had gone on to win their races. Incumbency and political party? Didn't matter.

This work has huge implications for influence. For one thing, it underscores, and to some degree justifies, the all-important role of the Gator when it comes to our perceptions of and decisions about each other. Gators make snap judgments, and once they have done so, they don't let go. Multiple studies indicate that having more time to ponder doesn't improve the accuracy of thin slice social predictions, and some studies have found that giving participants more time actually made their predictions *less* accurate.

We're making consequential decisions like whom to vote for and whether or not to sue based on little more than gut reactions, even if we're telling ourselves a different story. So understanding, predicting, or influencing other people's behavior should start with their Gator's snap judgments. Always.

Selective Attention and Biased Reasoning

The Gator and the Judge are theoretical—not anatomical—constructs, but if you're a science nerd you might find it interesting that they do loosely correlate with the brain regions you'd expect. The Gator is more related to primitive brain regions like the cerebellum, which coordinates movement, and the limbic system, where emotions are processed. The Judge is more related to the neocortex, where reasoning happens. And, even more interesting, neural anatomy confirms that Gator regions influence Judge regions more than the reverse. There are far more neural fibers sending messages from the limbic system to the neocortex than there are going in the opposite direction. Even anatomically, the Gator is the heavyweight.

Although you might not have considered this question before, you know from experience that you can't influence your gut reactions through conscious effort. The Gator doesn't take requests. You can't *reason* yourself into falling in love, despising ice cream, or enjoying parsnips (which are clearly odious). It's possible to override gut reactions, but it's not easy. When disgust researcher Paul Rozin asked adults to eat a piece of chocolate shaped like dog doo, 40 percent couldn't do it. (Toddlers, however, had no Gator conflict and happily ate poo-shaped food.)

An important aspect of this lopsided interplay is that the Gator acts as a filter that determines what reaches the Judge's conscious awareness. This means that not only does the Gator take over when the Judge gets tired, but it is the Gator who decides which cases and what evidence the Judge considers in the first place. Even in situations where the Gator isn't the whole show and the path of influence flows from the Gator to the Judge, the evidence has already run through two Gator filters: *attention* and *motivation*.

Selective attention

Detailed visual processing is costly. Neuroscientists Stephen Macknik and Susana Martinez-Conde write, "Your eyes can make out fine detail only in a keyhole-sized circle at the very center of your gaze covering one-tenth of one percent of your retina; the vast majority of the surrounding visual field is of shockingly poor quality." So why does so much of the world look like it's in focus? The Gator is guessing at it, filling the gaps with high-probability images. The Gator guesses at everything in a similar way, letting everyday, unremarkable responses rely on hunches, instincts, and habits. To conserve resources, the Judge's perceptions are saved for the unexpected: unexpected threats (a police siren behind you), unexpected opportunities (an attractive stranger), and even the unexpectedly familiar (Subaru Outbacks showing up everywhere now that you've bought one).

The Gator filters information by influencing the way we seek it. The most important way this happens is through *confirmation bias*. We unconsciously search for information that supports what we believe, or what we want to believe, or what we expect to find. Internet searches mirror the way we seek information in the rest of the world. When I search "Can homeopathic remedies help headaches?" the first page of results looks promising. Ten articles, including one from Kaiser Permanente and another from *The Times of India,* confirm my implicit hypothesis that homeopathic medicine can indeed help with headaches. Great. However, when I search "Is homeopathy just a placebo effect?" the first page of results yields ten articles, including one from the National Institutes of Health and another from the *Hindustan Times,* confirming this time that my completely contradictory hypothesis was also correct: Homeopathy is just a placebo.

While we tend to seek out information confirming that we're right, we also tend to avoid information that might prove us wrong or make us unhappy. You see the nutritional sticker on those muffins, but you look away before reading the calories. Or somewhere in the back of your mind you know you should get tested for the genetic disease that runs in your family, but you keep putting it off.

In a series of fascinating studies on willful ignorance, decision researchers Kristine Ehrich and Julie Irwin offered two groups of participants the same products but gave them different information about those products. Half the participants were told how the items fared on ethical attributes like child labor and sustainable sourcing while the other half were given the option of asking for the ethical information: They could choose to get it or not. The authors found that when participants were given information about an ethical issue they cared about, they did consider it when making purchase decisions—as you would expect. However, caring about ethical issues made them *less* likely to seek out information they would then be morally bound to consider. Can you guess which participants were *least* likely to search for ethical information? Those who really liked a product, like that beautiful desk made of wood that might or might not have been harvested from a rain forest. As long as people didn't know about an ethics violation, they couldn't be held accountable for it, even to themselves. The Judge cherry-picks information that helps us do what we want to do and believe what we want to believe. And those desires come from the Gator.

Sometimes this selective approach to information stretches

into outright self-deception. My colleagues and I have found that when you give people a reason and an opportunity to fool themselves, they do, for as long as they can. Details of our studies varied, but the basic setup was this. You bring a group of people into the lab and give them an IQ test or a trivia quiz that they will score themselves. Half the participants have access to an answer key while taking the test. The fact that those people do well is no surprise; a lot of them cheat. What *is* surprising comes next.

Now you show everyone a second test, equally difficult, and ask them to predict their score. Cheaters can see there's no answer key, and everyone can see the problems are as difficult as before. The cheaters should realize they won't do as well this time, but they don't want to believe it was the answer key that helped them score high on the first test. They feel smart thanks to their high scores, and this bit of self-deception is so powerful that they're willing to wager money on their performance. When they lose money after performing worse than they expected on the second test (which of course they do), you'd think this reality check would bring them down to earth. But it doesn't. We found they needed three reality checks in a row—consecutive tests they couldn't cheat on—to move beyond their self-deception. And when we let them cheat again? They fell right back to their delusional ways. Self-deception is an easy trap to fall into, and a difficult one to pull yourself out of.

Biased reasoning

I've just explained how the subset of information that gets through to our conscious awareness is biased. It turns out that the Judge's information processing is biased too, because *rea-*

soning itself is an influence process. An internal case is being argued.

Consider the following custody decision, from a study by public policy researcher Eldar Shafir. If you want to try this as an experiment, do it with a friend. Each of you takes on the role of a judge. One decides which parent should be *awarded* sole custody of the child; the other decides which parent should be *denied* sole custody of the child. The attributes below are all you know about the parents. Make your decisions before you discuss.

Parent A	Parent B
average income	above-average income
average health	minor health problems
average working hours	lots of work-related travel
reasonable rapport with the child	very close relationship with the child
relatively stable social life	extremely active social life

Most people award custody to Parent B. And most people deny custody to . . . also Parent B. Why? Because the Gator encourages us to play it safe by choosing things that are particularly good or by rejecting things that are particularly bad. When the information is processed according to which parent to *choose*, you look for the best attribute and your attention is drawn to Parent B's relationship with the child. When the information is processed according to which parent to *reject*, you look for the worst attribute and your attention is drawn to Parent B's work-related travel.

This choose-versus-reject bias plays an important role in the hiring process. When you're screening résumés, you're subconsciously hoping to reject because further consideration means more time and hassle. However, when you're interviewing applicants, you're subconsciously hoping to choose because identifying the right candidate means your job is done. Thus, your Gator preferences influence how the Judge processes the information. Cognitive biases like this are similar to social biases like racism, sexism, or homophobia in that you can't extinguish them simply by deciding to, even if you know they are wrong. You can put guardrails on behavior to prevent biases from steering you toward the wrong course of action . . . but only if you know it's happening. And most of us don't.

Biased reasoning can get activated when the Judge starts rationalizing the Gator's gut instincts—and it's very good at this. The tired, hungry judge in the parole hearing probably doesn't just look at a prisoner's face and say, "Lock him up. I've got a bad feeling about this guy." The judge listens to the evidence and chooses *reasons* to support the intuition that this inmate poses an ongoing threat to society. What was the nature of the offense? Is there any history of violence? Is the prisoner unwilling to accept responsibility? Whatever reasons that existed for locking the prisoner up in the first place can be drawn upon again. The Gator exerts a gravitational pull on the Judge that takes a lot of energy to resist.

I'll invite you to experience this tug of the Gator on the Judge in a moment as you consider a question about wildlife conservation. Deciding how important it is, what should be done, and what you personally should do, if anything, is very much a Judge process. But like all Judge processes, it's influenced by the Gator—your experiences, your preferences, and your reactions to the information being presented. Both the

Gator and the Judge are responsible for what you're *thinking* (consciously or not) and what you're *doing,* but only the Gator is responsible for how you're *feeling*.

Look at this picture of a Bengal tiger. There's one pixel for every Bengal tiger alive. About twenty-five hundred total.

By most accounts, this image succeeds in conveying the *feeling* of that number, and the tragedy it entails. (You'd get an even stronger feeling if you saw the photograph in color.) This emotional response is further influenced by your Gator familiarity with the species, the fact that the tiger is one of the charismatic megafauna you've grown up with, learning its name along with elephant, giraffe, and zebra. What a sad picture. Something must be done!

Now imagine there are two conservation programs and you must decide which one gets funded. There's the Bengal tiger program, and there's also an Indochinese tiger program. Here's

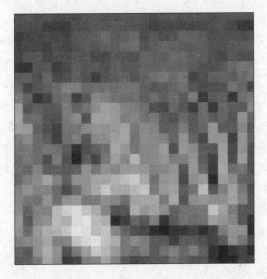

a picture of the Indochinese tiger, again with one pixel for each of the approximately six hundred alive.

This time it's the Judge who informs you that the image is a tiger, because you have to take my word for it. You see the pixels, but you don't *feel* the presence of the tiger, or the tragedy of its loss, the way you did for Bengal tigers.

As you consider which program to fund, you may *feel* (Gator) more inclined to fund the Bengal tiger program, so you look for reasons (Judge) to justify that preference. Bengal tigers are more famous than Indochinese tigers, so there probably always have been more of them. Bengal tigers are iconic, so their preservation will help raise funds for other conservation efforts. And if only six hundred Indochinese tigers are left, they're probably doomed anyway. Sad, but we should focus on species we can still save.

The Judge could have made a persuasive argument favoring

Indochinese tigers, who need more help and are probably getting less of it—but the Gator didn't want to. When the Judge is considering evidence and trying to reason its way to a conclusion, it's impossible to ignore the perceptions, judgments, preferences, and emotions of the Gator. The Gator will influence which facts the Judge focuses on, which alternatives are considered, and which decisions seem smart or fair. This means the Gator has the upper hand. Big-time. It also means reason can be difficult to distinguish from rationalization.

Suppose you were deciding between chocolate cake and fruit salad. If the choice feels like a no-brainer, the Gator takes care of it. But if you're uncertain, the Judge weighs in. The lawyers make their cases.

Your Honor, your pants are too tight, and you had a doughnut for breakfast.

Objection, your Honor. You did go for a run this morning afterward, and it's my understanding this cake is homemade.

Objection to the objection. Your new boss is right here. Just show a little self-control. Et cetera, et cetera. Until the Judge bangs the gavel and makes a ruling.

Reason and logic are types of arguments. *This means they are influence attempts.* As in the case of *Chocolate Cake v. Fruit Salad,* faculties of reason can be recruited to support either side of any argument. You have the Judge arguing both sides, but only a subset of all possible facts, skewed by the biases of the Gator, will be considered. Preferences, preconceptions, stereotypes, and shortcuts ensure that the process of evaluating those facts will be biased. Every time. The best we can say is that the Judge *tries* not to be biased.

Despite its good intentions, the Judge is a bullshit artist. It's so hardwired to provide "reasonable" explanations for unconscious Gator behavior that when it doesn't know the answer, it will simply make one up. If this sounds outlandish, let's look at the bizarre results of some brain experiments.

In some rare cases of severe epilepsy, the corpus callosum—the primary cable that connects the brain's right and left hemispheres—is surgically severed to keep seizures from spreading from one side to the other. After that connection is cut, a word, object, or picture presented to one hemisphere (through an image shown only to the opposite eye) doesn't consciously register with the other. However, it turns out that this total absence of information poses no obstacle to the Judge's ability to rationalize. Enter the bullshit artist.

While conducting research on these patients, neuroscientist Michael Gazzaniga would ask them to explain actions that had been directed and carried out by the brain's right hemisphere. But language is a conscious, Judge operation that draws on the brain's left hemisphere. So it should have been impossible to explain those actions, but Gazzaniga says, "The left hemisphere made up an answer that fit the situation." In one example, he flashed the word "smile" to a patient's right hemisphere and the word "face" to the left hemisphere, then asked the patient to draw what he'd seen.

"His right hand drew a smiling face," Gazzaniga recalled. "'Why did you do that?' I asked. He said, 'What do you want, a sad face? Who wants a sad face around?'" We use the "interpreter," Gazzaniga says, when we seek explanations for events, triage the overwhelming tide of incoming information, and construct narratives to make sense of the world. In other words, our brains are hardwired to come up with explanations for what we're doing, even when we don't have the faintest freaking idea why we're doing it.

Most of us, for most of our lives, with most of the people we know, have been approaching influence backward. We've been imagining that influencing people's behaviors requires changing their minds. This is only sometimes true and rarely enough. Those appeals based on logical, rational arguments are way less persuasive than we think. We've also been making the mistake of taking people's conscious attention for granted when it's in extremely short supply.

The scientific literature on the relationship between the Gator and the Judge makes a compelling case for shifting our focus so that we're applying our influence efforts first and foremost to the Gator. This accounts for how people really make decisions, rather than how we think they do. After capturing someone's attention and making it easy for them to say yes, you may still need to craft a rational argument. But you already know how to do that, and there are plenty of books out there to help you hone that skill. Our aim in this book is to learn about influencing other people by speaking to the Gator, because that's where we've been consistently coming up short.

The Path of Least Resistance

In the 1980s, researchers discovered that eating more fruits and vegetables could reduce cancer and heart disease, the two leading causes of death. The World Health Organization recommended that daily intake of fruits and vegetables should be at least 400 grams, or about five servings. To raise awareness of this recommendation, the US National Cancer Institute partnered with the Produce for Better Health Foundation to create the 5 A Day campaign. It was rolled out nationally in 1991, with millions of dollars spent on TV spots, news stories, and posters. By 1995, studies showed that public awareness of the need to eat five servings a day of fruits and veggies had quadrupled, from 8 percent to 32 percent. The 5 A Day campaign was deemed a huge success and adopted by thirty-two other countries around the world.

But ongoing research yielded deflating results: Despite their dramatically heightened awareness, people did not change their behavior. Actually, they did, but not in the way public health officials had hoped. Between 1990 and 2000, the consumption of fruits and vegetables in the United States actually *declined* by 14 percent. Results in the UK were similarly disappointing.

It turned out that 5 A Day was only one of a multitude of public health communication campaigns that were successfully delivering their message but failing to deliver results. As Po Bronson and Ashley Merryman wrote in *NurtureShock* in 2009, "The federal government spends over one billion dollars a year on nutrition education programs in our schools. A recent review by McMaster University of 57 such programs showed that 53 had no impact at all—and the results of the four good ones were so meager it was barely worth mentioning."

So, what's going on here? A message like "5 A Day" is certainly catchy and simple. It's Gator-friendly in that regard. And by the campaign's own metrics of success, it did increase public awareness. At the time it was celebrated as a triumph because it seemed to change people's *minds,* which is incredibly hard and exceedingly rare. But they were shooting for the wrong goal if they wanted to change *behavior.* Gators are fast, yes, but they are also lazy and that's the secret of their efficiency. When you're not meeting the Gator's threshold for ease, your great idea is landing outside the bite zone.

From this perspective, we can see that the 5 A Day campaign was doomed from the start. It expected people to remember the message at moments when they might be hungry, distracted, or in a rush. It expected them to reliably resist temptation in situations when hunger would be weakening their Judge's resolve. It assumed they could break ingrained habits just by realizing that they should. Eating more fruits and vegetables requires work. It's not just a matter of selecting them in the grocery store, but also of taking time and effort to prepare them. Additionally, as we'll explore in chapter 6, telling people what's good for them can make them want to resist your unsolicited advice.

The bedrock principle of influencing behavior is this: *People tend to take the path of least resistance*. Ease is the single best predictor of behavior. Better than motivation, intentions, price, quality, or satisfaction. There's a little-known marketing metric for measuring ease called the Customer Effort Score that comes down to a simple question: How easy was it?

How customers answer that one question explains one-third of their willingness to buy again, to increase their business with the company, or to rave about it to other people. While one-third may not sound like much, it's actually huge; the Customer Effort Score is 12 percent more predictive of customer loyalty than customer satisfaction is.

Ease makes people happy, and effort can really piss people off. In a study of seventy-five thousand customer service calls, researchers found that 81 percent of customers who reported having a difficult experience said they intended to complain to friends or post negative reviews, while only 1 percent of customers who reported having an easy experience said they would do the same.

Once you open your mind to this idea, you'll start finding evidence for it everywhere, including in your own behavior. You probably shop on Amazon more often than you go to Target because it's easy to find what you want, easy to get it quickly, and easy to return it if it doesn't work out. You probably use a ride-sharing app instead of calling a taxi because it's easier not to search for the phone number. Or figure out the address. Or dig through your purse for your wallet.

About 10 percent of car buyers decide not to be car owners anymore because ride-sharing is easier than owning a car. No hassling with insurance, maintenance, or finding a parking spot in a busy city. If you're looking for love these days, you probably use a swipe dating app because it's easy. Traditional dating sites require you to make complicated trade-offs. How much should you weigh the importance of smoking relative to age, or sense of humor, or how far away they live from you? That's difficult. Much easier to let the Gator mindlessly swipe left and right.

If you want people to do more business with you, make it as easy as possible. The Domino's 2015 AnyWare campaign made it as easy as possible to order a pizza. Since they knew your address, credit card information, and favorite pizza, they said, "You don't have to place an order—just text or tweet us an emoticon of a pizza." Shazam! Your favorite pizza shows up at your door. This campaign increased their sales by more than 10 percent that year, and by 2018, they had surpassed Pizza Hut to become the largest pizza company in the world.

One easy place to begin influencing people to do something is to help them remember to do it. The Judge is already occupied, always, so we shouldn't count on anyone remembering anything. Even ourselves. I recently brought my cat, Dave, on a flight, and forgot to take him out of the carrier as I loaded it onto the conveyor belt at the security line. He had already gone through the X-ray machine and freaked out the TSA agents before I realized he was still in there. I love Dave to bits, but love didn't matter. Of course, I had *planned* to take him out of the carrier, but my intentions didn't matter either. And I had even removed my shoes and placed my laptop in the bin—because the TSA agent reminded me to. Dave was unharmed, but I caused a commotion and heard the passenger behind me say, "Oh my God, can you believe she did that?"

Understanding some quirks of the Gator makes it easy to believe.

One of the cheapest and most effective nudges is the simple appointment reminder. Text-message reminders increase show-up rates for doctor's appointments, speed up loan repayments, improve medication adherence, increase vaccination rates, and help students turn assignments in on time. They also reduce failures to appear in court; these no-shows happen often and trigger punitive charges as well as arrest warrants. In a large field study in New York City, researchers sent text message reminders to people accused of low-level offenses, reminding them to appear in court. These simple nudges increased attendance from 30 percent to 38 percent. For those who did show up, two-thirds of the cases were dismissed, resulting in seventy-eight hundred fewer arrest warrants from just this one experiment. Sometimes a design change can make things easier to remember. Like the ding! reminding you to fasten your seatbelt, saving countless lives. Or the week of placebos in a month's pack of birth control pills, reinforcing the daily habit and, well, preventing countless lives. And providing unquantifiable relief.

Just as ease explains a vast number of things you do, *effort* explains a lot of the things you *don't* do. If you're expecting to exercise when you're busy and tired, or to ignore that cookie when it's calling your name, or to put down your phone and turn out the light, well, is that reasonable? You can't expect the Judge to overcome the Gator when you're depleted—tired, busy, stressed, hungry. Nobody has self-control in those situations, not even judges, as we've seen.

Our understanding of the Gator also tells us that our chances of success could be much greater if we just made it easier to follow through, or harder not to. You commit to exercising with a buddy, knowing you won't want to let her down. You store the cookies in an opaque container. They'll still be there, but they won't jump out at you when you open the cupboard. From time to time I block social media on my phone. I may forget and try to open Twitter anyway, and although the unblocking procedure would only take a minute, it *feels* hard, so it works.

Those feelings are important. The Customer Effort Score doesn't measure actual effort; it measures *perceived* effort, which matters at least as much. When researchers wanted to help people follow through on their intentions to work out more often, they stocked the gym with cliffhanger audiobooks on devices gym members couldn't take home with them. In order to find out what happened, they had to go back to the gym. Getting there and working out didn't really require less effort, but it *felt* easier when the Gator was nudging them forward instead of tugging them back.

———

If you're trying to influence someone to do something that feels really big, it can help to start small. I learned this by jumping out of an airplane. As I swiped my credit card for a tandem jump, my Gator brain was pleading with the Judge:

I'M GOING TO DIE!

You're not going to die. You're here by choice. You're paying a lot of money.

YOU'RE SENDING ME TO MY DEATH!

That's silly, this is a business. Dead customers would mean no business.

MURDERERRRRRR!

Once I had pulled the soft cotton jumpsuit over my clothes and watched the safety video, my instructor and jump partner came over to introduce himself and walk me to the plane. Alex was a thickset army veteran with gray hair and the kind of wide smile that puts people at ease. He had the quiet self-assurance you witness in someone who has been meditating for a long time or found God.

But what Alex had been doing for the past five decades was stepping out of airplanes two miles up in the sky and hurtling earthward. Again, and again, and again. As a competitive sky-diver Alex had specialized in accuracy landings on a target the size of a quarter. He had medals for this. I felt a bit calmer, knowing I was in good hands.

But as we crossed the pasture to the small plane, I wondered if I would be able to jump or if I would be riding back down with the pilot. Would I be a hero to myself or a coward? You're scared of the free fall, but you know that if you can manage that one moment of bravery there's no turning back. As the plane climbed to our jump altitude, I answered Alex's questions. Yes, I had a daughter. (Would I ever see her again?) Did I know skydiving was about becoming a banana? "All you have to remember is to do this." He arched back his hand like a banana. "Hips forward, arms back, head up. Banana." Banana, banana, banana. I could do banana. But would I be able to jump?

Alex asked another question. Yes, I replied, now I would fully concentrate on his instructions. He told me to sit here, pull this, hold that, scoot my butt over, lift my arms as he clipped us together, breathe, put my right foot here and my left foot there, and hold the door frame with my right hand. Then we were somehow falling through the air. I was laughing. I was a banana. One of us pulled the chute and we slowed. I burst into tears. "Are you okay?" Alex shouted into my ear. I nodded.

The earth curving beneath us was the most beautiful thing I had ever seen.

Step by step, Alex had led me toward the ultimate decision. But jumping out of the plane hadn't felt like a big choice, or even a choice at all. It just happened. And as each baby step took me closer to that final one, my terror never got triggered. My Gator brain was okay with each baby step. I might not be able to jump out of a plane, but I could scoot my butt over. I could push my hips forward. I could be a banana. Broken down into little moments like that, it didn't feel hard at all.

When your great idea means asking someone to take a leap of faith, you can be like Alex, leading them gently toward it, one baby step at a time.

Maybe you have a great idea for an app. Would someone with experience in this area be willing to meet with you? Could you ask for their advice? Would they be willing to suggest someone else to reach out to as well? Would it be okay if you followed up with them? Now that you've acted on their advice, would they like to hear how it went? Would they like to get more involved?

Every journey starts with a baby step. How can you make the first step as close as possible to effortless for everyone— including you? How do you do the same for the next step, and the next, and the next one after that?

CHAPTER THREE

The No That Saved the World

The word that saved the world was "no." Or more precisely, *nyet*.

In Moscow's secret command center Serpukhov-15, sirens howled and screens flashed LAUNCH. It was past midnight on September 26, 1983, and the Oko early warning system had detected five American Minuteman intercontinental ballistic missiles blazing toward the Soviet Union with their payload of nuclear warheads. Duty officer Stanislav Petrov knew what he was supposed to do: pick up the phone immediately and notify top command of the missile attack. They would have only minutes to decide how to respond before those missiles hit their targets, and Soviet doctrine dictated full nuclear retaliation. World War III.

Petrov's Gator brain told him something didn't add up, however, and he needed time to think. He was an IT specialist who had been working with the Oko system during its development, and it had been deployed only recently. Could this be a false alarm? It reported high reliability for the alert, but satellite operators weren't getting a visual confirmation. Cloudy skies? Maybe. But Petrov kept asking himself why he wasn't seeing more missiles. He had been told many times that a first strike by the United States would aim to obliterate the Soviet Union before it could retaliate. Hundreds or thousands of missiles, not five.

This was the height of the Cold War and tensions were high. Just a few weeks earlier, the Soviet Air Force had misidentified Korean Airlines flight 007 as a spy plane, shooting it down and killing all the passengers. That error had been tragic. An error in this case would be inconceivable. Stanislav Petrov couldn't be sure whether this was an attack or a false alarm. He considered his orders, he considered what would surely happen if he followed them, and he said *nyet* to notifying his superiors.

Twenty-three minutes later, when the missiles did not strike, he collapsed in relief. Petrov would later say he was sure that if any of his colleagues had been in command on that shift, they would have triggered the alarm—and a holocaust. It was estimated that two hundred million people—40 percent of the American and Soviet populations—would have died in the direct attacks. And two billion people would have starved when global agriculture was snuffed out by nuclear winter.

The "No" Challenge

Though worlds may not be hanging in the balance, "no" can be a lifesaver. Reluctance to say it leaves us overcommitted. Difficulty hearing it leaves us overly cautious and afraid to ask—burning out while playing small. And until we start trying to say no, most of us don't even realize it's a problem.

So no is where we begin.

In the fall of 2018, I'd gotten reasonably good at saying no to things I didn't want to do; however, my professional horizons were expanding and creating new challenges. I was thrilled to be flying all over the world giving talks, but these opportunities left me overwhelmed and stressed. My coach Mandy summed it up. "You want to say yes to everything and everybody. The enthusiasm is adorable, but it's burning you out." So I decided to let "no" be my default response for the entire upcoming month, which I dubbed NOvember.

No to speaking invitations! No to meeting for coffee! No to an upsell at the salon! No to rude people! No to nice people! No to a stranger asking for advice! No to a family member asking for money! No to a writing workshop! No to a scary senior colleague! The hardest no was to adopting a one-armed cat named Bandit. I did say yes to some things during NOvember, of course, but not before seriously considering the alternative. And as the month progressed, I started to feel less stressed and more in control of my decisions, my time, and my life. By the time the end of NOvember rolled around, I felt so empowered that I decided to continue tracking nos to help me stay more mindful of yeses.

This monthlong adventure was an extension of a 24-Hour "No" Challenge I pose to MBA students on the first day of class. Most people, and especially nice people, have internalized social norms around politeness that put us in an impossible bind. We try to say yes when someone makes a request or invitation because it would be impolite not to. Yet when we ourselves are in need, it seems rude to bother other people by asking for assistance. Somehow, we have been taught to be both generous and self-sufficient without considering how much this depletes us.

I invite you to take on the "No" Challenge to create some

more space in your life. You don't have to do it for a whole month. Just say no to all requests and invitations for the next twenty-four hours—no to working late, no to having a beer after class when you're tired, no to providing your professional advice for free, no to joining the board of the nonprofit you support, no to moving a friend's furniture just because you happen to own a pickup truck, no to the emotional labor that keeps falling to you, no to the friend who asks you to sing a song at his wedding. No to your partner who's cooking an elaborate meal and has asked you to dash to the store for fresh basil. Yes, I challenge you to say no to every person and to every one of their requests and then watch carefully to see what happens. How do you feel? How do others react? What do you *really* want to say yes to? And don't worry. If you're sure it was the wrong decision, you can always change your mind. But you have to start with no to expand both your comfort zone and your power.*

Don't take this challenge as an opportunity to say no to guilty pleasures. This is not Lent. But do practice saying no even to people close to you, even to things you want to do, even to things that are small. The No Challenge is about being kind to yourself and giving yourself permission to take up more space in the world. It's an experiment that will allow you to see how often your Gator's gut reaction is based on compliance. Compliance is usually the easiest thing in that moment.

As you practice saying no, try not to explain yourself any more than you have to. "No" is a complete sentence, and "No,

---

* Just to be clear, I don't want you to ruin your life. Don't say no if today is the day you get offered your dream job. Don't say no if you've been hoping to marry your partner and today is the day they propose.

thank you" is a polite complete sentence. Be warm, clear, and firm. If you don't seem sure when you say no to someone, they may persist in asking, which can make saying no even harder. You can explain the challenge if you need to, and, like I said, you can even change your mind. But you must start with no. Most people who take on this challenge are surprised with the results. It won't be as bad as you think. People won't hate you. You may find it exhilarating. And empowering. And practical. And worthy of repeating in your everyday life.

Although the "No" Challenge is straightforward, this doesn't mean it's easy. And sometimes you do need to respond with more than "No, thank you." Here are a few scenarios and how you might handle them with clarity and warmth.

- A friendly stranger asks you for advice or to join her for coffee.
  You're busy, so you could say, "Thanks, I wish I had time to say yes to invitations like this, but my schedule makes it impossible."

- An acquaintance invites you to a social event, and you would go if you could.
  "Thanks for asking, and I would absolutely love to do something like that with you another time."

- A friend asks you to lend them money or invest in their business.
  "Sorry, but I just don't mix money and friendship." (It's easier to say and hear no when it's part of a policy, although this requires applying it consistently.)

- A salesperson tries to sell you something you don't want.
  "Thanks, but I'm not interested." If they persist, you can shift to "The answer is no, and that's not going to change." (Now warmth is no obligation.)

- Someone expresses romantic interest. You don't feel the same way.
  "My intuition says no." If they ask why, you could say, "It's a gut feeling, and I always listen to those."

Saying no at work can pose special challenges, particularly in direct reporting relationships. But you can always say no while offering an alternative.

- An employee asks for a raise or promotion you don't think they're ready for.
  "I don't see that happening yet, but let's meet to discuss what it will take to get there."

- Your boss assigns a task when you're already swamped.
  "I'd be happy to do it, but I'm already behind on a couple of other projects. Should we reprioritize what I've got on my plate?"

Or you can just be lightheartedly frank as you ask for mercy in a case like the following.

- Your boss asks you to take the lead on a massive, boring project because you're so good at administration.
  "Thank you for the compliment, but that would be my abso-

lute nightmare. My soul would shrivel. Is there any alternative?"

You might be tempted to tell white lies to get out of saying yes, but usually you'll do better by just saying less instead. You don't owe anyone an explanation. Elwyn Brooks White, who went by E. B., was a star journalist at *The New Yorker* who would later write prizewinning children's books like *Charlotte's Web* and *Stuart Little*. He declined most invitations because he had social anxiety, but his mental health was no one else's business. He was known to slip out through the window and down the fire escape to avoid visitors. And he was known for writing letters like this:

> Dear Mr. Adams,
>
>   Thanks for your letter inviting me to join the committee of the Arts and Sciences for Eisenhower. I must decline, for secret reasons.
>
> Sincerely,
E. B. White

Boundaries

Adam Grant's bestselling book *Give and Take* is based on the premise that there are three kinds of people—givers, takers, and matchers—and on research findings that the most successful people are likely to be givers. You may be surprised and heartened to learn that generosity is associated with higher incomes, better grades, higher productivity, and more frequent promotions. I was. But to assume you need to do more giving is to overlook a key point: Grant's research shows that the *least* successful people are *also* likely to be givers. Givers are more likely to burn out, to fall behind at work, or even to be the victim of a violent crime or the plaintiff in a lawsuit.

A crucial difference between givers at the top of the ladder of success and givers at the bottom is how they handle boundaries. Grant notes, "Instead of trying to help all the people all the time with all the requests, successful givers reserve their generosity for givers and matchers, they block out time to get their work done, and they help in ways that energize them and make a unique contribution." Givers who don't learn to say no get sucked dry by over-giving and become easy prey for opportunists. They go along to get along and silence their misgivings for the harmony of the group. When they're getting burnt out, instead of easing their load by saying no, they take on additional burdens like adding meditation and gratitude journaling to their list of to-dos.

When we're rewarded by parents, teachers, professors, and bosses for being "good," we crave the dopamine hit of applause, a thank-you, a perfect score. But the people-pleasing habit can lead to chronic scarcity. Not enough time, not enough sleep, not enough money, not enough bandwidth to think clearly. Stress and exhaustion even temporarily lower IQ and bias people toward unpleasant memories, hampering their ability to make good decisions. These effects extend beyond ourselves; studies show that those managers who felt most swamped ran teams with the worst performance and lowest profits.

When my students reflect on their reluctance to say no, they're primarily concerned with other people's feelings. But there are other reasons we continue to say yes when we shouldn't. Fear of missing out is a big one. When offered an exclusive or limited-time opportunity, we might get a big bout of FOMO. I've wasted a lot of time and a lot of money this way and am embarrassed to say I'll probably continue to do so. Reciprocity comes up regularly too. If we say yes, the other person will owe us a favor. It's not a dumb reason, but it's pretty transactional. And finally, a lot of us really love to help. If life has been good to us, we want to pay it forward. Or if life has dealt us a tough hand, maybe we want to protect other people from suffering like we did. Kindness is admirable, but if we're waiting for other people to ask, then we're distributing our generosity unfairly.

The "No" Challenge will help you figure out what self-imposed burdens you can learn to avoid. It will also help you manage your opportunity costs. What will you have to say no to if you say yes to this? What can you say yes to if you say no to this?

When you don't set boundaries around your generosity, your kindness saps your strength, diminishing your ability to be influential. Saying no creates vitally important limits. Don't let yourself become someone whose cheery façade masks your exhaustion and leaves you prone to lashing out. Don't ignore your inner compass just to please someone else.

Through Rejection to Resilience

As we get more comfortable with saying no, we get more comfortable hearing no. From our insider's perspective we can see that, in most cases, rejection has little, if anything, to do with the person who's making the request and a lot to do with us. At the most basic level, saying no helps us take care of our own needs, but a hidden benefit of saying no to others is the implicit permission you give others to say no, too. Now we're moving into a shared space where we're all adults, communicating in a straightforward, open way. One of my students put it this way: "I learned that when people ask for something, they're not pressuring you; they are just asking. They understand it's possible you can't do it, and they are okay with that. I used to feel like when I asked for something it was a life-or-death situation, but now I can see that it's not that at all."

Despite its benefits, saying no can cause suffering, and we want to protect others from that. We all carry around horrible memories of times we've been rejected. This is because it's painful—and not just metaphorically. Naomi Eisenberger had a theory that we process rejection as physical pain, so she conducted a slightly mean experiment to see what happens in people's heads when they get left out. If you were a participant in her study, you would be lying in the long tube of an fMRI scanner while playing a simple videogame of catch with two other participants. (Or so you'd think; they would actually be members of Eisenberg's research team.)

Once the friendly game of three-way catch had been established, the other two players would stop throwing the ball to you but keep throwing it to each other. You'd try to rejoin the game, without success. You'd wonder what was going on. *Why am I getting left out?* While this was happening, the fMRI scanner would show that your brain was registering this feeling in the same areas that register physical pain, the anterior cingulate cortex and the right ventral prefrontal cortex. As far as your brain was concerned, being cut out of the game literally felt like a slap in the face. Rejection is one of the easiest and most reliable ways to generate a neurobiological stress response: a spike in cortisol levels, pulse rates, and blood pressure.

Our bodies respond to rejection like physical danger because rejection has put our species in physical danger. For early Homo sapiens, banishment from the tribe meant certain death, so rejection had to be avoided at all costs. Learning to play nicely with others was a survival mechanism reinforced by the brain's most powerful and unforgettable tool: pain. This forceful early warning of impending disaster allowed us to take corrective action before things went too far.

But just as we build strength by stressing our muscles, we can condition ourselves for bravery by facing rejection. When I was in college, I took a summer gig in one of the world's most uncomfortable jobs: door-to-door sales. I worked for a small enterprise called The Students Group selling dry-cleaning coupons in the suburbs of Denver, Colorado. The company was run by a middle-aged salesman named Jack who drove us around in his van, dropping us off with a high five and then collecting us hours later at a preestablished rendezvous point. Our objective was to knock on as many doors as possible before sunset.

The night before my first day in the field, I couldn't sleep. By this point in my life, I no longer considered myself a shy person, but the idea of knocking on strangers' doors and asking them for money still felt really scary. Jack said I should make ten pitches an hour. "Sell as many as you can!" My personal sales target was more modest: Do not die of shame and embarrassment.

Once the van let me out and drove away, I jogged up to the first door, knocked, and a friendly-looking woman with a ponytail answered. "Hi," I said, launching into the spiel Jack had taught us. "I'm Zoe, and I'm from The Students Group. We're a group of students raising money to pay for college." She listened politely as I told her about the coupon books, then said, "No, thank you," because she didn't really go to the cleaners. Jack had coached us to respond in those situations by asking for a donation to our college fund, so I did. She politely declined, saying she had to get back to her dinner. She shut the door.

I stood on her porch for a moment and took a deep breath. I had just asked a total stranger for money, heard the word "no," and then watched her close the door in my face. It was over. As I trotted toward the next house, I felt waves of relief. *I did not die. Success!* And the conversation had been warm and respectful—enjoyable even. I had faced one of my greatest fears and lived to laugh about it. I was now an official member of the sales reject club, but rather than feeling like a loser, I felt empowered. I even went on to make a handful of sales that night and walked away with a pocketful of cash.

Surviving door-to-door sales helped me learn one of the biggest lessons that students now take away from my class: No is not fatal. And as you release your fear of hearing no, you gain the freedom to ask for things. Internalizing this lesson, I stretched my comfort zone by asking in more and more contexts. I knocked on doors for political campaigns. I cold-called for charities. I even approached attractive people and asked them out. In all these pursuits, a negative response is the norm. But the practice of hearing no in low-stakes situations put me more at ease when the time came to make more important requests. Small rejections can inoculate you against the paralyzing fear of rejection.

When Jia Jiang graduated with an MBA from Duke, he wanted to be an entrepreneur. Like so many of us, however, his fear of hearing no was holding him back. To face this fear head-on, he started a video blog called *100 Days of Rejection Therapy*. His endearing, perplexing, and absurd videos document what happened as he approached complete strangers, day after day, with off-the-wall requests: to speak over Costco's intercom, to become a live mannequin at Abercrombie and Fitch, or to borrow a dog from the Humane Society. I love his rejections so much that I challenge my students to replicate them. Jia's tolerance for rejection and vulnerability reveal the delight and playfulness that can emerge out of the most awkward situations.

My favorite rejection attempt took place in a Krispy Kreme doughnut shop in Austin, Texas. Jia walked in and tried to order Olympic symbol doughnuts, bracing himself for rejection. The blond woman behind the register pushed up her glasses. "How soon do you need them?"

"Um, fifteen minutes." (He was really trying to get rejected.)

But rather than telling him why it couldn't happen, the Krispy Kreme employee—her name was Jackie—started trying to figure out how to make it work. "What are the Olympic colors again?" Fifteen minutes later Jackie presented Jia with a unique doughnut creation, a hand-cut cluster of circles that moderately resembled Olympic rings. And when Jia reached for his wallet, she told him, "This one's on me."

No matter how often I see it happen, I'm still surprised by the lengths to which strangers will go to be helpful just because they are asked. When Jia was making his crazy request, he was preoccupied by the logistics: the difficulty of fulfilling his request and of bucking protocol. Jackie could have said no—nobody's entitled to Olympic symbol doughnuts the company doesn't make—but she enjoyed the challenge. Why not?

You can try Jia's challenges if you like or invent your own. Sometimes—more often than you'd expect—you'll fail to get rejected, despite your best efforts. But when you do, you'll find yourself increasingly able to handle it. We possess a kind of "stress immune system," so facing fears repeatedly without serious harm can inoculate us against stress. When researchers place mice in a large empty box to simulate an open field in which a predator could swoop down on them, at first the mice lose control of their bowels, their stress hormones spiking as they freeze in terror. When they're able to move, they just slink alongside the walls. But if they're placed in that box every day, they soon habituate to the stress. They stop freezing and defecating, and if a new toy is placed in the center of the box, they'll go check it out. Their body is still releasing stress hormones, but the stress is manageable.

It's the same with skydiving. Before a jump, novice skydivers are terrified and their stress hormones show it. (I'm sure mine were spiking before Alex focused my attention on the baby steps.) By just the third jump, however, skydivers' hormonal stress level is no higher than it would be in a traffic jam. Studies of so-called toughened individuals like elite athletes have found that their bodies adapt to stressors by releasing a big hit of stress hormones that comes on strong and fast but fades just as quickly. This helps explain how people in stressful jobs like stock trading keep going back to work day after day. Those gut-wrenching plunges of the market become just another day at the office.

If we take it as social rejection, "no" is painful to hear and difficult to say. We almost never want to say, "No to you, personally and forever," and we certainly never want to hear it. Many skilled influencers have learned to hear no as simply "No to this, for now," unless told otherwise. The most successful salespeople will check back six or seven times after hearing a no. You might read this and think, "I don't want to be that creepy!" but they wouldn't be so successful if they were creepy. And those creepy salespeople you have met? They're not that successful. No one would ever be willing to talk to them six or seven times.

The best salespeople are great relationship builders whose clients want to do business with them again and again. If you say no, they'll ask your permission to check back with you in the future. If you say no to that, they won't bother you again. They're people who treat you with respect, people you're happy to interact with even if it doesn't make sense to say yes this time. The reason they don't come to mind when you think of the archetypical salesperson is that interacting with a master salesperson doesn't feel transactional. It just feels like a friendly conversation. And it is.

The person who connected me with Jia Jiang was an undergraduate student named Davis Nguyen. He was a quiet, kind person who took influence very seriously because he understood what it was like not to have any. He had watched his mother beg for food in a country where she didn't speak the language, and he was determined to thrive and to support his family someday. Rather than practice rejection through fun but silly requests, he decided to get rejected chasing his big dreams.

Davis challenged himself to reach out to a different one of

his heroes each day, sharing what he appreciated about their work and asking, "Can I help?" He expected them to say, "You're annoying, please stop emailing," but no one did. Jia Jiang accepted his offer to write a guest post for his blog, and an author said yes to his speaking invitation. Most people didn't respond at all or just politely said, "No, thank you." Davis was getting more comfortable with rejection but was still too nervous to contact Susan Cain, one of the people he admired most in the world. She had written a book on the power of introversion (*Quiet*) that would remain on the *New York Times* bestseller list for seven years and had given a TED Talk that would become one of the most viewed of all time, yet she remained humble and modest. A true role model.

When Davis heard Susan was thinking of developing an online public speaking course for introverts, he decided it was time. It would be a crazy long shot, but Davis himself had developed a series of public speaking workshops called "Speak for the Meek" and maybe Susan could use his help. He reached out to offer to help outline, develop, and promote her course—whatever she needed—for free. It took a month to hear back, but after a long phone conversation and then a visit, she agreed to take Davis on as a volunteer intern for the summer. He threw himself into the job and he thrived. At the end of the summer, Susan surprised him by paying him for the work he had done and asking him to come back the following summer. They continued collaborating, and she even interviewed him on the first episode of her podcast.

Susan became Davis's mentor, and when she invited him to work with her full-time after graduation, it was a dream come true. He loved her and loved working with her. But do you know what he said? "No, thank you." Davis had another dream job offer—and Susan encouraged him to take it. And they remained friends.

———

You might feel inclined to say no to the 24 Hours of "No" challenge or to trying to get rejected. That's totally fine. Say no to any of the ideas in this book. You are the boss of you. Maybe you need a more difficult challenge. Maybe your freedom requires a much bigger, more proactive no; you may need to say no to a commitment you've made, or to some kind of consent you've given. Remember, it's okay to change your mind or to have been wrong. You don't need to believe "my word is my bond" if it's going to shackle you to a soul-sucking endeavor. Maybe you need to say no to an energy vampire: a job, a relationship, or a secret you're tired of keeping. Maybe you can say no to a piece of guilt, shame, or righteousness. Maybe you can liberate yourself from a social norm or from one of your own great ideas. The fact that an idea came to you doesn't obligate you to give birth to it and nurture it through college. When you say no, you assert your fundamental human right to decide how to live your life.

You also set in motion some strange alchemy. Saying no helps you be more open to hearing it, and when that happens, your requests lose that edge of neediness or fear of rejection that can repel other people. They become relaxed invitations. Now when you ask for something, people are more inclined to say yes. When you're clear about your own parameters and comfortable establishing them, you convey confidence and inspire trust. All the parties involved feel more relaxed, more free, and more open to the mutual benefits of influence.

Just Ask

I begin the workshop by pulling a twenty-dollar bill out of my wallet.

"I have twenty dollars to give away this afternoon. Who would like to persuade me to give it to them? This is real money and real life." After some polite laughter, a volunteer raises her hand. I walk over. And wait.

With an awkward smile she makes small talk before explaining why she should get the twenty dollars. She needs a phone charger. She'll make a donation to UNICEF. She's going to buy me flowers.

"I believe you," I respond (if I do). And we wait. Now she isn't sure what to do. She has tried to persuade me, but I'm still holding the money. Eventually, I turn to the other people in the room. "What has she not done yet?"

"She didn't ask."

You'd be surprised how often volunteers in this situation think they have asked for the money when they haven't. And I don't part with it until they finally say, "Will you give me the twenty bucks?" or "Can I have the money?"

Along with saying no, the easiest thing you can do to become more influential is just ask. Ask more often, ask more directly, and ask for more. People who ask for what they want get better grades, more raises and promotions, bigger job opportunities, and even more orgasms. This might seem obvious but apparently, it isn't.

Most people don't realize how often they're not asking until they start asking more often. When our MBA course ends and students share the biggest thing they've learned—after we've done so much together—the most common answer is "Just ask." The full realization comes from practice. What if you're not sure how to ask? Just ask the other person. Seriously. One of the simplest and most surprising influence hacks is that if you ask people how to influence them, they will often tell you.

Most of us are reluctant to ask because we fundamentally misunderstand the psychology of asking and we underestimate our likelihood of success. In one series of experiments, employees were more likely to turn in mediocre work than to ask for deadline extensions, fearing their supervisor would think them incompetent if they asked for extra time. But they had it backward: Managers saw extension requests as a good sign of capability and motivation.

In another series of experiments, Frank Flynn and Vanessa Bohns directed participants to go up to strangers and ask for a variety of favors—everything from filling out a ten-page questionnaire to escorting them across campus to a building that was hard to find. Before making the request, participants were invited to predict how many people they would have to ask before one said yes. Again and again Flynn and Bohns found strangers were surprisingly willing to help. On average, they were two to three times more likely to grant favors than participants had expected.

When we're the one making a request, like Jia Jiang at the Krispy Kreme, we tend to dwell on the obstacles—all the ways that saying yes could make the other person's life more difficult. The recipients of our requests, however, tend to focus on how hard it is to say no. By focusing on the cost of helping, requesters overlook its potential benefits. Neuroscientists have discovered that generosity can stimulate the brain's reward circuitry, triggering the dopamine rush of a helper's high. You know that feeling. You help somebody out, they're grateful, and you feel great. Multiple studies show that volunteers are happier and healthier than non-volunteers, and people tend to feel better about spending money on others than on themselves.

This link between generosity and happiness runs deep and starts early. In one cute experiment, researchers coded the expressions of joy among toddlers receiving Goldfish crackers or giving them away. They were glad to receive the tasty treats, even happier to give away Goldfish from the researchers' supply, and most delighted of all to give away their own Goldfish. We can't take the benefits of generosity for granted; they don't always outweigh the costs. But they are concrete enough that when we don't ask, we limit the potential joy in the world— and not just our own. If you're holding back from asking because you want to be liked, consider that you're not giving other people the chance to feel good about saying yes to you. And consider that more of them would like to say yes than you think.

As we saw with the twenty-dollar bill, you may also need to ask more directly. Because sometimes what you think is asking seems more like hinting. Norms about directness vary among genders, industries, and cultures, and they depend on the closeness of the relationship and the power dynamics of the situation. If you jump in and ask too directly, you might be considered rude. But if you're too indirect, your hopes and dreams will go unnoticed. No one can read your mind. The truth is they're not even trying; their minds are focused on their own hopes and dreams.

So how direct should you be? You could start by asking less directly first, then more directly if the other person doesn't respond. Or you could use a hypothetical question I call a *soft ask,* like "How would you feel about . . . ?" We'll explore that further in chapter 6, but after the other person tells you how they'd feel, you'll know whether or not you should go ahead and do it.

In addition to not asking often enough and not asking directly enough, you're probably not asking *for* enough, either. Why not consider making some outrageous asks? You never really know what someone else will perceive as outrageous, and it turns out that outrageous asks can work out in your favor even when the answer is no.

Robert Cialdini, who would become one of the best-known researchers of interpersonal influence, ran an experiment in 1975 known as the "juvenile delinquents at the zoo" study. His research assistants approached passersby on the Arizona State University campus asking if they would be willing to volunteer to chaperone kids from the city's juvenile delinquent program on a two-hour trip to the zoo. Seventeen percent of them agreed on the spot. (I'm constantly amazed by how nice people are.) This wasn't the outrageous ask, though. Research assistants asked other passersby to volunteer at the juvenile delinquent center for two hours a week for at least two years. After those people declined, which they all did, they were asked about chaperoning the trip to the zoo. The people first approached with the outrageous ask were three times more likely to say yes to the zoo than were those who had been asked only about the zoo.*

There are two reasons that people are more likely to say yes to a smaller request after having said no to a larger one: *relative size* and *reciprocity*. Chaperoning a group of troubled teenagers on a trip to the zoo might be a pretty serious commitment, but it's nothing compared to spending two hours a week with them for the next two years. So, that's relative size. When you step down from an outrageous ask to something smaller, the other person sees this move as a concession on your part and feels inclined to reciprocate. Research on negotiations shows that people feel better about the outcome if they have gained a concession from the other party: They like you more for having made the concession, and they feel better about themselves for having negotiated it.

The best reason of all for asking (and for making your ask big or outrageous) is that you'll never know what people will agree to if you don't ask. You could go for a huge ask in order to create room for a future concession only to find that the other person says yes right away. Even when my students are *trying* to get rejected, they get what they ask for about a third of the time.

When you're making up your own mind about whom to ask, consider asking men. We tend to ask women for favors and help, so we're taking women for granted and underestimating men. Shaquille O'Neal is famous for his generosity. "When I'm

---

* In 2020, Oliver Genschow replicated the juvenile delinquents at the zoo study at the University of Cologne, finding similar results. But in that case, 9 percent of people said yes to the outrageous ask for the two-year commitment, confirming again that people are incredibly, incredibly nice.

at restaurants, I am a big tipper," he told Jimmy Kimmel. "I like to show people my appreciation. So when they come up to the table, I say, 'The quicker I get my order, the bigger your tip will be.' Then, when we're getting ready to leave, I'll ask them: 'How much do you want?'"

What was the most anyone had asked for? Four thousand dollars.

And what did he say to that? "Okay, no problem."

CHAPTER FOUR

The Curious Qualities of Charisma

The Twin Paradoxes of Charisma

When I ask people which influence skill they'd like to develop, the most common response by far is "charisma." When I ask them to define it, they tell me, "It means people pay attention to you" or "It means you have a lot of presence." But *why* do we pay attention to charismatic people? What are they *doing*? A dictionary definition of charisma is "compelling attractiveness or charm that can inspire devotion in others," but as a tool for influence, that language is awfully vague. Yes, charisma gets people to pay attention to you, but it's not just *any* kind of attention. You wouldn't say a guy running through the office in his underwear is charismatic. People who try to make themselves the center of attention just become annoying.

The first paradox of charisma is that trying to be charismatic has the opposite effect.

Most of us, most of the time, aren't consciously trying to be the center of attention. But we can fall into this trap subconsciously, focusing on ourselves in ways that are anti-charismatic. Humor me for a moment and try this exercise.

In each row below, guess which group uses the word "I" more often.

Leaders . . . or followers?

Older people . . . or younger people?

Richer people . . . or poorer people?

Happy people . . . or depressed people?

Angry people . . . or fearful people?

Better students . . . or worse students?

Men . . . or women?

According to analyses of formal and informal conversations, speeches, emails, and other written documents, people in the groups listed on the right-hand side tend to use "I" and other first-person pronouns more frequently and by a large margin. The pioneer of this research is James Pennebaker, a social psychologist who describes his work in a delightfully nerdy book called *The Secret Life of Pronouns*. He found that people who feel they have less power or lower status tend to use more self-referential language. Sometimes the gap has a basis in reality—followers must take orders from leaders, and the poor are less powerful than the rich. But unconscious linguistic patterns derive more precisely from *feelings* of personal power—or lack thereof.

An analysis of Academy Award acceptance speeches showed that actors used first-person pronouns more frequently than directors did. If you're an Academy Award–winning actor you're not exactly low-status, but directors are still the boss of you. This relationship between pronoun use and status isn't unique to English. Pennebaker found the same pattern in letters written in Arabic by lower-ranking Iraqi officers to their more senior colleagues. When someone lacks power, status, or agency, they tend to focus on their own experience: "I," "me," "my," "mine."

You might assume that when someone's attention is self-focused, they're talking in a narcissistic or self-aggrandizing way. But often it's the opposite. Consistent self-focus usually arises from feelings of insecurity. When you feel vulnerable, you can't help directing your attention inward. What's more, you're probably unaware that your frequent use of first-person pronouns is a tell for your mental state.

Think back to a time when you were physically vulnerable—in pain, ill, very hungry, or cold. Your conscious attention (the Judge) was focused on your own experience because you were stuck in a situation you were desperate to escape. Your mind was saying, *Help me. I feel sick*. Or, *My arm hurts*. When your own difficult situation occupies all your mental real estate, it shouldn't be surprising that this is reflected in your unconscious (Gator) use of pronouns. This self-focus also applies to emotional pain, including anxiety and depression.

When Pennebaker and his colleagues analyzed pronoun choices in essays written by depressed college students, they found that these students used "I" a lot. Their self-referential language didn't spring from some fixed personality trait; it merely reflected their mental state, which, of course, is subject to change. In this same study Pennebaker found that students who had been depressed but no longer were used "I" less often. The bottom line here is when you are feeling vulnerable, physically or emotionally, it's difficult to get out of your own head.

This makes it hard to be fully present with someone else. Or to be charismatic.

First-person pronouns aren't the only words we use that act as attentional boomerangs, returning the focus to ourselves. Diminishers—verbal attempts to connect through submission—do this, too. These are the human equivalent of a dog rolling over to expose his belly or neck. We tend to use them in situations where there's an imbalance of power or status, and we do it more often when we're on the low end—when we feel our safety or well-being may depend on being liked. Higher-status people don't need to care what others think of them, although some who do care diminish themselves in order to avoid coming across as arrogant or controlling.

What does diminishing language sound like in conversation? "I was just wondering," "I thought maybe," "Can I ask a stupid question?" and "I'm sorry, but . . ." (lots of "I"s here, too). Diminishers express caution and vagueness, as in "kind of," "sort of," "it seems," "generally," "more or less," and "it's possible that." Sometimes you hear diminishing language in "upspeak," that submissive, friendly lilt that turns statements into questions. You know what I mean?

"I'm sorry" is so overused as a diminisher that comedian Amy Schumer created an entire skit to satirize it. An all-female panel of world experts is incapable of actually describing their work because its members are constantly apologizing for everything. I'm sorry for the mic feedback, sorry for being interrupted, sorry for clearing my throat, sorry for correcting your pronunciation of my name, sorry for being such a diva because I'm allergic to that soda and asked for water instead. The apologies culminate with one of the panelists apologizing for having her leg burned when someone accidentally spills boiling-hot coffee. The "Sorry" skit is simultaneously hilarious and painful to watch because so many of us can relate to it.

Although no one will dislike you for diminishing yourself, they're not going to like you for it either. Like boomerangs, diminishers keep bringing attention right back to you. Diminishers are hard to listen to, easy to interrupt, and astonishingly common. Even James Pennebaker, the expert on language and power, found he was diminishing himself when emailing his higher-ups.

He noticed this when he had to ask several people in his department at the University of Texas to move their offices. When appealing to a colleague with higher social status, Pennebaker wrote, "I've been trying to avoid this, but I think I may need to ask you if you would be willing to give up your office." You can feel the diminishing effect of those three "I"s in one sentence. And you can appreciate how difficult it is to listen to people who write and talk this way. Their communications require additional decoding. The fact that Pennebaker is uncomfortable certainly comes across, but beyond that, what is he really saying? Is he asking for something, or is he saying he might have to at some future time?

You may notice you tend to be self-focused not just when you're speaking and writing, but when you're listening too. We all are. My mind bounces from *When have I experienced something like that?* to *What will I say next?* and it doesn't help that much to *try* to listen. When I do try harder, my mind starts jumping to *How should I demonstrate that I'm listening?, How do they want me to respond?, How can I show empathy?,* or *How can I help?* I, I'm, me, I, I.

Even when I'm motivated by compassion (*I want to show*

them I'm a good listener because I care about them), that's still a lot about "I." Comedian Mindy Kaling does a funny bit on this phenomenon. Describing what it's like to meet someone at a party, she talks about compulsively trying to focus on them. "I don't think they're interesting. I don't want to keep this going. But the worst thing in the world for me is for them to think that I think they're boring or want to extricate myself in some way from this conversation. . . . So, then this person leaves the party telling their spouse, Mindy Kaling is obsessed with me. She talked to me for two hours."

While listening to another person, our conscious mind (the Judge) might be asking, *How are they feeling and what are they thinking?* while our unconscious mind (the Gator) might be asking, *How are they feeling and what are they thinking about me?* One way to overcome this difficulty is to explore some deeper ways of listening, which we'll learn more about in chapters 6 and 6½.

In the meantime, if you'd like to reduce diminishers from your vocabulary, know that most can simply be skipped. Just go ahead and say it. When James Pennebaker conveyed the same office-moving message to a graduate student of lower status, he felt no need to diminish himself. He simply wrote, "Would you be willing to move your office?" Mindy Kaling knows she could be straightforward and charismatic at the party, too: "You can simply just say, Well, it was great to meet you. I'm going to go mingle."

This pivot in your use of language reflects a deeper shift. We've seen that self-focus is anti-charisma: How can anyone connect with you when you're so busy paying attention to yourself? The solution is simple, if not easy. Shift your focus to the other person. Here's what this can look like.

DIMINISHER	PROBLEM	SOLUTION
"I could be wrong, but . . ." "It kind of seems like . . ." "This is just an idea."	Uncertainty about the facts or the future is fine, but uncertainty in the way you express yourself makes people tune out. You could always be wrong and people know that already.	Engage them with a question. "Is it possible that . . . ?" "What if . . . ?" Or spark curiosity. "Here's a crazy idea."
"I wanted to let you know . . ." "I was just wondering . . ." "I thought maybe . . ."	Your attention is on you, and in the past, and full of verbal clutter. It's hard to listen to.	Shift the focus to them and the future and the clutter will fall away. Instead of "I was wondering if you might be willing," "Might you be willing . . . ?"
"Sorry for being late." "Sorry for interrupting." "I'm so sorry to hear that."	"I'm sorry" means you're feeling bad, so you're asking them to focus on your feelings when you meant to focus on theirs.	"Thank you for your patience." "Forgive me for interrupting." "How awful!"

The second paradox of charisma is the inverse of the first: You attract other people's attention by giving them yours.

When you focus your attention on someone else, they feel seen or understood. You're fully present with them, and they can tell. It makes a palpable difference. Spiritual teachings on being present focus on dissolution of the ego, or escape from the entrapment of your own mind. Great teachers of stage presence use the same principle. I learned this lesson from Martin Berman, a professional actor who could perform what felt like a miracle. He could wring an Oscar-worthy performance out of anyone simply by reading a scene with them. The secret he taught his students was simple: *Always remember that the most important person on the stage is the other actor.*

It has been said of many highly charismatic individuals that they can make you feel like you're the most important person in the world in that moment. One visitor described his one-on-one meeting in San Quentin with Charles Manson in similar terms: "When you meet people who are highly persuasive, oftentimes they take a tremendous interest in you." He said Manson made him feel as though he were the only other person in the room (which he was, but you know what I mean).

Shifting your focus to the other person

Questions are an easy way to transfer your focus from yourself to the other person. You can replace diminishers with questions, or you can ask the other person about themselves. We all know that people like to talk about themselves, but did you know we like to talk about ourselves so much that we'll actually pay money to share inconsequential information with strangers? Neuroscientist Diana Tamir, who studies the pleasure of self-disclosure, finds that talking about ourselves activates the same areas of the brain as money, sex, and chocolate, which explains why we like people who ask us questions. In a series of studies, people could choose to answer questions about other people for pay, or answer questions about themselves for free. The topics were trivial, but the experience of answering questions about themselves was so enjoyable that they chose to forgo about 20 percent of the money they could have earned, just to let people know they liked snowboarding and hated mushrooms on pizza.

Since we enjoy talking about ourselves, we appreciate people who invite us to do so. Alison Wood Brooks and her colleagues have found that when people are getting to know each other, those who ask more questions are better liked, and speed daters who ask more questions are more likely to get second dates. Question askers were liked even more when some of those questions were follow-up questions, which were perceived as expressing deep interest. I find it noteworthy that eavesdroppers didn't like the question askers more—only the question answerers did.

Could this affinity lead to real intimacy? Arthur and Elaine Aron set up a study in which pairs of participants took turns asking each other thirty-six questions. These began with simple queries, such as "Who would you like to have as a dinner guest?" and slowly progressed to more personal questions, such as "When was the last time you cried?" Finally, at the end of the experiment, each person focused their attention on their partner with no questions at all. They looked at each other for four minutes without talking. Just pure attention. Legend has it that one of these pairs got married.

You don't have to go that deep. You can remind yourself to focus your attention outward just by using people's names more often. For one thing, it's a useful cue for your subconscious mind: *It's not about me, it's about them.* And, of course, you attract the other person's attention this way too. After all, hearing our own names has the power to arouse us from sleep. Dale Carnegie advised us to use other people's names back in 1938 when he wrote his classic *How to Win Friends and Influence People,* and neuroscience has since confirmed that your name has a unique signature that activates self-referential parts of your brain. *That's me. He's paying attention to me!*

I thought of Dale Carnegie when my upstairs neighbor Kevin kept using people's names *over and over* in every conversation. "Hey, Zoe, how are you doing, Zoe?" He was an optometrist who seemed to know everybody in the whole town. We called him the Mayor of Somerville and we were always happy to see him. Even though his naming habit was weird and we teased him about it, it worked. We all liked him, in part because we felt that he liked us. If you asked anyone, they'd say that friendly, happy, goofy Kevin had lots of charisma.

Being charismatic doesn't require you to be nice (although of course you can be both charismatic and nice). And being charismatic doesn't mean you can't talk about yourself. The pronoun research can help you spot clues to when you might be using the kryptonite of self-focus on your charisma, but don't go overboard stripping "I" from your vocabulary. Just use this new insight as a cue to consider, from time to time, who might be the center of your attention. And then, if you choose, shift that attention away from yourself.

Relaxing Your Voice as a Marker of Confidence

In 2015, Elizabeth Holmes, the biotech darling of Silicon Valley and founder of Theranos, was an icon of female empowerment. At age thirty-one she was recognized by *Forbes* as the world's youngest self-made billionaire. Holmes was intelligent, attractive, and tough; she showed other young women how to succeed in the cutthroat, male-dominated tech start-up sector. That is, until John Carreyrou broke the story that the Theranos blood tests, with their promise of improved global health, were complete fabrications. Holmes had lied to investors and to her board; she had lied on TV and to the public. In hindsight, what should have tipped us off?

Public opinion converged on a red flag: Elizabeth Holmes's voice. The young, thin, blond woman was famous for sounding more like an old man with a pack-a-day habit. Surely no woman with a growl like that should have ever been trusted. Witnesses came forward and claimed they knew her "real" voice, which was higher and more feminine.

Despite being pretty busy with politics, British prime minister Margaret Thatcher worked with a coach to deepen her voice. Thatcher and Holmes weren't dumb; various studies have shown listeners judge people with lower-pitched voices as stronger, more competent, more attractive, more dominant, and more likely to be good leaders. But I believe Elizabeth Holmes, Margaret Thatcher, and everyone else who has been taught to lower their voice to become more influential has misunderstood something important about *why* lower voices are more influential.

Have you noticed that when you're tense and self-conscious, your shoulders slump and you might cross your arms protectively over your chest? This affects how you're coming across visually, of course, making you look less than confident, but just as important from an influence perspective, it affects how you *sound*. When we're nervous, we tend to do things that constrict our throats, making our voices rise in pitch, or creating the creaky vocal fry that so annoys some people. If high, constricted voices are associated with fear or tension, it should be no surprise that they're less persuasive. Speaking in your *natural* low register has the opposite effect: It's a display of confidence. It requires relaxing your diaphragm and throat, which you simply cannot do under threat. Your natural low register is the comfortable, confident voice that makes you sound more present and makes it easier for people to pay attention to you. This applies regardless of your gender.

With a little practice, speaking in your natural low register can help you *feel* more present too. At first it might feel weird, though, like any new behavior. You might start practicing on the phone, so you can stand up or lie down, whatever helps you feel comfortable. Closing your eyes can help. So can slowing down a little bit. If this is awkward, practice with strangers before turning to friends. Notice whether people seem more open to what you have to say. I remember when I was first becoming conscious of this, my then partner said for the first time, "I could listen to your voice for hours."

Actors, singers, dancers, and other performers use a postural training exercise to help the voice relax by releasing tension in the body. All you need to do is stand with your eyes closed, your arms at your sides, and imagine an invisible thread connected to your breastbone reaching straight up into the clouds. Now imagine the thread being pulled up softly as you take a few slow, deep breaths. Your shoulders gently fall back. Your rib cage expands. Your arms get heavy. Experience what this feels like in your body. This relaxed, open posture helps free your voice to fall into its natural register. You may even find that opening your posture and relaxing your voice makes it easier to let go of diminishers. You will look and sound more charismatic, and people will find it easier to pay attention to you.

Charisma in the Spotlight

Packed in tightly with a hundred other fans in Club 3121, I savored the anticipation of a dream coming true. I had adored Prince since grade school and was about to see him live in concert. As the drum began to thump, the legendary artist sauntered across the stage in a long satin jacket and platform heels. He took the mic in both hands and paused as he looked—I was sure—straight into my eyes. He purred the first line of his opening number, "Before we get started, are we all alone?"

I grabbed my friend's arm. "I'm about to faint."

As I spoke those words, the woman on the other side of me slumped to the floor, unconscious. I learned from the paramedics who carried her away that fainting at Prince concerts wasn't unusual. His charisma was more than some people could handle.

But it hadn't always been that way. In fact, lack of charisma nearly killed his career before it got off the ground. Industry insiders agreed that young Prince Rogers Nelson was a talented musician, but no one knew what to do with his awkward performance style. He seemed most comfortable with his back to the audience, and when he did speak between songs, he couldn't manage more than a whisper. When talent scouts from Warner Bros. came to his second-ever solo show in 1979, they signed him to the record label but refused to send him on tour.

When Prince's single "I Wanna Be Your Lover" reached number one on the charts and he *still* wasn't touring, Rick

James, the reigning King of Funk, invited the up-and-coming artist to join his tour as the opening act. As Rick James remembered it, when Prince got on the stage in his trench coat and bloomers, "the guys in the audience would boo him to death."

But Prince refused to give up. He had earned his musical chops by practicing his instruments for hours and hours a day, and he approached stagecraft the same way. Prince studied Rick James and other performers he admired, paying close attention to every word and gesture. He changed the way he moved and, most important, he learned to focus his attention on the audience. He did these things repeatedly, until they became habitual. He told stories and asked questions, engaging the fans with call and response. By the end of the tour, Prince was transformed and the audience was transfixed. Rick James admitted feeling jealous. Charisma isn't something you *are*. It's something you *do,* which places it within your control; you can become more charismatic by adjusting the way you interact with people.

We've already looked at some tools that are useful in one-on-one interactions, so now let's look at some that apply to public performances, including public speaking, which is scary for most of us. Some of my sweetest moments as a teacher have been watching students try out the small adjustments that make them irresistible onstage. One student's vocal cord surgery had left her speaking in a whisper. She had assumed that because it was difficult for people to hear her, they weren't interested in what she had to say. But with a microphone and a little coaching on how to direct her attention, she had us hanging on her every word. Another student kept us spellbound with a story about his mother even though he was speaking in Hungarian and we couldn't understand a word he said. Then there was

Sukari Brown, a visiting prospective student who didn't feel like she belonged.

Sukari hated public speaking, but she volunteered to try it anyway and told a story about watching the film *Black Panther*, which had come out a few months earlier. I coached her to make a few small adjustments so she could draw us in. Focusing on members of the audience one by one, Sukari invited us to reflect on what it's like to see people who look like you always relegated to playing drug dealers and sidekicks on the big screen. She paused, we leaned in, and she asked us to imagine what it's like to see, for the first time, people who look like you playing heroes, full of pride and power. She told us how she went back to that theater to watch *Black Panther* five times. We felt her dignity, her anger, and her hope. We gave her a resounding round of applause, and she basked in it. In a note she sent me afterward, Sukari wrote, "Up until that point, I questioned whether I belonged there—at Yale, in the seminar, and even pursuing an MBA. After my heart stopped freaking out and my breathing returned to normal, I realized I *can* do this. I DO belong here."

When you feel like you belong onstage, then you do. Here are a few ideas and tools that can help you get there. This is all I taught Sukari.

The Stage Is a Time Warp

Spending an hour with your crush can feel like a minute, while a minute in the dentist's chair can feel like an hour. I'm paraphrasing, but this is how Einstein explained his theory of relativity. The passage of time depends on your frame of reference. If you've ever experienced a car accident or a fall as happening in slow motion, you've experienced that time warp. While the accident is happening, the Gator is in hyperdrive. It's paying so much attention to every detail it's as if you've increased the number of frames per second in your movie, which is exactly how a slow-motion scene is shot. When people sharing the same experience have different frames of reference, though, time can get weird.

Standing in front of an audience creates a time warp. Time moves at a different speed for speakers than it does for audience members, which can make it difficult for them to sync up with each other. Feeling nervous—as almost every public speaker does—triggers the Gator brain's heightened awareness, its moment-by-moment attention; people in the audience have no reason to be nervous, so they have no heightened awareness. Enter the time warp.

After inviting a volunteer from my class to stand up and speak to the rest of us for one minute (with any stress unavoidably compounded by the knowledge that we'll be judging them as a speaker), I'll check in with the audience. How was the tempo? Too fast, too slow, or just right? Almost always, the audience says it was too fast. Being nervous makes time feel as though it's slowing down, which causes nervous speakers to speed through their presentations, leaving audience members struggling to keep up. It takes a lot of effort to pay attention, so the Gator gets distracted. They start checking the time, checking their phones, and checking out. If a speaker can't slow down to match the audience's tempo, they won't have the audience's attention and won't be able to deliver their message. Slowing down can be strangely difficult, though (which also makes it funny to watch). Speakers trying to slow down sometimes drawwwww ooooout theeeeeir sylllllablllles. Or. Talk.

Like. A. Robot. But what really helps them solve the time warp problem is *the power of the pause*.

In class, we spend a lot of time practicing this. I'll coach speakers to add pauses at every period and comma in their presentation, decelerating until they're sure it's too slow—but the audience says it's just right. Pauses are moments to connect with the audience, to focus attention on listeners while their thoughts are catching up to the present moment. Pausing not only conveys confidence, it requires it.

Full-body pauses—moments when you're not walking, fidgeting, or making any dramatic hand movements, but you are breathing easily, your hands comfortably by your side—are especially helpful. Not just during your presentation but also before and after. This key to charisma is so simple that almost no one teaches or practices it, yet it works for speakers and performers of all kinds.

Here are some opportunities for a full-body pause in a formal talk or performance situation.

- When someone else is speaking or performing, you pause with your whole body and *focus your attention on them.* Maybe an audience member is asking a question. Maybe a junior employee is speaking up at the meeting. Maybe your bandmate is playing a solo. Whoever should have the audience's attention should have your attention too. You'll be tempted to look around at other people, or look down or away. If you do, you're fracturing the group's attention, and fractured attention is harder to collect when it's your turn to speak. When it's someone else's turn to be charismatic, don't distract others or let yourself get distracted.

- When it's your turn to speak or perform, thank the person introducing you, if there is one, then *shift your focus to the audience*. Take a full-body pause for one complete breath, smile, and you'll have the audience's full attention when you begin. When you're on a panel or in an informal meeting, the pause needn't be so obvious, but taking that moment to shift your attention will catch theirs. Now all eyes are on you.

- When you finish your turn in the spotlight, take a moment to thank the audience before you leave. If there is applause, pause to bask in it for at least one breath, *letting the audience's attention rest fully on you*. You have been focused on everyone else, charisma blazing, and they felt it. Now, humbly and gratefully, you receive. We tend to imagine that rushing offstage shows humility, but it conveys a tacit apology—*I'm sorry I wasted your time*. Instead, take a moment to appreciate your audience with a pause that says, *Thank you for your time. I'm grateful for it, and I enjoyed being with you, too.* You might nod, bow, put a hand to your chest, or even blow a kiss if you're that kind of person and it's that kind of event.

A pause, whether it's momentary or stretched out, can realign the passage of time between you and your audience. They catch up with what you've just said. It's one of the two big secrets to stage presence.

The second one is shining.

**This secret is based on the third paradox of charisma.
To connect with many people, connect with one.**

When Prince made eye contact with me, I don't know if he was really focusing on me, or the woman who fainted, or the man next to her, or someone else entirely. It didn't matter. The individual connection was so powerful that we were all transfixed. This technique—connecting with many by connecting with one—is *shining*.

Here's how we practice it in class. I ask for a volunteer who hates public speaking. We're going to see how long it takes for this person to connect—really connect—with every member of the audience. It's not an easy task. In fact, shining is such an advanced skill that few professional speakers or performers have mastered it. But even a novice can learn the art of shining, and it helps to have a village to practice with.

If you step up to volunteer, you'll tell a story in your native language. Something you've heard or told many times, like a fairy tale or a religious parable. It can be a personal story, but only if you've rehashed it a lot. To shine, you must be comfortable enough with your material that you can speak extemporaneously, or rehearsed enough that the words flow automatically. When the Gator is speaking the words, the Judge can be telling the rest of the body what to do. For the purpose of the exercise, it doesn't matter whether the audience understands your words or not. You could shine without even making a sound.

Shining is the electric connection that gives someone the feeling of being the only other person in the room. It has the intimate flavor of the exercise in which both partners gazed into each other's eyes without speaking. It's what made the woman at the Prince concert lose consciousness.

Shining differs from every other public speaking strategy because it requires the willing participation of another person. You can't shine alone; you can't shine with someone who's looking down at their phone; you're only shining if they feel you shine. And they want to feel you shine because it makes them feel more alive. As the performer you'll feel this way too—simultaneously connected and vulnerable and powerful. As you're reaching out with your attention, you're also opening up to let theirs in.

This is how you do it. Lock your gaze on one person in the audience and open your heart as you speak to them and only them. Offer this person the gift of your focused energy until they feel the connection between you. The message you're sending is *Here I am. Here you are. Here we are, together. Hello.* The energy being exchanged is something like love. Or maybe that's exactly what it is.

When we practice shining, everyone in the audience begins with their hand raised, and they keep it raised until they feel the speaker connect with them. Then their hand goes down. The speaker's goal is to get all the hands down. The time warp plays a role here, too. Speakers are surprised by how long it takes to connect, but it doesn't feel that way for the audience. And when a true connection has been made, time not only synchronizes; it can almost feel like it has stopped. When they achieve that level of connection, both speakers and audience members are surprised to see additional hands going down in other parts of the room. The vicarious connection can be as palpable as a direct connection.

It's not easy to shine when you first try it. And some audience members set a high bar for feeling a connection and won't put their hand down until you've touched their soul. Proximity helps. If the audience member doesn't put their hand down after a couple of sentences, you'll want to move on and try to connect with someone else. But remember your pauses and take a step closer instead. And another step if you need to. As you approach, eventually their hand will go down. No one can ignore the feeling of connection when a brave and vulnerable human being is standing right in front of them, ready to shine. Shining is so powerful that even a reluctant or novice speaker can connect with every member in a class of thirty people within five or ten minutes.

Next time you're speaking to a group, look out at the audience. You'll notice that some folks out there are shining, too. Maybe they're smiling or nodding, laughing at your jokes. They draw your attention by giving you their focused and delighted attention, and some shine so brightly that it would be easy to ignore everyone else. When you make eye contact with these people, you feel their energy amplify your own.

You can be one of those people shining from the audience too. Sit near the front, follow the speaker's eyes, open your heart, and radiate your energy toward the speaker. Really listen. The speaker will feel it and will make eye contact with you because your presence is drawing their attention. Shining from the audience is a gift for the speaker, and that connection makes it easier to ask a question or to approach them afterward, if that's something you want to do.

If you're an experienced speaker who's already comfortable onstage, you can take shining to the next level by challenging yourself to connect with those audience members who don't seem open to it. They might be checking their phone, or just keeping their eyes down taking notes (though they might be listening intently), or looking drowsy or skeptical or bored.

These people might not notice when you look at them, but they'll notice when you walk over or if you address them by name. You're not judging them for not being present, you're welcoming them back. This is a gift to the group because the connection you establish with a reluctant audience member can reach everyone in the room. The audience is like a string of fairy lights with only a few bulbs glowing. When you shine with the person whose attention is wandering, the whole string suddenly lights up. Faces glow, eyes brighten, everyone feels it.

Charisma is all about connection.

Moments of Truth

You've just arrived and the party's already in full swing. The music's thumping and the guests are clustered into groups, leaning in to hear each other. There's no round of applause to greet your entrance; no one falls silent to admire your new out-fit. The party just goes on. If you had been there earlier, the host might have been talking to you rather than to the guy in shiny pants. But you didn't arrive then—you arrived now. And you can't just stand there blocking the door.

Feeling awkward, you scan the crowd so you can look pur-poseful when you walk somewhere. A friend waves you over. You come and stand at the periphery of the group, listening to the woman with pink hair who's laughing so hard she can barely finish her story. You don't interrupt or barge in with your own story when she gets to the punch line. You don't pull your friend away. You don't ask everyone's name as if the party were just getting started. Instead, you join the flow, laughing along with the rest of the group. Maybe you comment on the story or ask a follow-up question. You introduce yourself when people are ready to meet you. You tell your story when they're ready to hear it.

You know the rules of party etiquette. But when you want to capture someone else's attention in everyday situations, it's easy to forget that their life is a party that's already in full swing. Whether or not they choose to pay attention to you—and how they respond if they do—depends on your timing. *When* you ask can sometimes matter more than *how* you ask or even what you're asking for. *Moments of truth* are situations in which someone is particularly likely to be open to your influence. Since the Judge's conscious attention is always already focused on something, it helps to ask yourself what it's focused on, and to see if you can reach out when your idea is going to be relevant. Maybe you have the solution to a problem they're facing. Here's what I mean.

My second-favorite marketing campaign based on a moment of truth was a promotion by Cebu Pacific airlines. Hong Kong was in the middle of monsoon season, hours of daily rainfall leaving everyone wet and miserable. Instead of trying to compete in the crowded digital media market, Cebu Pacific's advertising team slipped out during a break between downpours to stencil messages on city sidewalks with water-repellent spray. The spray worked like invisible ink, disappearing as it absorbed into the dry cement. Thousands of people walked over the messages without seeing them—until the rains returned.

When the next deluge soaked the sidewalks and pedestrians huddled under their umbrellas, they saw Cebu Pacific's message appear beneath their feet as if by magic. "It's sunny in the Philippines." Scanning a stenciled QR code took them to the Cebu Pacific website, which was offering a monsoon sale for beach destinations. This promotion increased sales by 37 percent, which, if you're in marketing, you know is a massive success. The secret messages grabbed everyone's attention by appearing just when the offer of a tropical getaway would be most welcome (in a downpour) and in a place where people's attention was already focused (on the sidewalk, to avoid stepping in puddles). A moment of truth is a time or a place or both—the whole context. And in this case, the QR code made it easy to take action right then, when they would be most motivated.

Moments of truth are relevant in any kind of communication. When might your boss be more open to discussing a raise? When might your partner be more open to discussing a move? If you have a message to share with the world, how can you connect it to current news or current events, issues people are already paying attention to?

When there isn't something in the zeitgeist to latch on to, you might be able to create your own moment of truth. A flair for drama comes in handy. When the eccentric Brazilian billionaire Chiquinho Scarpa announced he had been inspired by the pharaohs to bury his five-hundred-thousand-dollar Bentley in his garden, he drew a hailstorm of criticism on social media and from the press. The day of the burial was a media circus, buzzing with journalists, camera crews, and helicopters overhead. As the Bentley was being lowered into its grave, Scarpa suddenly called the proceedings to a halt and invited the crowd inside his mansion, where he made a prepared statement.

Although everyone recognizes that it's absurd and wasteful to bury this beautiful car, Scarpa said, most of us have chosen to bury something far more valuable: our organs. This, he added, is truly the most terrible waste of all. Then Scarpa made his big announcement: the launch of Brazil's new National

Week of Organ Donations. In that moment he went from national scoundrel to national hero, turning hordes of haters into fans. Organ donations increased by 32 percent in just one month.

We'll discuss the importance of framing in the next chapter, but it turns out that the best frames often depend on timing. Researchers have found that we make decisions differently depending on whether an opportunity is coming up soon or is in the distant future. Decisions about the near term tend to be based on concrete considerations like process and feasibility. *How could I make it work? Do I have time? What else would I miss?* Considerations about the distant future tend to be more abstract, focusing on desirability. *Why would I do this? How much would I enjoy it? What would it contribute to my life or someone else's?* When inviting someone to do something for you, you might focus on logistics and concrete details when talking about the near future and focus on impact when talking about the distant future. If you're asking your CEO to give a talk next week, explain how you'll minimize the hassle—because that's what they care about then. If the talk is next month, describe what a big difference it could make—because that's what they care about then.

Understanding this dynamic creates another opportunity to activate the power of timing: the *implementation intention*. It is one of the most successful interventions for changing behavior and has helped people do all kinds of things they want to do but often forget to do, like exercise, get annual health checks, recycle, and vote. An implementation intention is basically answering the question *"Okay, so when and how are you going to do that?"*

In 2008, Todd Rogers had just graduated from Harvard, and he wanted to use behavioral science to influence politics. He knew that most get-out-the-vote campaigns had no effect whatsoever, but he had a hunch that implementation intentions might help. His research team called more than two hundred thousand registered voters. The implementation intention script asked if they were planning to vote, and then asked what, specifically, were their plans. When would they be voting, and where would they be coming from? What would they have been doing just before that? The answers didn't matter, but the questions did. By considering the questions about how they'd implement their intentions, voters formed a plan and identified a cue that would serve as a Gator brain alarm clock on election day. If the plan was to vote on the way home from work, the alarm would go off when they got in the car to go home. *Ding! Time to vote!* An internal moment of truth. And it worked. Rogers's intervention increased voter turnout by 4 percent—a margin large enough to have changed the outcome in four out of five battleground states. Today both major parties use this strategy in their get-out-the-vote campaigns.*

I'm a fan of using timing as an influence tool because it keeps you from being a pest. Instead of trying to pull people away from whatever they're doing, you're finding a moment of truth in which to introduce something relevant. You're seamlessly joining the conversation at just the right time and contributing to it instead of interrupting.

Oh yeah. Remember when I told you that Cebu Pacific's

---

* But can you guess what has the biggest effect of all on voter turnout? Yep. Easy access to a polling station. Ease trumps pretty much everything.

"Sunny in the Philippines" was my second-favorite moment of truth marketing campaign? My favorite was a print ad for Durex condoms that ran during the month of June. Very simple. Just a few words on a lavender background: "To all those who use our competitors' products: Happy Father's Day."

CHAPTER FIVE

The Life-Changing Magic
of a Simple Frame

Derren Brown has played Russian roulette with real bullets, successfully predicted the National Lottery numbers, convinced a shy person to push a stranger off a building, influenced an American White supremacist to give up his life for a Mexican illegal immigrant, persuaded business executives at a motivational seminar to steal £100,000 in an armed bank robbery, and conspired with the friends and family of a selfish loser to stage the end of the world and the zombie apocalypse that would turn him into a hero (afterward, in real life, he became a teacher for kids with special needs). My daughter Ripley and I once tried to replicate a simpler trick in which Derren buys jewelry with blank pieces of paper instead of cash, but for us it did not work. Derren Brown is a psychological illusionist who knows more about influence than pretty much anyone.

I'm a huge fan, so I was in the audience for *Secret,* his American stage debut.* When Derren pulled from his pocket "an ordinary handheld banana," we laughed. He said he was

---

* When you attend a live show you're sworn to secrecy, so, Derren, I hope you'll forgive me for breaking my vow and revealing just a tiny piece of it.

glad to see us—just not quite as glad as some of us might have thought. We laughed some more. He placed the banana on a stand near the front of the stage and warned us that at some point a man in a gorilla suit would walk across the stage and take the banana from the stand, but we'd probably miss it.

Game on! I was *not* going to miss the gorilla because I knew all about the invisible gorilla experiment. Christopher Chabris and Daniel Simons had asked participants to watch a short video of basketball players dribbling a ball and passing it back and forth. The task was to count the number of times the players wearing white shirts—not those in black—passed the ball. Because study participants were so focused on counting, they didn't notice the guy in a gorilla suit walk through the game, stop in the middle to beat his chest, and walk away. When they watched the video again after being told about the gorilla, they were dumbfounded. How could they possibly have missed something so dramatic? The researchers dubbed this phenomenon *inattentional blindness*.

So I was paying close attention. No inattentional blindness for me. While Derren talked I glanced back at the banana a hundred times to make sure it was still there, and it was—right until the moment Derren asked us, "Did anyone see the gorilla take the banana?" Nobody had. Then a gorilla arm reached out from offstage to hand back the banana to Derren, and he gave us another chance. I promised myself I *would* catch the gorilla this time, and I did.

Moments after Derren carried a large easel over to the right side of the stage ("Just keep your eyes focused on the easel"), the gorilla snuck out from behind the curtains on the left to steal the banana! There was laughter and excitement as audience members called out the discovery—we'd out-tricked the trickster! The gorilla shrugged, then removed the head of his costume to reveal . . . Derren Brown. We'd missed the real switch, once again.

Derren Brown is a whiz at directing attention through a process called *framing*. Both directly and indirectly, he tells you what to look for, influencing what you see—and what you miss. Framing is magical stuff. It determines people's experiences and even shapes how they think. In Chabris and Simons's original gorilla experiment, framing the task as a counting exercise made participants oblivious to everything else. In *Secret,* Derren Brown gave us frames to direct our attention during every moment of the show—even the ninja moment when he told us, "Just keep your eyes focused on the easel," to make us look away. A frame doesn't *say,* "Pay attention to this and ignore everything else!" But it creates this effect by putting an idea at the center of our attention and giving us a reason to focus on it.

If I asked you to come up with a list of things that are white, that would be easy, right? But what if I framed the experiment a little differently by adding, "like milk and snow"? Try it. There are countless white things on earth, yet once you have milk and snow at the center of your attention, it's a lot harder to come up with other white things, like clouds and coconut flakes. Milk and snow are so iconically white and create such a strong frame that they inhibit alternatives. To put it another way, effective frames can be so sticky that it becomes hard to see things from a different perspective. One such frame helped transform a small tech start-up into the world's most valuable company.

Just a few years after he co-founded Apple in a garage, Steve Jobs wanted to recruit John Sculley to become the company's new CEO. This was no small request. Sculley was CEO of

PepsiCo, the two-billion-dollar snack and beverage behemoth, which meant Jobs would be asking one of the most successful businessmen in the world to take a huge step down. Not surprisingly, Sculley said no. But the two men became friends, and from time to time Jobs would press his case. One day, when they were seated on a balcony overlooking Central Park, Jobs turned to his friend and asked, "Do you want to sell sugar water for the rest of your life? Or do you want to come with me and change the world?"

As Sculley recalls, "I just gulped. I knew that I would wonder for the rest of my life what I had missed."

In the same way the word "snow" inhibits other white objects from springing to mind, the idea that he was "selling sugar water" was going to make it hard for Sculley to think of his job at Pepsi any other way. Once Jobs created that frame, it stuck. Sculley agreed to join, and the rest, as they say, is history.

Framing is how spellcasting works in the real world. Just by describing something or giving it a name, you call it into being. A well-chosen frame can determine what's relevant, what's important, or what's good. When you frame someone's experience in a compelling way, you shape their expectations as well as their interpretation of events. Here's an example of how I might use framing at the beginning of a presentation.

"My promise to you for this session is that you'll leave with at least one new strategy you want to put into action immediately, and that strategy will have the potential to make a meaningful difference in your life or work. Does that sound like a fair expectation for our time together?"

Most people nod. Now we've agreed on terms. I've set a low bar for satisfaction, which will be a boon for all of us. If I hadn't done so, after my talk they might focus on what they've sacrificed (*That was a lot of time*) rather than what they've gained (*I can't wait to practice shining in my presentation tomorrow!*). I've also framed the strategy as important, because it could make a meaningful difference in their life right away. Of course, I'll have to deliver on that, and I will.

Next, I'll give them a frame for what's relevant, which will help them to focus, and to refocus when their mind wanders. I don't take their attention for granted—it's hard to stay attentive to even the most engaging speakers.

"I'll be sharing an assortment of strategies today and I don't know which one will provide the "aha" moment for you, so be listening for that. When you hear it, write it down so you don't forget. If some of what we're talking about doesn't connect for you, or maybe you knew it already, that's fine—those are the strategies that are going to work for someone else. But I do invite you to listen for tools or ideas you can share with other people when you go back home or go back to work. I'll try to make this stuff as concrete and straightforward as I can so that you can apply it for yourself and also teach it to other people. Okay?"

Thumbs-up. I use that way of paying attention—listening for something to teach or share with others—to help me stay focused when I'm a listener myself because it makes me curious about a broader collection of ideas. As we wrap up the talk, I'll remind them about the one tool I promised at the outset. Did they find it? Yes? Excellent. We set an implementation intention so they'll remember to use it, and we part ways confident that their investment of time and attention was truly worthwhile.

Bigger and Better

I lay the groundwork for framing with my MBA students by challenging them to play a game called Bigger and Better. The rules are simple. You start with a paper clip and trade it up for something bigger and better. Then you trade that item up for something even bigger and better, and so on. ("Bigger and better" is subjective.) I tell the students they can make as many trades as they want, and ask them to bring their biggest, best item to class the following week.

The Bigger and Better game has been around for a long time but if you've heard of it, it's probably because of Kyle MacDonald. Between the summers of 2005 and 2006, Kyle traded up from a red paper clip to a fish pen to a weird doorknob . . . and on and on, until eventually he traded up to a house in Saskatchewan, Canada, where they made him mayor of the town for a day and erected a giant statue of a red paper clip in his honor.

MBA students have only a week to play, not a year, and no instructions from me about how to do well at this game. The goal is to have fun and see what they learn, and whoever shows up with the biggest, best thing wins a prize. A handful of players will have been suckered by neighbors into accepting junk like a broken microwave, a fourteen-foot oar, or a huge, smelly overcoat. Some will be frustrated at having so little to show for their efforts: a used accounting textbook that no one else wanted, or a collection of coffee mugs with stupid sayings. Some "biggest, best" items will surprise us. We've had a living tree, a ten-foot statue of Anubis, and a week at a condo in Hawaii. I didn't know what to think when someone brought in a piece of marble from Saddam Hussein's palace. And I was floored by Manus McCaffery and Tom Powell.

Manus had challenged Tom to get a car. Tom had laughed, "Or maybe we should set our target for twenty bucks?"

Tom was moving to Manhattan, and Manus didn't have a driver's license, but the audacity of trading up for a car excited them. Because the game would be more fun if it served a higher purpose, they decided that if they miraculously managed to get a car, they would give it away. The game was afoot.

Over the next three days, Manus and Tom shared their crazy mission with New Haven business owners and neighbors. "We're playing this game called Bigger and Better. It's for a good cause and we need your help. Would you like to hear how the game works?" And because it was Halloween, they decided to wear fuzzy animal onesies.

They would make ten trades in all. They traded the paper clip for a gift certificate from a cheese shop, which they traded up for a box of cupcakes, which they traded up for a brooch, which they traded up for a travel mug, which they traded up for a gift card from a crêpe restaurant, which they traded up for a gift card from a nightclub, which they traded up for a bottle of cologne, which they traded up for a fancy camera bag, which they traded up for a fifteen-hundred-dollar oil painting. The final item was too big to fit into our classroom, so they invited us to come outside.

A Volkswagen Jetta was parked in front of the school, "Bigger and Better" scrawled across the windshield.

That last step—asking a car dealer to trade a used car for a painting—had felt like insanity. Manus and Tom weren't expecting to succeed, but they were prepared to call every dealership in the state. Can you guess how many they had to call?

One.

Caroline Heffernan, sales manager at Unique Auto Sales, had supported good causes in our community before, and hearing Manus and Tom frame their ask in a generous way inspired her to step up again. When our class met Caroline to thank her, she thanked us. Rents are high in our town, money is tight, and public transportation isn't great. Helping someone by providing a car is a game-changer. She blushed as she told us how good it felt to help people who were struggling.

Having achieved their outrageous goal, Manus and Tom reached out to IRIS, a local refugee resettlement agency, to donate the car to a refugee family. That mission was personal for Manus, whose own family had lost their home in Hurricane Katrina and found themselves dependent on compassionate strangers.

We got to meet our new neighbor when she came to receive the car. She was a young mom who had been working as an accountant in Afghanistan before her family was displaced by war, and now she was commuting two hours a day by bus to work in a factory. A car could be life-changing.

Two useful lessons emerge from the Bigger and Better game.

First, we're always framing, whether we know it or not. And second, frames have consequences. In class that year, most students had framed the Bigger and Better game in transactional terms—asking to swap for things other people didn't need, or touting the merits of whatever it was they had to offer. Manus and Tom took a different approach. They dreamed big, raising the stakes for themselves and for the people they met. Then they went out and framed their trade requests as an opportunity to play a game and be part of something beautiful. Even Derren Brown would have been proud to see the transfiguration of a humble paper clip into a car.

When you decide to try framing things more consciously, it can be hard to know where to begin. There exist an infinite number of possible frames, but the three most useful are *monumental, manageable,* and *mysterious*. Each can be motivating in its own way.

Monumental frames

A monumental frame tells the Gator, *Pay attention, this is a big freaking deal!* It motivates people through importance, size, scope, the fear of missing out, or all of the above. Monumental frames inspire enthusiasm and commitment. Manus and Tom framed the Bigger and Better game as monumentally exciting by setting their sights on a car—there was barely a shimmer of a chance that their crazy plan would succeed, yet their frame was so exciting that everyone wanted to be a part of it. And by helping to fulfill their dream, Caroline Heffernan gained legendary status too: Not only do we tell her story, but I hear its echoes from friends who tell other friends who tell other friends. Together Manus and Tom and Caroline made history at Yale and in New Haven.

Organizations often try to frame their work as monumental in their mission statements. Take General Motors' mission statement: "To create a future of zero crashes, zero emissions and zero congestion." Saving lives, saving the planet, and saving time. Who wouldn't be on board with that? They're inviting us to be part of something truly important. Even if you don't share the company's specific aspirations, their vision might inspire you to dream bigger. What would *your* ideal future world look like? What big problems would *you* like to eradicate completely and forever?

Consider, in contrast, Rolls-Royce's mission statement: "For over 100 years, motor cars of the Rolls-Royce brand have stood for truly outstanding engineering, quality, and reliability." Underwhelming, right? A hundred years is a big chunk of time, but it doesn't say anything about what's important here; and "truly outstanding" is just saying, "Take our word for it, we're really, really great."

You might expect mission-driven organizations to have inspiring mission statements. Sometimes they do. The Nature Conservancy is committed to "conserving the lands and waters on which all life depends." Preserving "all life" is monumental, full stop. Habitat for Humanity's mission statement is "Seeking to put God's love into action, we bring people together to build homes, communities and hope." For believers, what could be more monumental than putting God's love into action? And for nonbelievers, isn't it still inspiring to imagine building homes, communities, and hope?

On the other hand, consider the Museum of Modern Art in New York, which is "dedicated to being the foremost museum of modern art in the world." The world is big and "foremost" might be important, but for whom? Maybe employees? If you're a visitor or donor, do you care whether this museum beats out other museums (whatever that means), or would you be more inspired by some other frame?

Framing can also make or break political messaging and public policy campaigns. The reframing of the American tax code in 2001 shows that it's not *whether* you frame an issue as monumental but *how* you do it that counts. For a long time, Republicans had been looking for a way to get rid of, or at least weaken, the inheritance tax. This was far from a middle-class concern: Only the wealthiest 2 percent of Americans—those with estates valued at over $675,000—were subject to any inheritance tax at all. But Republican lawmakers wanted to raise this threshold in order to shield their big donors from inheritance taxes, so they needed to muster popular support. They reached out to pollster Frank Luntz, described by *The Atlantic* as America's top political wordsmith.

Luntz accepted the challenge and recruited hundreds of participants to his market research lab. There they were asked to consider various combinations of words and respond by turning a knob to the left (bad) or to the right (good). Respondents were also asked to react as quickly as they could. After a bit of practice, they could move the dial reflexively, recording their visceral responses with hardly any conscious thought at all. The Gator was in direct communication with Luntz's team.

When the inheritance tax was framed as an "estate tax," Luntz found that participants felt it was a good idea, regardless of their party affiliation. An *estate* sounds monumentally large, so if you have one you must be filthy rich and probably should be paying taxes, right? But when Luntz tested an alternative frame, the "death tax," nearly 80 percent of participants disliked it, including a majority of Democrats. Taxing someone for *dying*? That's just not right! And what could be more monumental than matters of life and death? Luntz reported his findings in a widely circulated memo. "If you want to kill the estate tax," he advised, "call it a death tax."

The new frame proved effective with lawmakers as well as voters. Over the next twenty years, Congress increased the $675,000 exemption threshold several times. By 2021, individuals could pass down to their heirs up to $11.7 million tax-free, and married couples could double that amount.

Manageable

A monumental frame can motivate people and inspire them to action, but some problems already feel *too* big, too daunting. In these cases, you might frame them as *manageable* instead. A monumental frame emphasizes *why* (It's important!), and a manageable frame emphasizes *how* (It's not that hard). You've already learned that ease is the best predictor of behavior; that's why a *manageable* frame is so powerful. Frames like "just pennies a day" work by making the prospect of a sizable contribution to your local public radio station, for instance, feel manageable. *You've got this*. Cheaper than a cup of coffee. Baby steps.

When a problem feels too big to handle, the Gator is tempted to ignore it. But ignoring a big problem, such as credit card debt, only allows it to grow. What if you were to give people the choice to pay off credit card expenses by category? Would it make the debt feel more manageable and motivate them to pay it off faster?

Grant Donnelly, Cait Lamberton, Stephen Bush, Mike Norton, and I set up an experiment in which credit card customers could see how much they owed in categories like "entertainment," "restaurants," etc. Rather than thinking, *Can I pay off the whole balance? Nope*, customers could be asking themselves, *Can I pay off my transportation expenses? Hm, maybe*. Achieving small, immediate goals creates a sense of momentum and persistence in the pursuit of larger ones. In the case of credit card debt, the small, immediate goal can be to pay off the cable bill, while the higher goal can be to become debt-free. We ran our field study with the Commonwealth Bank of Australia, inviting half their credit card customers to allocate their debt repayments by category. The 2,157 people who did choose to allocate their payments by category paid back their debts 12 percent faster than the control group.

A manageable frame can be particularly effective when you want to help people who are facing fears, grief, or doubts. It can be counterproductive and hurtful, however, to diminish their feelings with assurances like "There's nothing to worry about." Instead, let them know that they're not alone and that their feelings are totally normal—which can make them feel more manageable.

This kind of frame is particularly helpful when you're in a position of power or even just older and more experienced. I'm in a unique position to be able to normalize my students' fears because I was a student myself for a long time and because I've known so many students who have been in similar situations. Graduation is coming and you have no job? That's normal. Panicked on the PhD job market? It's normal. Lots of crying? Normal. It sucks, it's awful, and it's normal. You can't solve these problems, but you can help people live with them. You can normalize by sharing your own problems and experiences, and again, this helps even more when you have authority or status. When a student comes to me in pain, I don't hide that I too have been depressed, gotten divorced, doubted myself, done stupid things, lost loved ones, gone to therapy, or freaked out. All normal. Problems feel more manageable when you have the comfort of knowing you're not alone.

Monumental or Manageable?

In June 1988, NASA scientist James Hansen testified before Congress on the greenhouse effect, the natural process that allows gases in the atmosphere to trap heat radiating from the earth. In the right proportions, greenhouse gases like carbon dioxide and methane support life on the planet, but human activities like burning fossil fuels can throw off the balance. In his testimony, Hansen used the phrase "global warming" to describe the causal relationship between the greenhouse effect and the rising temperatures scientists were observing around the globe. His testimony was widely covered by journalists and news organizations, who picked up on the term "global warming."

Hansen had created a monumental frame—global warming involves the entire planet, after all—but it failed to reflect many people's day-to-day experiences, and frames don't work unless they resonate. If the globe is warming, why did it snow so much this year? And is warming really that much of a problem? If you live in a cold climate, you might be grateful for more warm weather.

Fossil fuel companies and their political allies did their best to stoke skepticism, and Frank Luntz—the same researcher who had reframed estate taxes—used his dial testing apparatus again. This time his goal was to reframe global warming to emphasize scientific uncertainty on the issue and make it sound less frightening. The new term he settled on? "Climate change." This frame was sticky because it seemed more accurate: Earth's climate was certainly changing, no debate about that. But, for the normal person who equates climate and weather, a changing climate didn't feel like something new. It seemed natural. The weather was always changing, wasn't it?

"Climate change" also made rising global temperatures feel manageable. Nature is always changing, and haven't we always dealt with it? In 2001, President Bush had used the phrase "global warming" frequently in his talking points. By 2002, however, as Republicans converged around the term "climate change," Bush's use of "global warming" decreased to only a few mentions. The Bush administration had a new frame, and so did everyone else.

"Climate change" marched on, oblivious to what anyone called it.*

Nearly two decades later, researchers at a neuromarketing agency decided to test alternative frames to find the one that would have the best chance of motivating people to take action on global warming. They recruited participants from across the political spectrum and measured their Gator brain physiological reactions as they listened to six different phrases describing the climate situation. Electrodes attached to the scalp measured brain activity, electrodes attached to the palms measured sweat, and a webcam tracked facial expressions. The combined results reflected the intensity of each person's emotional response. "Climate change" elicited the weakest response, followed by "global warming." The winning frame? "Climate crisis." That phrase elicited reactions 60 percent stronger for Democrats and 200 percent stronger for Republicans than "climate change" did. A "crisis" is monumental yet potentially manageable. "Climate crisis" says it's not too late—yet—but if we don't take massive action immediately, it soon will be.

In 2018, Al Gore and his Climate Reality Project launched an initiative calling on news organizations to reframe "climate change" to "climate crisis," to communicate how dire the situation had become. That term, and "climate emergency" became the preferred frame for major news outlets across the world, and for António Guterres, secretary-general of the United Nations. Google searches for "climate crisis" were five

---

* Climate change hit home for Frank Luntz in 2017 when he awoke at three o'clock in the morning to an emergency warning blaring and flames outside his window as the Skirball Fire raged. He was safely evacuated, but the fire burned more than 400 acres in the Bel Air neighborhood of Los Angeles. After this experience, Luntz would turn to assisting efforts to mitigate the climate crisis, which was becoming a bipartisan issue.

times higher in 2019 than they had been in 2018, and "climate emergency" made the shortlist for Oxford Dictionaries' word of the year. How these urgent frames will influence behavior remains to be seen.

Mysterious

Try reading the following sentence: *The mnid deos not raed ervey lteter by istlef, but the wrod as a wlohe.* Strangely easy, isn't it? That's your visual processing system making guesses. The third powerful frame, *mysterious,* is effective because it disrupts this guessing process and the expectations that go with it. Mysterious frames speak directly to the Gator by introducing change or uncertainty—exactly what the Gator is attuned to. New threats. New opportunities. Intrigue.

Words and phrases like "new," "suddenly," or "breaking news" are mysterious frames that spark curiosity about what has changed. Words like "mystery," "secret," or "reveal," or topics framed as questions spark that same underlying uncertainty that piques our curiosity. Mysterious frames attract the Gator's attention. When it can't fill in the missing details, it alerts the Judge to take on the case. But *this requires mental resources.* So, the flip side of this phenomenon is that once a cognitive process has been completed, we don't need to focus on it anymore, and it's no longer top of mind.

In the 1920s, doctoral student Bluma Zeigarnik was chatting with her adviser, Kurt Lewin, and some academic friends in a café in Berlin. Impressed by their server's flawless memory—he could deliver complicated orders to large groups without ever writing anything down—they decided to test it. After covering their plates and cups with their napkins, they called the server back, asking him to list the items he had just delivered to the table. To his own surprise, he had forgotten many of them. You may have experienced the same mnemonic oddity when you crammed for an exam. You remembered the facts you needed for the test, and then poof! They vanished from your mind. If you had needed to retake the exam a few days later, you would have been as clueless as the restaurant server.

When Zeigarnik decided to investigate this phenomenon in lab experiments, she found that participants were able to recall more details of incomplete tasks than completed ones. Subsequent researchers dubbed this need for completion the "Zeigarnik effect" and confirmed it repeatedly. Incomplete tasks or unresolved questions engage—and sometimes hijack—our attention. Once the uncertainty is resolved, however, working memory clears the decks to make room for new information. The Zeigarnik effect explains why you forge ahead to finish a dumb movie or a boring article, why you obsess over trying to remember the name of that actor even though it doesn't matter, and why I fall for clickbait like "Did Neanderthals die because they didn't have jackets?" (Apparently not.)

Relatedly, progress toward a goal feels rewarding—and even more rewarding as you get closer to completion. It's one of the reasons coffee shops offer punch cards to track your progress toward a free coffee, videogames have a series of levels to complete, and it's hard to stop reading a listicle like "10 Big Financial Mistakes" at number four.

Combining Frames

These three powerful frames—monumental, manageable, and mysterious—can also combine forces. There's no need to limit yourself to one. When Manus and Tom started trading that first paper clip, they not only let participants know they had an opportunity to participate in something monumental. (We're trying to trade up for A CAR! It can change someone's life!) They also made it clear that what they were asking for was totally manageable. (All you need to do is trade one thing with us.) Combining those two frames turned out to be very effective.

One of my favorite examples of combining all three powerful frames comes from a book about how to organize your house. Personally, I can't imagine a less appealing topic. But when I saw a small volume by an author I had never heard of named Marie Kondo, titled *The Life-Changing Magic of Tidying Up,* I was drawn to it. Life-Changing = Monumental! Magic = Mysterious! Tidying Up = Manageable! All three frames in just six words.

The result of Marie Kondo's masterful framing? An international mega-bestseller published in forty languages. More than eleven million copies sold. And a television show about cleaning your house. Such is the power of mastering these three simple frames. Did Marie Kondo need to deliver on those promises as well? Naturally. And did she? Absolutely. Could the book have done as well if it had been published under its subtitle, "The Japanese Art of Decluttering and Organizing"? You decide.

Framing in Action

Now that you're familiar with the three big frames, you're going to start seeing them everywhere, and you'll notice their effects on you. Here are some lists to help you get started on using these frames yourself.

MONUMENTAL	MANAGEABLE	MYSTERIOUS
The large: everyone, everything, galaxy, global, planet, population, universe, world **The extreme:** always, billion, bliss, catastrophe, chasm, cosmic, crisis, devil, epic, disaster, divine, ecstasy, epidemic, eternal, existential, freak, law, legend, millennium, million, never, revolution **The dramatic:** army, battle, betrayal, clash, courage, danger, dare, desire, enemies, explode, fearless, kill, murder, power, rebel, rivals, survival, threat, war	**The simple things to do:** habit, hack, game, project, tweak **The small amounts of time:** day, hour, instant, minute, moment **The effectiveness:** be, can, DIY, do, help, how to, make, solution **The small numbers:** 1, 2, 3, top 10 . . . **The togetherness, sharing the burden:** our, together, us, we	**The uncertain:** if, impossible, improbable, why **The changing:** kindle, new, spark, transformation **The creative:** art, imagine, innovation, original, unique, wonder **The secrets to be revealed:** confession, cult, dark, debunk, hidden, invisible, lies, myth, science, secret, surprise **The supernatural:** enchant, magic, manifest, monster, spirit

In summary, framing is a simple tool for unlocking the secrets of massive power. (See what I did there?)

What Business Are You In?

Here's how a new frame dramatically changed how I approach my work.

When Danny Meyer, the restaurateur behind famous eateries like the Union Square Cafe and Gramercy Tavern, came to speak at Yale School of Management, he suggested a new frame. "You're all in the hospitality business," he told us. It was an invitation to see our work with fresh eyes.

In my early career as a professor, I was still trying to prove that I knew what I was talking about, so I bragged that my job was "teaching Jedi mind tricks." That made the class sound mysterious and made me a Jedi master—sort of. The reality was that I was trying to be the star of the show, the director, and the stage manager all at once. My MBA course has a lot of moving parts, and I would rush into class each day focused on logistics. I thought building a tight-knit community in just a few weeks required stringent social norms and rules, so I leaned on my teaching assistants to enforce them. There were gobs of assignments to be handed in and graded, and I was frazzled whenever anybody missed a deadline.

A teaching assistant I really liked complained to me, "After taking your class I thought it was going to be fun to work with you, but you're really not motivating me to do a good job." I was frustrated. Should it be my job to motivate her to do her job? Students were swarming me before and after class, and I was too busy to listen to them either. I was saving my focused attention for teaching, when I could shine. In every other moment, I was overwhelmed.

Danny Meyer's hospitality frame prompted me to ask myself, *What would it look like to be hosting the class rather than teaching it?*

This new frame changed everything. I was able to genuinely shift my attention from myself to the students; at a party, it's the guests who are important. It shifted the course's power dynamics; a host isn't in charge of her guests, she's serving them. And a host isn't telling anyone what to do, she's just inviting people to take part in something wonderful.

The frame also released me from my own exacting standards. A Jedi master is supposed to be perfect, but a host can burn the pie or have cat hair on the sofa. A student is supposed to please the teacher by attending every session and completing each assignment, but a guest can show up late, leave early, or spill wine on the carpet without the host taking it personally. Grading still had to happen, but we didn't need all those rigid rules.

Even as the new frame helped me focus better on the students' experiences, it freed me from feeling responsible for them. A host can't guarantee that every guest will have the time of their lives; that's out of her control. But she can light the candles, turn on the music, and try to make sure nobody drives home drunk. She can say, "It's wonderful to see you. I'm so happy you're here." And she can mean it.

When I hired new teaching assistants, I would enlist their help. "This is our party, and we are the hosts." Instead of rushing in at the last minute, we showed up early, smiling and welcoming our guests. We worked hard to memorize their names. An attentive host seeks out the person who's sitting alone, so I reached out to students who were falling behind. Not to chastise, just to see how they were doing. Since a host helps guests get to know each other, I switched from individual to group office hours—more about them and less about me.

I let students know we could talk about anything. I would stick around after class with no agenda and no rush even when we had to shift to a virtual platform. I continued office hours even after the term was over, for anyone who wanted to join. I stopped requiring or even taking attendance; as a host, you want your guests to come because *they* want to. On any given day, by their own free choice, about 90 percent of the students would show up for class. Many never missed a single one.

Our class is still a class in the end. But when I see students as my guests, work ultimately feels *to me* more like a party, and I become a better, happier teacher. Maybe you want to ask yourself how things might change if *you* were in the hospitality business. If not that, ask yourself, what "business" do you want to be in?

CHAPTER SIX

Inner Two-Year-Olds

> Because wise rulers love the people, they lead without
> using force. While protecting the people, they do not
> control them.
>
> —Lao Tzu, *Tao Te Ching*

It tells you a lot about our family that my dad once caught a live baby rattlesnake, mailed it to his mother in a Coke bottle, and she was delighted. Dad's a rebel who comes by it honestly. His first notable rebellion was when he decided at age six to quit piano lessons by running away from home. He collected supplies for weeks and then climbed through the window with a knapsack and his little sister, Kathy. The children hid out in the woods until their parents called the school and eventually the police. They would have stayed longer if Kathy hadn't betrayed them by shouting out, "Daddy!" when she heard their father's voice.

One of my most memorable childhood moments with Dad involved racing through the woods at night, splashing through the creek and diving for cover as the spotlights of a police chopper scanned the underbrush for us. We hadn't done anything too terrible, just setting off fireworks so big and so illegal Dad had had to order them from China on the black market. Dad didn't mind breaking rules, norms, or even laws when he could do it without hurting anyone, because he has always believed you should be the boss of your own life.

He'll resist you even if you actually are his boss and he likes his job. He'll resist you even if you're his wife and he loves you to bits. When my stepmom quite reasonably demanded that Dad stop setting up targets in the woods and limit his shooting to the gun range, he secretly purchased a large metal box called a bullet trap. During lightning storms when my stepmom wasn't home and thunderclaps would distract the neighbors, Dad would set the bullet trap in the fireplace and we'd shoot at it with his .22 caliber pistol. Although he may be more rebellious than some, that tendency doesn't make him unique. In fact, you could say that his impulse to resist sort of makes Dad a conformist. It's normal to perceive restrictions, and even persuasion, as a threat.

Our brains emphasize threat detection because our survival has depended on it. To avoid calamity, the Gator is constantly scanning the environment for potential threats. Threat detection happens quickly so that you can react quickly. Which sometimes means overreacting quickly. Have you seen those online videos of cats freaking out about cucumbers? Because it looks sort of like a snake, a cucumber placed behind a cat while it's eating will send the cat exploding off the floor and ricocheting off walls and tables when the long, green object catches its eye. So mean but so funny.

Human brains aren't that different from cat brains. Not only do we identify threatening images faster than other images, but our brains can alert us to those threats before we even know what we're seeing. Phobia researcher Arne Öhman used electrodes to monitor participants as they viewed a series of pictures. Some pictures were benign, like flowers, and some were potential threats, like spiders and snakes. Each image was displayed for only a thirtieth of a second—far too quickly for most people to consciously recognize what they were. But the Gator reacted. When a snake or a spider image whizzed by, viewers began to sweat.

Try this experiment. Take a look at the blurred images below and see if you can identify the bird, the cat, the fish, and the snake.

If you see nothing there at all, no worries; I don't either. But when people are forced to guess, their instincts skew toward danger. Were you able to guess the cat (D), the fish (C), or the bird (A)? What about the snake (B)? When threat detection researchers Nobuyuki Kawai and Hongshen He showed volunteers these images, about half could identify the less threatening

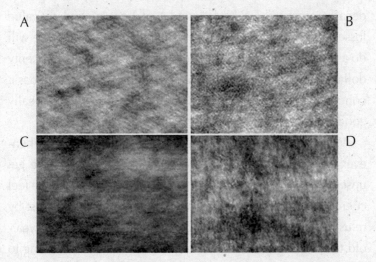

animals. But a full 75 percent could tell that B was a snake. The researchers tested varying degrees of blurriness and at all of them, people were most accurate at identifying snakes. Because snakes are potential threats.

The Gator is extraordinarily sensitive to danger. Even if you have the best intentions, someone you are trying to influence might feel you're threatening to take away their time, attention, money, or other valuable resources. This is why some people will say no when it seems to make no sense. Or before they've even been willing to listen to your great idea. Their Gator is tipping the scales.

It's not just threat detection that sparks resistance to influence. You're also up against a universal bias called *loss aversion*. When people evaluate opportunities for what they might gain versus what they would have to give up, they weigh losses far more heavily than gains. Daniel Kahneman and Amos Tversky's research on this phenomenon fueled the discipline of behavioral economics in the 1970s and ultimately led to a Nobel Prize in 2002. Over myriad experiments during the past five decades, researchers have found that people tend to value losses about twice as heavily as similarly sized gains. We will do as much to avoid losing ten dollars as we will to gain twenty dollars. For influencers, the ratio is less important than the basic concept: For a change to feel worth it, it has to be really, really good. This mental calculus favors the status quo.

What people most hate to give up is their freedom. Whenever a perceived liberty is taken away or threatened, we get upset and do whatever it takes to try to restore it. When we feel coerced to act in a certain way, we may respond not just by refusing but by doing the opposite thing. Our inner two-year-old takes charge. At the faintest hint that someone is trying to control us, the two-year-old screams, YOU'RE NOT THE BOSS OF ME! DON'T TELL ME WHAT TO DO! This phenomenon is called *psychological reactance*.

In a classic reactance experiment with actual two-year-olds, researchers invited children to the lab and asked which of two toys they wanted to play with, the easily accessible toy or the one behind a tall, Plexiglas barrier. As you might guess, they consistently picked the toy behind the barrier, regardless of which one it was. We want freedom of choice, and when someone tries to limit it, we're inclined to push back. When Derren Brown said, "Just keep your eyes focused on the easel," he knew that command would prompt our inner two-year-old to look around instead.

See what I mean?

When I worked for a company that was losing money, we understood when they cut our bonuses. But we got furious

CHICKEN GAME:
DON'T LOOK AT THE CHICKEN

when corporate bean counters decided to quit stocking hot chocolate packets in the break rooms because hot chocolate was more expensive than coffee. For a brief time hot chocolate was the topic of every hallway conversation.

Then I realized that not only had *I* not been drinking hot chocolate, I couldn't actually remember ever having seen *anyone* drink hot chocolate. Why was I so angry? Each time someone complained, I asked if they had been drinking it. They all said, "Well, no. *I* don't drink it, but it's still outrageous." It's not that we couldn't stand losing the hot chocolate. We just couldn't stand losing our freedom to choose hot chocolate if someday we might want to.

Behaviorist B. F. Skinner observed that people don't mind giving money to the government in the form of lottery tickets because it's a matter of choice. Being forced to pay taxes, however, makes a lot of us angry even though we depend on the roads, schools, and other services they fund. Having to pay taxes is like being forced to wear a mask during a pandemic— a win for the common good that comes at the risk of provoking a backlash.

In 2010, a movement called Meatless Monday was trying to nudge people to eat less meat. Some people think a meal isn't complete without meat. But what if they could experience delicious, filling, meatless meals one day a week? Maybe they'd become more open-minded. It was a baby step.

The Google Food team decided to try Meatless Mondays at their company headquarters in Mountain View, California. They would test it first as a pilot project on Mondays in September when two Google cafés would stop serving pork, beef, and chicken (though they would serve fish). There would still be twenty-two other cafés serving meat every day on the Google campus, so most employees didn't mind. But those who did weren't shy about their feelings. The food team got messages like this:

> Stop trying to tell me how to live my life. If you don't
> want to provide us the traditional food benefits then
> shut all the cafes down. Seriously, stop this *** or I'll go
> to Microsoft, Twitter, or Facebook, where they don't f***
> with us.

The reaction didn't stop at email. Disgruntled employees hosted a protest barbecue right outside the Meatless Monday café. Google got the message, and the company's experiment with Meatless Monday came to an end.

Looking back on it, a big part of the problem was the frame. While "meatless" was accurate, it was emphasizing loss. *We're taking your meat away.* Google was restricting the freedom of its employees. The subtext was a problem, too. *Why* were employees being told to go meatless? Maybe for health reasons, for the good of the animals who would otherwise be eaten, or to benefit the planet. But honestly, any of these explanations can get tricky and leave people feeling judged, which makes them more likely to resist. Or to dig in deeper just to spite you. What could a more effective approach to promoting a plant-based diet look like?

Ethan Brown has five dogs, two horses, a cat, a turtle, and a potbellied pig named Wilbur. When he was growing up, his family owned a dairy farm and he loved animals. He also loved meat, particularly burgers. His favorite sandwich was Roy Rogers's Double R Bar Burger: a quarter pound of ground beef smeared with melted cheese and layered with thinly sliced deli ham. Mmmm. Delicious. But Ethan was a philosophical child who wondered why we cuddle dogs and cut up pigs. He gave up eating animals, then gave up being vegetarian, and then gave up eating animals again. It was hard.

Ethan knew he would never go back to eating animals, though, when he learned that industrial livestock might be hurting the planet as much as fossil fuels were. He was working on hydrogen fuel cells at the time, a new, more sustainable source of fuel to replace petroleum. He wondered, what if there could be a new, more sustainable source of meat to replace animals?

Ethan Brown would reframe meat. What if meat meant the combination of proteins, fats, and flavors that look and taste a particular way but don't necessarily come from animals? He reached out to two professors at the University of Missouri who were already experimenting with plant-based proteins in their lab. With a growing team of researchers, Ethan would figure out how to strip protein molecules from plants and reconfigure them to create the taste and the texture of chicken, beef, and pork. They made brats and burgers, strips and sausages. They even mimicked blood using beet juice. Production of their plant-based meat would require 99 percent less water and 93 percent less land, and would emit 90 percent fewer greenhouse gases than the production of animal meat.

Having been a meat lover himself, Ethan anticipated the resistance his vision would trigger. He understood that when food is framed as healthy, some people translate that to mean it tastes bad or that their ordinary eating habits are being frowned upon. And he understood that meat eaters (like everyone else) don't like to hear that their choices make them bad people.

Keeping all this in mind, Ethan decided not to frame the benefits of the meatless burgers around virtue. Instead he focused on deliciousness, naming his new product Beyond Meat. Like meat, only better! Vegetarians might resist a frame like that, but Ethan was trying to reach meat eaters. He stocked Beyond Meat in the butcher section of the grocery store rather than in the health food aisle. He decided to forgo the colorful cardboard packaging of veggie burgers and sold Beyond Burgers in a cellophane-covered tray so they looked like other meat products.

To underscore the message that they weren't trying to force anyone to be healthy, Ethan and his team partnered with fast-food restaurants to offer plant-based alternatives to their regular fare. Not low-calorie rabbit food, but gooey cheeseburgers, hot meatball subs, and smoky breakfast sausage sandwiches—plant-based versions of what people were already craving. Beyond Meat never claimed the moral high ground, and its marketing involved no pressure.

Other brands paid celebrity spokespeople to promote their products, but Ethan and his team took the opposite approach. They reached out to famous athletes to *ask* for money instead. Kyrie Irving, Chris Paul, and Shaquille O'Neal all came on board as investors in the company.

In 2018, few Americans had heard the term "plant-based meat," but by the end of 2019, more than 40 percent had tried it—and the majority were meat eaters. Beyond Meat tripled its sales that year to $98.5 million. By 2021, Beyond Meat products were being sold in a hundred thousand restaurants and grocery stores in eighty countries. Pizza Hut was selling Beyond Pan Pizzas and McDonald's had announced a new McPlant Burger, developed in conjunction with Beyond Meat.

Ethan Brown had become a millionaire many times over and would be delivering the commencement address at his alma mater. By anticipating resistance to "meatless" and "healthy," and by directing attention instead to "deliciousness," Ethan succeeded in providing customers with a healthy, more sustainable alternative to eating animals.

Meatless Monday and Beyond Meat illustrate how psychology plays an important role in any influence attempt. Are people experiencing your big idea as pressure or as an invitation? As a painful loss or an irresistible gain? In this next section, we'll look at what you can do when someone is objecting—or you think they might object—to your suggestion. You'll learn how you can open yourself to their resistance without getting caught in a struggle and how you can come back after hearing no without bothering them.

Handling Objections Like an Aikido Master

The core principle of aikido is to respond to an attack by redirecting your opponent's momentum while trying to protect both of you from injury. *Aikido* means "the way of harmonious spirit." It is in this spirit that I offer you the following strategies for handling another person's objections, which you might otherwise experience as a mild form of attack. If you respond with your own attack, they're likely to fight back, becoming more committed to their own views and decisions. Here's what you might try instead. This isn't a step-by-step process; it's a menu to pick and choose from, as many options as you like.

Witness and explore their resistance

I've mentioned that a master salesperson might return many times after hearing no. What makes them welcome (instead of annoying) is that they've asked for and received permission and they've learned to be present with other people's resistance. If the other person isn't ready to say yes, they don't take it personally. Instead, they're receptive and curious. They don't push back or give up; they lean in and listen even if what's being expressed isn't pleasant or easy to hear.

Bearing witness to resistance means observing it without judgment. By not pushing back or jumping in or making the situation about you—by simply focusing your attention on the other person, listening, and expressing what you observe or intuit—you create space for them to say what they're feeling and get it off their chest.

Resistance wants to be witnessed. If you think you know what the other person will object to or you sense resistance around a particular issue, an aikido move is to put it into words before they do: "You might be thinking we won't have enough time." Or "This may sound like a lot of money." Or "I may seem a little young for a director role." By reading the other person's mind and articulating the objection, you free their attention from the voice in their head so they can listen to you. You've also shown yourself to be a smart and reasonable person, since you see their point of view.

This doesn't mean you have to guess right every time. It can be helpful just to say, "I can see you have some doubts." By showing that you're considering their feelings, you're establishing a sense of kinship. If the other person has already expressed an objection (say, someone already tried your idea and it failed), then they'll be expecting you to counterattack. Instead, you can take a breath and calmly wait for them to share more, or you can bear witness by reflecting their feelings back to them: "Wow, what a disaster." "That must have been so frustrating." "If I were you, I'd feel that way too"—which, of course, is always true.

Taking a step further, you can gently explore the nature of their resistance. Getting curious about it, rather than defensive, encourages them to let their guard down. You might say, "Could you tell me more about that?" Or "And then what happened?" Or "I think I know what you mean but say more." This open-minded approach can be disarming as well as informative.

If "tell me more about that" isn't appropriate, you can invite the other person to open up by reflecting back their statement as a question. If they say they just don't feel like it, you can reply, "You don't feel like it?" This aikido move says, *I want to be sure I understand you.* Because people want to be understood, they're likely to elaborate if it seems like you don't understand them, and you'll get information that could be useful. You can also probe to see if there are other issues that they haven't brought up yet: "And what else is on your mind?" "That's probably not your only concern. Is there anything else we should be talking about?" "What other concerns do you have?" You can practice this approach whenever someone is complaining, even if those gripes have nothing to do with you. People will love you for it.

Affirm their freedom of choice

Technically, people always have the freedom to choose. Even if you hold a gun to someone's head when you ask for their wallet, they still have to choose to hand it over. But people won't *feel* free to choose if you're pushing your agenda on them. And if they feel coerced, they'll resist—either in the moment or later—by looking for a way out.

When I'm hoping to influence someone, I like them to know that they're in control, free to choose either way. My motive here is both generous and selfish. It's generous because feeling in control makes people happier. It's also selfish because, as we've discussed, making it more comfortable for people to say no makes them more willing to say yes. This doesn't mean they'll always comply, but it means that if they don't, they probably have a good reason. Furthermore, if they do say yes without coercion, they'll feel responsible for their choice. This makes them feel better about the decision they've made and helps that decision stick. Research shows that after complying with a gentle nudge to lie, for instance, people become more receptive to believing the lie. (This isn't how we want to influence people, but it's interesting, isn't it?)

You can affirm someone's freedom of choice by asking for permission to ask. People are constantly thrusting things at us: meeting invitations, blog links, books we might like, helpful pieces of advice. You don't want to be one of those people, aside from the fact that everyone's instinctual response to unsolicited stuff is *no*. (In one study, a free money sign made people walk on by or cross the street to avoid the researchers giving away fifty-dollar bills.) Instead, share with someone the briefest possible version of your great idea and ask if they'd like to hear more: "Is that something that might interest you?" "Would you like me to send you a link?"

Requesting permission to ask sounds like this: "Could I ask your advice?" "Can we talk about what went wrong?" "Could we have a conversation about my career path?" "Could we meet to discuss my pay?" You can also ask when a good time would be. If they agree to a time, they're also agreeing to listen with as much of an open mind as they can muster. You might also ask how they'd prefer to communicate—email, phone call, videoconference, meet up for coffee, etc. Some people have strong preferences and would feel they had already sacrificed something if they had to communicate in your preferred mode instead of theirs.

Asking consent before sharing advice is an aikido move because while people are naturally resistant to pressure, they're also naturally curious. They might not have been seeking advice, but when you say, "I might know something that would help. Would you like to hear about it?" curiosity makes it hard to refuse. This is the Zeigarnik effect in action again. And when they do say yes, they'll be more open to your idea because listening was their choice.

This might seem a little odd, but you can also affirm their freedom of choice by actually stating that they're free to choose. Of course, you're not granting them freedom of choice; they've got that already. And you're not saying you'll be equally happy no matter what happens. You're just affirming the fundamental truth that they are already free. In addition to not pressuring them, you're letting them know you're not pressuring them—

which suggests you won't be pressuring them in the future, either. You might try some of these phrases to let them off the hook: "No pressure." "Feel free to say no." "I know you must be busy, so I won't take it personally if you say no." "Please don't say yes unless you're completely comfortable." "It's completely up to you." Or even, "I'm not the boss of you." I use these phrases a lot in part because they're useful, but also because I really mean them. I want people to say yes only if it really feels right.

When there's a hierarchical difference, you'll want to be sensitive to how you affirm the other person's freedom of choice. If they have higher status, then saying "It's completely up to you" could fall flat. They already know the decision is up to them. But in that case a statement like "I know you must be busy, so I won't take it personally if you say no" might be welcome. They are busy, they appreciate your recognition of that, and they probably prefer not to hurt your feelings. When you're reaffirming the freedom of someone of lower status, you'll want to be careful not to accidentally pressure them. If you say, "It's up to you" but your tone of voice conveys, *But I'll be very disappointed with you if you make the wrong decision,* that won't feel like freedom.

Softening resistance with a soft ask

After someone refuses your request, it's difficult to get them to change their mind. (This is related to the psychological wrinkle we discussed a little earlier: People tend to give additional weight to their own decisions once they've made them.) A better approach would be to gauge how they're feeling by asking a hypothetical question that doesn't lock them in. I call it a *soft ask*.*

A soft ask sounds like this: "Is this the kind of thing you might be interested in?" Or "If I were to ask you _____ , what would you think?" Or "How comfortable would you feel doing _____?" Or "I'm not trying to push you to decide, but where would you say we are right now between one and ten, if ten is all in and one is never going to happen?"

Soft asks are effective for lots of reasons, but mostly they offer a low-risk way to gain valuable information. There's no point in wasting your time or theirs discussing something that's never going to happen. There's also no point in wasting time if they're already all in. Additionally, soft asks protect feelings on both sides when there's a rejection. Let's say you're attracted to a friend and want to explore the possibilities. If you pose the question hypothetically ("How would you feel about going on a date sometime?") and they tell you they'd rather just stay friends, that will hurt a little but it won't cost too much. It was just a thought, and the two of you can probably still hang out. But if you ask a direct question like "Will you go out on a date with me?" and you get a direct refusal, this will make it harder for the two of you to stay friends.

A soft ask is also a smart move when you're requesting a work reference or a letter of recommendation. Instead of asking, "Would you write me a letter of recommendation?" ask, "Would you feel comfortable writing me a strong letter of recommendation?" or "Would you feel comfortable giving me a strong reference?" This approach makes it easier for the other person to say no, and you definitely want that to be easy. Why?

* If you've worked in sales, this is related to the concept of a "test close."

Because the soft ask protects you from getting a lukewarm recommendation that could torpedo your chances. And if your recommender does say yes, they'll support you as enthusiastically as they can, having freely committed to doing so.

The Kindly Brontosaurus

If a master salesperson goes back to a prospective client six or seven times after getting a no, how many times do you think the *average* salesperson goes back? Three times. How many times do you think the average person (not working in sales), checks back after hearing no? Yep, zero. Persistence is an underappreciated virtue.

One beloved influence model for my students is the *Kindly Brontosaurus*: a gentle herbivore that doesn't take no for an answer. This is a deceptively passive technique, and it's simple—pretty much all you have to do is wait. But you're *not* waiting invisibly in a corner with your fingers crossed. No, like a conspicuous dinosaur, you'll remain optimistically in view: *Hello! It's me here. (Still.) Just checking in!* The Kindly Brontosaurus is patient, polite, and persistent. You ask for what you want, then you step back. You check back in. You wait, and you check, for as long as it takes. Nobody can get angry at—and no one can ignore—the Kindly Brontosaurus. And it's hard to keep refusing such a benign being. Persistence and nonaggression can be an irresistible combination.

Journalist and author Jessica Winter describes how the Kindly Brontosaurus secures a seat on a packed flight. When the agent tells you there's not a chance, you amicably reply that you're sure something can be worked out. Then you step back. Winter writes:

You must stand quietly and lean forward slightly, hands loosely clasped in a faintly prayerful arrangement. You will be in the gate agent's peripheral vision—close enough that he can't escape your presence, not so close that you're crowding him—but you must keep your eyes fixed placidly on the agent's face at all times. Assemble your features in an understanding, even beatific expression. Do not speak unless asked a question. Whenever the gate agent says anything, whether to you or other would-be passengers, you must nod empathically. Continue as above until the gate agent gives you your seat number. The Kindly Brontosaurus always gets a seat number.

When my former student Tiago Cruz received an offer to work at a large consulting firm after graduation, he made a crazy ask: Might it be possible to get a company car? New MBAs don't get company cars in any firm I've ever heard of, but Tiago is the kind of person you want to say yes to, and they did. Later, however, they apologized. Actually managers weren't allowed to have company cars. Tiago said, "Ah that's too bad! Well, hopefully we can work something out." He checked back in the next month, saying how excited he would be if they might be able to figure out a way to do this, even though it was crazy. Still no. The next month, still no. He was relentlessly, persistently friendly. And hopeful. Checking back in, month after month, until, to my utter surprise, the company worked something out.

One of the best ways you can show respect while still being persistent is to ask if you can ask again. And when. Then, when you're following up, you can say, "You mentioned it was okay for me to check in with you on Friday afternoon. Is this still a good time?" Pay attention to both nonverbal and verbal cues when you follow up. This is the moment to find out whether you're welcome or you're being a pest.

You won't persist after every no (please don't do this in romantic situations), and you won't want to waste your time. Top salespeople persist only after figuring out who might be open to the idea *and* able to commit to it; then they invest in those relationships. In their jargon, they won't put in the time unless they've qualified a lead. They don't keep going back to everybody.

What handling objections might sound like

When we cover objections in class, students practice by role-playing. If you find a partner to practice a real-life scenario with, they'll play the role of you and you'll play the resistant person. Usually, students pick a job or school-related situation to practice, like a problem with a boss or teammate. But Niv Weisenberg wanted us to help him handle his wife's resistance to getting a puppy. He was quiet and funny, the kind of person you want to see succeed, and we were all rooting for him to get that puppy (because . . . puppies).

Aikido practice with Niv sounded something like this.

Witness and explore their resistance

HE: Could you help me understand what the biggest obstacle is, in your mind, to us getting a puppy?

SHE: It's the work, but not just the training. It's like having a child.

HE: Like having a child?

SHE: The walks, the training, the having to get home to let her outside. The crying at night when she's being crate trained. And traveling becomes more complicated.

HE: It does sound like a lot of work. And it sounds like you're assuming you'd have to take it on.

SHE: Well, yeah. Because you've never had a dog and you have no idea what you'd be getting into.

HE: I can understand you not wanting to take on a lot of extra work. Is there anything else that bothers you about the idea of having a puppy?

SHE: Well, the dog couldn't sleep in our bed, for sure. You know I get cranky if I don't get good sleep.

Affirm their freedom of choice

HE: Ha, ha, I sure do. We'd have to figure out the work and the sleep. And of course we couldn't get a puppy unless you wanted to.

SHE: Yeah, okay.

Soften resistance with a soft ask

HE: Can I ask, hypothetically, if you didn't have to do anything to take care of the puppy, and it slept in another room and didn't wake you up, would you enjoy having a puppy around to play with?

SHE: You know I love dogs. That's why I took care of Zumi when my sister was traveling. But I was coming home from work at lunchtime to do it, and that was stressful. And you'll be starting a new job. Since we have no idea what that will be, or even where we'll be living, I don't see how you could commit to a puppy either.

Be a Kindly Brontosaurus

HE: Okay. Well, thanks for talking with me about this, and I think you're right that it makes sense to wait. Would it be okay if I check back in with you about the teeny, tiny, oh-so-cute puppy after we figure out our work and living situation?

SHE: That's okay. Meantime, get a job.

HE: Okay. I'm on it!

This was just role-play, and even in that conversation these aikido moves didn't magically move Niv's wife from a no to a yes. But Niv could sense that her opposition to getting a dog would soften a bit, and that she might be open to talking about it again at a better time. This is what aikido moves can do for you. Practice will diffuse some of your own resistance and give you some language to make these conversations easier.

In an earlier discussion about the power of no, I said that "No" is a complete sentence. This is true, but it doesn't necessarily mean no forever. By exploring other people's concerns, we can discover whether they might be open to collaborating or changing their minds in the future. When you respect people's intentions, their intelligence, and their fundamental liberty, your attempts to influence them will go more smoothly. As you become more expert, you might even welcome resistance and the way it teaches you more about the person you're negotiating with than a simple yes would (although a simple yes is nice, too).

Oh, by the way, Niv did persist, and he and his wife are both happy with their decision. This is Tink.

Deep Listening

Sometimes bearing witness to someone else's resistance can feel like too much because you have your own resistance to grapple with. You're trapped in your own head. We all are. Even in a friendly conversation, we're busy remembering our own similar experiences or figuring out what we're going to say next. In a disagreement, the mind amplifies these urges. The Gator filters out most of what you hear, and the Judge mounts a damning critique of whatever information seeps through. This mental process leads us to caricature the views of people who disagree with us, and to imagine them to be far more extreme than they actually are.

These distortions play out in every realm—personal, professional, and political. In the United States, Democrats and Republicans both believe that members of the other party hold more extreme views than they themselves do. When it comes to the contentious issue of immigration, for example, Democrats assume Republican voters want to close borders completely and Republicans assume Democratic voters want to open them completely. But both are wrong; there's a significant degree of overlap in views on immigration.

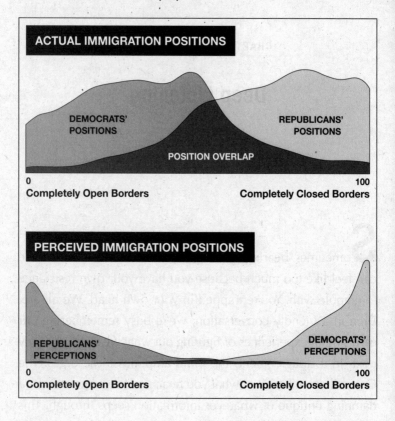

ACTUAL IMMIGRATION POSITIONS

DEMOCRATS'
POSITIONS

REPUBLICANS'
POSITIONS

POSITION OVERLAP

0
Completely Open Borders

100
Completely Closed Borders

PERCEIVED IMMIGRATION POSITIONS

REPUBLICANS'
PERCEPTIONS

DEMOCRATS'
PERCEPTIONS

0
Completely Open Borders

100
Completely Closed Borders

This phenomenon is known as the *false polarization bias*, and researchers have documented it in all kinds of domains. Members of religious and ethnic groups believe other people's perceptions of them are more negative than they actually are. People miscalculate how much members of the opposing side disagree with them on many hot-button issues like gun control, racism, and religion. And the more vehement our own views are, the more extreme we imagine views on the other side to be.

The key to bridging this gap is listening, and the underappreciated first step in listening is actually hearing another person's voice. Social psychologists Juliana Schroeder and Nick Epley have found that when we hear someone's voice rather than just reading their words, we find them more competent, thoughtful, and intelligent. We'd rather hire them—and this "we" includes professional recruiters. When someone disagrees with us, we can't discount their opinion as easily while hearing their voice; it reminds us that they're thinking, feeling, fellow human beings.

But how do you listen to another person when disagreement motivates you to turn inward? When I ask students to listen while a partner speaks just for one minute, they report all the usual distractions, which mostly boil down to *What am I going to say when it's my turn to speak?* But you can shift your focus to the other person by making your listening goals more specific.

The simplest goal is to *listen for what they're thinking.* Try to hear the other person's conscious thoughts instead of just your own. You're not a mind reader, but you can make inferences based on the other person's words.

To go deeper, you can *listen for what they're feeling,* tuning in to their Gator responses. You can do this by labeling their emotions "angry," "worried," "proud," or whatever you sense. Silently or aloud. Putting someone else's feelings into words has a stress-relieving effect on your own brain and can help you stay focused. Or you can try to let your Gator experience their emotions, making you feel closer to that person even if what you feel isn't the same as what they're feeling. (We'll get to accuracy in a bit.)

To go even deeper, you can *listen for the thoughts that are being left unsaid.* You're unlocking your inner Sherlock Holmes, using both reasoning and intuition. Henry Kissinger once described this kind of listening as the key to successful diplomacy, and it can be surprisingly helpful—although you still might be wrong. Listening this way can also run the risk of triggering feelings of superiority if you think you've discovered something the speaker may not realize or didn't want you to know. Try to hold that feeling in check. For now, you're just forming hypotheses—and you could be mistaken.

To go deeper still, you can *listen for the other person's unspoken values*. Why do they care about the things they're saying? If they're outraged, what underlying principle is being threatened or violated? If they're elated, what value is being fulfilled or vindicated? This deepest form of listening is particularly helpful with conflicts and complaints, but you can use it any time. You can usually find a whisper of those same values in yourself, which helps you develop empathy and connect with the person you're listening to.

After you've finished listening, reflect back to the other person what you heard or intuited, to see how well you understood and to gain a more accurate understanding. Putting someone's feelings into words helps them feel seen and understood and calms down activation in their amygdala, where the brain processes fear and stress. In this case you aren't just parroting back what they've said, you're adding your own interpretation—something they *didn't* say. This serves as an invitation to go even deeper in the conversation, so you can understand each other even better. This can be a gift that helps the other person understand themselves better as well.

A friend once described to me a moment in therapy that came after weeks of struggling with a painful family dynamic. Whenever domestic disagreements got heated, his wife and teenage daughter would each expect him to take their side, and he hated being caught in the middle. After listening attentively, my friend's therapist said, "It sounds like you care a lot about peace."

In the silence that followed, my friend had a profound sense of things falling into place. Until that moment he had been blaming his painful experience on his own ambivalence or weakness. A great weight lifted as he saw his own feelings more clearly, and without judgment.

You're not a therapist and you don't have decades of practice at this, but you don't have to be right; you just have to try. After you have listened to someone with a specific goal in mind—understanding their thoughts, or feelings, or what's been left unsaid, or their values, or all of these—and you reflect back your best guess without judgment, they'll appreciate that you're trying to understand them.

This is not a test of your abilities, it's a conversation. If you've been listening for values, you might say, "It sounds like you feel strongly about _____" (fill in the blank with learning, or justice, or creativity, or freedom, or whatever value you witnessed). If you're off-base, they'll clarify so you can understand them better. Reflecting back what you heard can transform the way a conversation feels on both sides. In a friendly chat, it builds intimacy. In a disagreement, it helps tamp down adversarial feelings while amping up collegial ones.

The Empathy Challenge

My students practice listening to understand people's values with an exercise called the Empathy Challenge. In this challenge, you listen to three different people who disagree with you on an issue you care about. You begin each of these conversations with the assumption—the frame—that the other person is smart and well-intentioned. As they explain their position, you listen for their underlying values. Finally, you look for common ground as you reflect those values back. That's it.

Before assigning the Empathy Challenge, I tried it myself. This was in 2016, two months before the U.S. presidential election. I couldn't understand why smart, well-intentioned people would be voting for the Republican candidate, so I set out to hear from them firsthand. Some of my progressive friends were annoyed by my project. "Why are we the ones who always have to listen?" But I knew I hadn't actually been listening; thanks to the false polarization bias, I had been caricaturing other people's views without having asked about them.

So, I set up three conversations with Republican voters.

The first conversation was with an Orthodox Jewish man living in New York. The Trump sticker on his car was a cause of regular harassment by strangers, and he was in conflict with friends and family, too. When I asked why he supported Donald Trump, he loudly enumerated his criticisms of Hillary Clinton. I held my tongue until he finished. Then I said, "Since you've kept this bumper sticker on your car even though people are honking and yelling at you, you must be a real fan of Donald Trump. I'm curious. Can you help me understand what you like about him?"

He started talking about his faith and about being persecuted for what you believe in. It meant a lot to him that Trump's daughter and her husband were Jewish. Then he told me a story he had heard about Donald Trump covering the medical expenses for an Orthodox Jewish boy who was gravely ill.

I had no way of knowing if the story was true. If my goal had been to try to win an argument, I might have challenged its accuracy. Instead, I sat quietly for a few moments before observing, "It sounds like you care a lot about helping other people."

"Of course I do. You have to."

"And it sounds like you have a soft spot for heroes."

He laughed. "I guess I do."

"Me too."

We talked more about life in an Orthodox Jewish community and about the class I was teaching. I could relate to being loyal to your heroes and wanting to help people who help people. If I had shared this man's beliefs about Donald Trump, I would have had a MAGA bumper sticker too. Our conversation ended amicably.

To my surprise, so did the next two. I had to bite my tongue a few more times, but going into those conversations with the expectation that the other person was smart and well intentioned was helpful. In the second case I agreed wholeheartedly with a Russian émigré's passion for freedom. In the third conversation I related to an attorney's deep need for authenticity.

These conversations didn't shift anyone's opinions about the presidential candidates; that wasn't the goal. But I was developing empathy and finding common ground that could have become a basis for agreement on other issues. And I was also learning that people who disagreed with me didn't necessarily agree with each other. Unique experiences informed their opinions, they had varying degrees of enthusiasm for the candidate, and they each connected with Trump's platform for different reasons—none of which turned out to be the ones I would have predicted. It's easy not to notice we're projecting opinions onto people when we haven't actually listened to them.

As my students took on the Empathy Challenge, sometimes their experiences were transformative. A pro-life student listened to a close friend explain why she was pro-choice. The friend revealed that she had been raped and gotten pregnant. My student realized that in those circumstances she might have considered getting an abortion, too. Another student healed a family conflict over an arranged marriage, and when the parents felt their values were being affirmed, they became more open-minded about letting their daughter stay in college. And the LGBTQ students who reached out to family members who had judged them found more love there than they had expected.

Both the listening exercises we do in class and the Empathy Challenge help us lean into disagreement peacefully and remind us to look for the source of people's strong opinions. We learn to accept that you might feel one way about the Black Lives Matter movement if your brother is a cop and you fear for his safety and another way if you're a Black man fearing for your own safety and having to bite your tongue all the time so you don't scare anybody.

These conversations aren't all kumbaya. Some get heated. But we are trying. Having empathy doesn't establish anything about who's right or wrong. We're just trying to understand each other as fellow human beings. By listening skillfully, modeling openness, and letting go of our agendas in order to relate to another person's experience, we show each other what empathy looks and feels like. By connecting in this way, we open hearts and minds—including our own—to influence.

CHAPTER SEVEN

Creative Negotiations

In a small village in rural Zambia near a big game preserve, Gloria Steinem sat down with a group of women on a large tarpaulin in the middle of a barren field. She had recently attended a conference on sex trafficking, and these villagers were mourning the recent loss of two young women who had been taken by sex traffickers. Instead of offering advice, Gloria asked a question: "*What would it take* to keep that from happening again?"

They told her: an electric fence.

An electric fence?

When the corn reached a certain height, the women said, elephants would come eat it, trampling the fields and leaving families hungry and vulnerable to exploitation.

"Okay. If I raise the money," Gloria asked, "will you clear the fields and do all the work to put up the fence?"

They said yes. So she raised the few thousand dollars required, and the women cleared the rocks and stumps by hand. The next time Gloria visited the village, she saw a bumper crop of corn, untouched by elephants. And since the fence had gone up, no young women from the village had been sex trafficked.

What would it take?

I call this the Magic Question, and it's my favorite influence strategy.

When I was an MBA student, I interned at a biotech company called Guidant that makes products for cardiac surgery. When Guidant launched a new stent system, their forecasts predicted it could capture most of the market. But they hadn't anticipated that the market itself would also be growing fast, and demand quickly outpaced supply. It was a good problem, but still a problem. In order for Guidant to fulfill its avalanche of orders, employees would need to work three shifts a day, seven days a week, including Thanksgiving and Christmas.

It was up to Ginger Graham, one of the company's senior leaders, to make that happen. She could have demanded mandatory overtime, but morale would have suffered. So instead, she explained the situation and asked, "*What would it take* for us to work together to fulfill these orders?" Employees brainstormed a wish list that included pizza deliveries, late-night taxis, babysitting, and Christmas present wrapping. When Ginger and her management team came through with those requests, employees came in around the clock and worked hard. Production hit new records, sales tripled, and everyone got a fat bonus. It didn't feel like the result of a negotiation; it felt like a joint endeavor. It was both.

Negotiating a raise or a promotion is so stressful that most people never do it. But consider how the Magic Question could reframe that situation so it doesn't feel so awkward or adversarial. It could point you toward an outcome you and your boss both want—you happily doing great work. What if you just asked, "*What would it take* for me to get to the next step in my career?" or "*What would it take* for me to be at the top of the salary band for this role?"

As a manager, how would you feel if an employee asked you these questions? You'd probably be glad to explain, "Here's what needs to happen." At some point, your employee might come back and say, "You said it would take this and that for me to get a raise. Here's what I've done. Now can you help me out?" If your conditions had been met, you'd support their case.

The Magic Question works with clients, with kids, anybody. You can use it repeatedly with the same person, even if you've taught them how the Magic Question works. My students, friends, and family use it with each other and with me because I teach it to everybody. We laugh when we hear it, but then we answer, "Here's what it would take. . . ." And it works. Like magic. It provides many of the ingredients you're looking for in a negotiation.

First, it's a catalyst for creativity. "What would it take?" is an invitation to ditch conventional ideas and consider a new approach.

Second, the Magic Question conveys respect. By posing it, you're acknowledging that you're not the expert on the other person's situation, or their needs, or their obstacles to striking a deal. *They* are. This defuses their Gator's threat response and opens up the possibility that this negotiation might produce easy wins for both sides. And respect, like kindness, is likely to be reciprocated, making everyone happier.

Third, the Magic Question can unearth important information. Without it, Gloria Steinem never would have known the sex trafficking problem in that village was really an elephant problem. Ginger Graham never would have thought of hiring a

Christmas present wrapper. Gathering information is essential for any negotiation, and if you treat the other party well, they can be your best source.

Lastly, not only does the Magic Question shift the conversation away from confrontation, it moves it toward collaboration. That's what creativity, respect, and information can do for you. Not only does collaboration make the process easier and more fun, it makes the solution more durable. Once the village women came up with the idea of the electric fence and agreed to their part of the bargain, they became invested in the outcome. They were also making an implicit agreement to protect their village from sex trafficking after the fence went up.

The Magic Question often leads to solutions that are simpler than you would have expected, requiring less than you would have been willing to do. But it's not always going to be simple; the Magic Question usually leads to more discussion. Which puts us back in the realm of negotiation.

A negotiation is just a conversation aimed at coming to an agreement. That's all it is. Everything you've learned about influence applies to negotiations. Timing, framing, handling resistance, all of it. Thus far, we've been talking about situations in which you have a great idea and the other person says yes or no, or you're just trying to get your point across, or you're trying to make a connection. Negotiating adds a layer of complexity; instead of a simple yes or no, you've got a discussion going back and forth.

So why do most of us hate the idea of negotiating? When I survey people, they describe it using words like "tense," "aggressive," "slimy," and "cutthroat." But it turns out they're describing their fears more than their actual experiences, which tend to be limited. Since most important negotiations happen behind closed doors, the negotiations we've observed are generally fictional. And since novelists and screenwriters love drama, their stories involve bullies trying to bulldoze each other in a zero-sum situation: I win, you lose, ha ha ha ha ha, you sucker. In reality, though, these aggressive negotiations are rare. And when they do happen, it's often because novice negotiators were afraid they would.

I see how this lack of experience plays out in my class. For weeks, students have been practicing how to be warm, assertive, and influential. We're becoming people others want to say yes to. But as soon as we pair off for a mock "negotiation," most students get tense and some forget everything they've learned. They dig in, use ultimatums, lie, and try to squeeze their partners dry. Or they capitulate and say, "Okay, you take everything!" Both are Gator threat responses. Playing hardball leads to either stalemate or capitulation. If there's a stalemate, nobody wins, and capitulation leads to fragile agreements that could fall apart. Contrary to what you might think, the bullying approach has a low success rate in real life.

When we debrief the exercise, it can be surprising to hear from the tough negotiators. Some were assuming that hard-nosed tactics and deceit are just part of how the negotiation game is played. Many thought they were playing defense, desperately trying not to get taken for a sucker. This is typical of novice negotiators, and most of us feel like novices because we haven't spent a lifetime negotiating international peace treaties, plea-bargaining criminal cases, or working on mergers and acquisitions. We might haggle over small purchases sometimes, but we'll probably only be involved in a few high-stakes negotiations. And even then we might have an agent or attorney doing the negotiating on our behalf. No wonder most of us are trying so hard not to be suckers: We feel like we don't know what we're doing.

We do, though. Remember, we've been negotiating since we were in diapers. And we're still doing it all the time, in everyday conversations with family members and colleagues and bosses about how to make things happen and who's going to get them done: "You can play videogames once your homework is finished." "What time should we get together for a drink after work?" "If I take on that new project, I'll have to stop working on this one; who can I pass it on to?" These moments don't feel like negotiations, but they are.

Even when we're negotiating with strangers or making deals involving money, it's not usually as bad as we expect. Although we might hate the *idea* of negotiating and find the process stressful, we usually feel good afterward. When I asked those same people who had described negotiations in general as "cutthroat" to tell me about their own most recent negotiation, 80 percent said they felt positive emotions like "happy" or "empowered," and almost everyone had been able to come to an agreement.

Most experienced negotiators look for mutually agreeable solutions. If the negotiation is over a pie, say, they're not trying to bake a small one, eat it all, and leave you staring at crumbs. They're looking to bake a big pie and sort out slices so everyone walks away full and happy. "You don't like pumpkin. Okay, how about apple? Great, that's what I'll do. So could you pick us up some ice cream, maybe butter pecan?"

You're already well on your way to being one of these negotiators even if you don't know it quite yet. In this chapter I'll offer you some advice on preparation, collaboration, and drawing a line with the rare bully so you won't have to worry about being a sucker. I've coached hundreds of students and friends to happy outcomes in their important negotiations like job offers, raises, promotions, business deals, and big purchases. And even in divorces, a good negotiation can leave everyone feeling less unhappy.

When people come to me for negotiation advice, often they're hoping I'll show them the kind of Jedi mind trick I used to brag about, something that will bend the other person to their will. But we already know that's not a good idea. If you try it, you're going to trigger resistance; and if you win, you'll trigger resentment. Yes, I'll show you some helpful strategies for the conversation, but the real art of negotiation has less to do with what you say than it does with the mindset you bring and the preparation you've done before the conversation gets under way.

Collecting the Ingredients for a Bigger Pie

Most potential negotiations fail before they begin because we don't realize negotiating is even possible. As you start negotiating more often, eventually it dawns on you that negotiating is *always* possible. You won't always succeed, but you can always try. You can say things like "I know it might not be possible, but is there any chance you could do some magic here?" When you're asking with warmth and a sense of humor, people don't get mad.

When you have this lightbulb moment about negotiating, you'll feel elation—and then maybe a twinge of regret over all the opportunities that went whizzing by unnoticed. Up to this point, most of us have been following the advice and role modeling of our parents, which varies widely. It's also unevenly distributed along socioeconomic lines. In *Negotiating Opportunities,* sociologist Jessica Calarco describes a years-long study in a middle school. She observed which children tried to negotiate extra help, better grades, or better situations. She also interviewed parents about what they were teaching their kids to do and interviewed teachers to understand how they made their decisions.

The findings were stark: Kids from middle-class families negotiated with their teachers seven times as often as kids from working-class families did. Teachers weren't biased in granting requests; they tried to say yes to everybody when they could. But as Calarco writes, "Middle-class students rarely took 'no' for an answer. Instead, they treated 'no' as teachers' opening gambit in a back-and-forth negotiation." Kids from middle-class families negotiated circumstances that allowed them to be more creative, feel more comfortable, and suffer fewer punishments. Kids from working-class families tried to figure things out on their own, spent more time struggling, and completed less of their work. Calarco describes middle-class parents as teaching their kids to be influential and working-class parents as teaching their kids to be deferential.

What we're seeing here is that privilege is at least partly negotiated. In order to open a world of possibilities and advantages, first you need to know that negotiation is possible. Then you need to be comfortable doing it. This isn't just true for kids in school. When Accenture, the management consulting firm, conducted a study of thousands of executives across the world, they found the biggest dissatisfactions with work centered on low pay and lack of opportunity—yet the majority of those executives had never tried to negotiate a raise or a promotion. (When they did, though, 72 percent got what they asked for and 25 percent did even better.) These were smart, successful people. Some were probably coaching their kids to negotiate with teachers, but they weren't doing the same with their own supervisors. Most people find job negotiations scary.

But they don't have to be. Once you leap the hurdle of realizing that everything is negotiable, the next step is getting past the zero-sum, win/lose mindset that activates the Gator's defenses and brings out the worst in us as negotiators—or keeps us from negotiating at all. If we employ the creativity that animates the Magic Question, we can see negotiations not as a win/lose proposition but as an opportunity for both sides to add value.

Baking a Bigger Pie Together

Negotiations professor Kimberly Elsbach observed screenplay ideas being pitched to fifty Hollywood executives over the course of six years to understand what was special about the pitches that led to successful deals. Studios can green-light only a small number of projects and a screenwriter's career can be made by one big hit, so the stakes are extraordinarily high on both sides. The biggest difference Elsbach found between successful and unsuccessful pitches was that the former were collaborative conversations. Both parties asked questions, shared ideas, and used "we" pronouns. It wasn't just a matter of personal chemistry; experienced pitchers were creating that dynamic. As one of them put it, "You want to stimulate them, you want to get their curiosity going. And then you want them to be a team player with you." In the best negotiations, you walk out with an even better idea than the one you walked in with.

Here are three questions that can help you get to that better idea, to the bigger pie.

The Value Creation Questions

You can look for opportunities to create value by coming up with even better ideas before, during, or after a negotiation. The questions to ask yourself, and to discuss with the other party when that makes sense, are:

How could this be even better for me?
How could it be even better for them?
Who else could benefit?

These are invitations to dream big. Since they begin with a private conversation between you and yourself, let your Gator's pleasure centers run wild (and don't listen yet to the Judge pointing out roadblocks).

How could this be even better for me? In a new job negotiation, the obvious thing to ask for is money—a higher salary, a signing bonus, relocation expenses, or more stock options. But maybe they could pay off your student loans! Wouldn't it be great if your new employer would cover travel expenses for a house-hunting trip in the new city—or even cover your rent while you look for a house to buy? Maybe doing your job better means getting funding to attend conferences in your field, or even having a budget to hire more people! Maybe you'd be thrilled if your new employer would cover the cost of, say, a second master's degree so you can become even more of an expert.

But don't limit yourself to lucre. Dream *big*. Maybe you'd be happier and more productive if you worked from home—or for that matter, why not from the beach, in Bermuda? Oh, and of course you'd need Fridays off in order to take those classes you're going to ask them to pay for. Or maybe your big concern about the potential move is finding a preschool for your child; the best one has a long waiting list, but could your new employer finagle you a spot? Or perhaps your partner needs a job. Maybe your big dream is to never go to another department meeting again unless you feel like it. Could that be possible?

You'll rarely get what you don't ask for and you can't ask for something that didn't occur to you, so it's worth spending time on this creative phase. And it's fun. You'll decide which of these things to ask for, and how many, based on your particular situation and how the conversation goes. You might add on a crazy ask or two at the end, depending on how it's going. You might dream up some wishes that will be easy to grant. And you can keep exploring ways in which this could be even better for you with simple questions like "What alternatives might there be?" and "Is there anything else you could offer?"

My students and friends have successfully negotiated all those perks in the lists above and many more. Don't prevent magic from happening by assuming it won't.

Dreams are crucial, but the best negotiations involve both creativity and preparation. So while you're using the Value Creation Questions to dissolve conventional boundaries, also be gathering evidence to support your case, asking advice about the specific process you're engaged in and learning about the person you'll be negotiating with.

This is where the Judge comes in, preparing you to face the resistance that may come up. In a negotiation at your current job, it might be helpful to find out about employee retention policies—is there money set aside to match competing offers? Useful benchmarks in any job negotiation include what others are being paid in that role, organization, or industry. You can get this data and also learn what other people have successfully negotiated for in the past from friends or allies in the industry; alumni from your school; the recruiter, if you're working with one; and even people you met with when you were interviewing, if you hit it off. And when you reach out to these people, ask their advice about negotiating. You may find them surprisingly candid and willing to help.

Now you're ready to explore the second Value Creation Question, *How could this be even better for them?* This question frees you to start thinking about what *you* could offer, and during the conversation you'll be listening to understand what they care about—their values and, more concretely, their priorities and concerns. This applies to the human being you're speaking with as well as the person or organization they represent, if there is one. Don't make the common mistake of imagining the representative always has the same interests as their company. Personally, they're getting a lot less out of the deal, so they may be keener to minimize the hassle than to maximize the outcome. Good to know.

Like the first two, the third Value Creation Question, *Who else could benefit?* begins with brainstorming on your own and then gathering more information during the conversation. Are there people you know or care about who could benefit? People the other party knows or cares about? Is there an opportunity here for you to serve as a role model? Could other people build on your agreement to do something even better?

In almost any negotiated agreement the key ingredients will

be similar: dreams and data. And if you're well prepared, you can't be a sucker. Take car buying, the most hated negotiation of all. You dream about your perfect car, you seek out models that have the features you care about, you do online research and visit dealerships. And when you have a clear idea of what you want, you search for that specific car at the lowest price around. You know before you walk in what options like upgrade packages, financing, and extended warranties cost. When you've identified your dream car and found it at a good price, the rest is easy-peasy.

If you're negotiating a big purchase, you research alternatives. If you're negotiating a divorce, you get legal advice. Dare to dream—and be prepared. Being prepared helps you be warm, confident, and present with the other person, as well as knowledgeable. Experienced negotiators ask twice as many questions and spend twice as much time listening as inexperienced negotiators do. Feeling creative and feeling in control increase happiness. Even if you didn't care about the other person's well-being, which of course you do, it would be smart to want them to feel good. Happy people are more generous and more creative, leading to better agreements and a greater likelihood of sticking to the bargain. In most cases, generosity inspires trust and reciprocation. (But we'll cover some exceptions too.)

Here's how the Value Creation Questions worked in a big, real-life negotiation. It started with a conversation with my coach Mandy Keene, who's the person who taught me the Magic Question.

When I was a postdoctoral researcher, I received my first speaking invitation. It was for an industry conference on health promotion, and although it wasn't my industry or my topic of expertise, they wanted me. Fantastic! I agreed to present my one piece of health-related work. My colleague Ravi Dhar and I had created a framework for applying behavioral economics nudges to the real world, and we had published a white paper with Erin Ratelis and Ro Kichlu in which we discussed how to apply this framework to support employee wellness.

After I had agreed to present our work at the conference, the organizers asked me to lead an additional session on "social influences on health," and I said yes even though I knew almost nothing about it. Before joining academia, I'd had to study plenty of things in order to teach them. Database programming. Italian. How to pick up guys. When the conference was still months in the future, it felt good to say yes. Now that it was almost time and I was unprepared, I was thinking, Damn! I told Mandy that preparing for these sessions was going to take days of work that I shouldn't have committed to when my real job was academic research—and trying to get a job in academia.

"So maybe you shouldn't have accepted the invitation, at least the second one," she told me. "But you did. Can you back out?"

"No. It's next week. I committed, I'm in the conference program, and canceling isn't an option."

"Then what's your outcome for this event?"

"I fulfill the obligation . . . and I learn a lesson to never do this again?"

"Mmmm. What *inspiring* outcome could you have? What could make your participation and all the prep you're going to do worthwhile?"

"I can't get a professorship out of it, but maybe I could get some consulting work."

Mandy asked how much, if I had to put a dollar amount on it. How much consulting would make this investment of my time worthwhile?

"Well . . . earning a ton of money would take a ton of work, and I can't make the time to do that. But an exciting amount that might be conceivable? Let's say fifty thousand dollars."

Having nudged me to think about how the situation could be even better for me, now Mandy asked the Magic Question: "What would it take for you to get fifty thousand dollars of consulting out of this event?"

That shifted my perspective. "To start with, I guess I'd need some business cards."

She laughed. "Okay. And what about your presentations, how will they help you get the consulting outcome you want?"

"Well, I should provide as much value as possible."

"And how will you do that?" (She was helping me toward an implementation intention.)

"Actually I have no idea what challenges the attendees are facing, or what this conference is like, but my collaborators Erin and Ro will be there so I could ask them."

I got to work on the preparations. Placed a rush order on the business cards, had a fun and enlightening pre-conference dinner with Erin and Ro, and prepared to deliver a talk that would be as helpful and practical as possible. I would still need to figure out what to teach in the second session and create slides.

With Erin and Ro's help, the first session was a success. As I was walking down the hallway afterward I heard a voice call out, "Zoe!" A woman from the audience caught up with me.

"Loved your presentation, and we should talk. My name's Michelle Hatzis and I work for Google. Can we have breakfast tomorrow?"

"Thanks, but I'm sorry," I said. "I'll be preparing a session for tomorrow."

She gave me her card and as she started to walk away, I heard Mandy's voice in my head. *What would it take . . . ?*

"Wait a second, Michelle. I changed my mind. Breakfast would be great."

And it was great. Michelle was wicked smart and funny. She was the new director of the Google Food team, and she was trying to figure out how behavioral science could inform the company's new global guidelines. She thought my framework might be just what they needed. It would be a big project, so we continued talking over the next few weeks until Michelle confirmed that she'd like to hire me as a consultant. A project like this would bring prestige and money and make a difference in people's lives. It was an exciting opportunity for many reasons, but it would require a big chunk of time.

When I asked myself, *How could this project be even better for me?* I wished I could spend less time on it so I could focus on academic research. And it would be way better if we could be working on publishable research—helping me in my academic job search—rather than working on company guidelines. Might that be possible?

When I asked myself, *How could it be even better for Michelle?* I wondered if she might be interested in doing research together. She was a researcher with a PhD who seemed enthusiastic about Yale. Maybe she'd like to be involved in our work there? When I brought these questions to Michelle, we began a series of discussions that resulted in a research and consulting partnership between Google and the students and faculty of the Yale Center for Customer Insights (YCCI), a think tank run by Ravi Dhar. We published our joint research in academic journals, a textbook, and *Harvard Business Review*. I didn't pursue the consulting income, but I would receive some contribution to my research budget through YCCI. And I don't know if the Google project helped, but Yale did offer me my dream job on their faculty the following year.

The answer to *Who else could benefit?* was a lot of people. For Google, the upside of working with Yale rather than just with me was high—lots of smart brains working on their challenges, so progress could accelerate. Google did write their new food guidelines based on our behavioral economics framework, so the company's then fifty thousand employees could make healthier choices. And Yale students got to collaborate with us on a series of research projects tackling challenges like how to nudge people to eat more vegetables, do less mindless snacking, and steer away from single-use water bottles. They gained consulting experience and added a Google project to their résumés. Some even landed jobs with Google.

Beyond Yale and Google, the publication of some of our work in popular media inspired other organizations to rethink their own food policies. And we modeled an example of a fruitful joint partnership between industry and academia, making it easier for other organizations to do the same. You'd think this would be common, but it isn't; I've never heard of a partnership as mutually beneficial as ours. Win, win, win, win, win . . . These benefits continued to expand. The architecture firm that designed Google's employee break rooms even decided to use our findings to help employees from other companies make healthier choices. And as life blended with work, Michelle became a close friend and one of my favorite people.

I had forgotten about the money target I had suggested to Mandy until years later. When I finally stepped away to focus on other projects, I added up the total contributions to my research budget that I had received from this partnership. It was exactly fifty thousand dollars. Magic.

The Value Creation Questions are great tools for people who want to work together like Michelle and I did. But they can be just as helpful when there's a problem to solve.

One of my students, Natalie Ma, created a problem by being *too* influential. She was using the Yale alumni database to ask for donations for our class fundraising project, not knowing that the school reserves the sole right to solicit alumni for money. When the development office sent me a friendly cease-and-desist note after they heard about Natalie's fundraising, I could have responded to their letter with an apology and a promise not to let it happen again. Instead I got curious. Anyone working in a development office is likely to be an expert in influence, after all.

I had coffee with two leaders from their team to discuss the situation. I wanted students to practice asking for money because it's scary and builds confidence. They could appreciate that, of course. They wanted to raise money for the school, but it was just as important to them that alumni didn't feel bombarded with requests.

We started discussing creative ways to solve the problem: What would it take to make the situation better for all of us, and who else could benefit? It was such a collaborative discussion that I don't remember who first proposed co-hosting a cold-calling night with my students reaching out to alums to raise money for scholarships. Students would get practice asking for money in one evening instead of over a period of weeks. Alums might enjoy talking with current students about their shared experiences with courses and professors. These friendly conversations would leave alums feeling more involved and more inclined to donate. Future students would get scholarships, the development office would hit their goals, and I looked forward to saying hi to some of my former students too. The problem-solving conversation didn't feel like working on a problem, or even like a negotiation.

When the students made their cold calls they raised tens of thousands of dollars, and it went so well we made it an annual tradition. It evolved into a party with pizza and beer and narwhal costumes. Natalie was such a star that I asked her to be my teaching assistant the following year. After graduation, she negotiated her way around the world on a yearlong vacation and ended up leading business development for a biotech start-up, negotiating millions of dollars in research investments to program viruses to fight infections. Win, win, win, win, win.

How could this be even better for me?

How could it be even better for them?

Who else could benefit?

Additional Ways to Stimulate Collaboration

One of the simplest ways to inspire collaboration is to give the other person choices. Even if you think you know somebody's best course of action, offering only one suggestion can lead them to feel pressured. Having options means they're in control, which soothes their resistance. It's also hard to evaluate something when you have nothing to compare it with. Is this good? Bad? Smart? Expensive? Fast? *Compared to what?*

Marketing professor Daniel Mochon found that people were far more likely to want to purchase a product like a television or a camera when it was presented with an alternative than when it was presented alone. Across various studies, when he offered only one option, up to 97 percent of people chose to wait rather than deciding on a purchase.

When you offer alternatives, you can still make a recommendation. An architect might say, "Here are two designs. I think the first is better because you'll get a lot of light in the common areas, like you wanted. But the second gives you a larger master bedroom." When the other person recognizes the merits of your suggestion in contrast to the inferior option, they see you as trustworthy and feel in control of the decision. You're also inviting collaboration and creativity; as you and they consider options together, you may come up with something even better.

In a complex deal with multiple issues to negotiate, like price, scope, delivery date, payment terms, and so on, you could offer a selection of bundles to choose from. For example, as an architect, you might offer a pay-as-you-go hourly rate, a more expensive package for complete designs and permits, and a far more expensive package to include project management of the construction. Design the bundles so you would be equally happy with any of them. You're offering what are known in the trade as multiple equivalent simultaneous offers, or *MESOs* (pronounced like the Japanese soup). They might pick an option, but even if they don't, the ensuing conversation will move the collaboration forward by helping you learn what they care about.

If you're offering good/better/best or small/medium/large types of choices, it helps to know that people tend to favor middle options; relative to the extremes, they seem practical and easy to justify. And middle options seem like they should be right for typical situations or typical people. In an experiment at a science museum, visitors were asked to choose a rain poncho. Average-sized people chose ponchos labeled "medium" regardless of the actual size of the poncho, even though they could see the ponchos and some of those mediums were quite tiny. Knowing that people tend to favor middle options, economists Carl Shapiro and Hal Varian identified what they call the *Goldilocks strategy*. You propose something you think will be ideal for the other person, along with one alternative that's far less than you think they need and one that's far more than you think they need. The middle option feels not too big and not too small: just right. You're not manipulating them into something they don't need; you're encouraging them to take action rather than putting it off.

Dealing with Difficult People

Most people are open to collaboration and prefer it to competition, so when you start a negotiation by conveying friendliness and flexibility, your behavior usually elicits similar warmth and open-mindedness in your counterpart. But sometimes they'll be difficult no matter how you approach them. People can be difficult for various reasons, many of those benign. They're scared and defensive. They're inexperienced, or they think hardball is just how you negotiate. They're not stingy at all but are already at their real bottom line. And a handful enjoy making you squirm. They'll do childish things like the "upper hand" handshake, twisting their hand on top of yours in a show of dominance.

Regardless of their motivation, you can't collaborate with someone who's unwilling any more than you can clap with one hand. So in a case like this, don't try to get creative with them or collaborate on great new ideas. The outcome of a negotiation with a difficult person (if you choose to follow through with it) comes down to identifying your leverage and communicating your wishes and boundaries clearly. Nothing more creative than that.

Leverage

In a negotiation, leverage is the power that each party can use to pressure the other side. What do they have that's desirable to the other party? What will they have to forgo if there's no agreement? What desirable things, including intangibles, will they have to give up if there *is* an agreement?

In Tina Fey's sitcom *30 Rock,* Alec Baldwin plays Jack, a bullying network television executive. Adriane Lenox plays Sherry, the Trinidadian nanny who works for him. Jack has reduced Sherry's hours but Sherry tells him her weekly rate remains the same.

JACK: You understand my confusion. I'm actually paying you more money to be here half the time.

(Sherry says nothing.)

JACK: . . . Say you're at the market buying potatoes, and that ten-pound bag of potatoes costs . . . four hundred dollars. But then the . . . grocery concierge tells you that a five-pound bag of potatoes costs four hundred dollars, well that would be shocking, right?

(Sherry says nothing.)

JACK: What I'm saying is that we value what you do but this rate is, uh . . . unreasonable.

SHERRY: So, what you wan' do?

JACK: . . . You think you have leverage over me, but you don't. I don't care about the baby. I've only known her for a few weeks and other than a fondness for Avery's breasts, Liddy and I have nothing in common. . . . What's more, I don't think Liddy looks like me, so evolutionarily that makes me want to eat her. In other words, either you take a pay cut or go and look for another job. Who has the leverage now, Sherry? Your move.

(The baby cries. Sherry prepares to leave.)

JACK: Please stay. I'll send everyone in your family to college.

In the outside world, Jack has more money, power, and status. He has power in their working relationship too because he can fire Sherry. That's leverage, and how powerful it is depends on how much she wants her job, which depends on her outside options and on how she feels. For reasons we can only guess at, Sherry is willing to lose her job rather than take a pay cut. And Jack doesn't want that to happen. He's a busy executive and if she walks away, she'll be leaving him with childcare duties to sort out, the hassle of finding a trustworthy new nanny, and maybe a big fight with Liddy's mother. So, despite appearances, Sherry's got more leverage. And she wins.

When you find yourself negotiating with a difficult person, or preparing to, focus on leverage. What do they have that you want? What do you have that they want? What does each side stand to lose (including pride)? Can you improve your alternatives? If you feel like you don't have much leverage, consider the possibility that you might be wrong. To the outside observer Sherry might not seem to have had much leverage, but in fact she had more than enough. Although they may not be aware of it, employees do have leverage over their managers, children have leverage over their parents, and you have leverage over anyone who cares about you, the relationship, or the potential deal, for any reason.

When you have leverage you don't need to do much, and that suits me well when negotiating with difficult people. Prepare so that you know what your outside options are, what you want, and where you'll draw the line. Then tell the other person what you want and let it sit there. Like Sherry did. This is the power of the pause in a negotiation. You don't need to bend over backward or respond to aggression; you don't need to get angry, and you definitely don't need to brainstorm with them. You may try to find a creative solution on your own or reach out to allies for support and advice, but with the difficult person you want to keep things simple.

Saying no without getting angry can almost be a spiritual practice. Sometimes I try to maintain a Kindly Brontosaurus equilibrium: "I'm sorry, I just can't." "Unfortunately, it's not possible." "It's just not realistic." And sometimes I channel my frustration into enthusiasm: "Oh, God no!" "You must be joking!" "Ha, that's the worst idea I've ever heard!" When a difficult person drops the ball at your feet, calmly toss it back: Pause. "So, what you wan' do?" Quietly establish your parameters and let them decide.

Face-Saving Plan B

If you're familiar with only one negotiation strategy, it's probably the walkaway bluff: "Either you take a pay cut or go and look for another job." But don't use it. It failed for Jack, and it's the technique I see failing most often in real life. It can blow up in your face because it threatens the other person's pride and yours. When you make an ultimatum, you're taking away their freedom of choice by putting them in a lose-lose situation: lose the opportunity, or lose face by submitting to you. We've discussed how much people hate to lose their freedom, so they may be willing to give up a good opportunity if they feel forced into it. And you may feel forced to follow through with your bluff if your pride gets in the way.

A friend told me about a beautiful pair of leather sandals he almost bought in Greece. The craftsmanship was so exquisite that he would have been willing to pay even more than the cobbler was charging, but according to the guidebook, in Greece you weren't supposed to pay full price; you were supposed to haggle. When the merchant refused to go lower, you were supposed to start walking away, triggering one final price discount. When my friend asked for a discount on the sandals, the merchant said he didn't negotiate prices. My friend asked again; the merchant was firm. Being difficult, apparently. My friend said never mind, forget it, and began to walk away. His bluff was met with silence. Out of pride, my friend kept walking. This happened forty years ago, but he still remembers those sandals.

The strategy that prevents pride from getting in the way is *Face-Saving Plan B*. This approach demonstrates strength in a submissive posture. You refer to an alternative—or just let them know you have alternatives—while saying you hope it won't come to that. And mean it. With this approach, their Gator threat response doesn't get activated. If they do agree to your suggestion, they're being generous. You'll feel grateful and they'll feel good about themselves. If they can't or won't, you'll still have your options open because you haven't painted yourself into a corner.

You can use Face-Saving Plan B in almost any difficult situation. A diplomat might say, "Listen, here's what I can offer you under the current administration, but we have an election coming up and after that I just can't make any promises." If you've experienced some kind of service failure as a customer and it's not getting resolved, you might say (if it's true), "I'm somebody who posts a lot of reviews online and I enjoy posting positive ones. I rarely post a negative one, but I'm so frustrated right now that I'm tempted to. Can't we please find some fair resolution?"

Say you want to use an outside job offer as leverage to increase your pay. A walkaway bluff could force you to leave, so instead you might say, "I have this other offer with a great salary, but I really like it here. If you could match the salary offer, I would definitely stay." If they match the offer, great. If they can't or won't, you've still left yourself room to make up your mind. No matter what happens when you use the Face-Saving

Plan B strategy, you still have options. And options are a good thing.

Many people who seem difficult are simply unable to say yes to what you're asking. But when you approach them with a great frame and with warmth and open-mindedness, they'll *want* to say yes. And sometimes they'll help you come up with a better idea. Manus McCaffery, the same student who negotiated up from the paper clip to the car, had a notable negotiation with, and regarding, Patagonia—the company and the geographical region. He and some teammates had been working with an NGO to get part of Patagonia, Chile, designated as a UNESCO World Heritage site, and they were going down there on a camping trip during fall break. So Manus approached the manager of the Patagonia store in New Haven to say, "Hey, we know your company is committed to conservation, and we are too. Here's the project we're working on, in Patagonia, no less. How would you feel about giving us some free gear? It's really cold down there!"

The store manager said he couldn't give them free gear, but he could offer them a discount of more than half off. Amazing! And actually, they could also host a fundraiser at the store. Oh, and the manager also knew someone who owned a brewery who might donate free beer. Manus and his teammates asked more local businesses to donate prizes for a raffle, invited friends who played in a band to perform, and we all went to the Patagonia store to party. We had a blast and of course we did some shopping, so the store benefited too. And then, because now everyone was friends and Patagonia was already support-ing Manus and his team, one of the directors from their corporate office offered them three thousand dollars in free gear after all. An even better outcome than Manus's original audacious ask.

The ripple effects of a good negotiation can extend far beyond what you initially imagined, and you never know what the seeds of your good ideas will grow into. In the village in Zambia, the women who had first gathered on a tarp in a field when Gloria Steinem had visited decided to keep meeting. Eight years on, the group had expanded to include women from neighboring villages and they had launched two workers' collectives, a women-run chicken farm, and a tailoring operation. They called their group *Waka Simba,* "Strong Women."

Negotiating While Female

At age twenty-four, Jennifer Lawrence had already won an Academy Award and been named by *Time* magazine as one of the 100 Most Influential People. She was talented, rich, beautiful, generous, and charmingly down-to-earth. Fans wore T-shirts proclaiming her their spirit animal. She had it made—and she had made a lot of it herself. A headstrong tomboy who struggled with social anxiety, she had dropped out of middle school and then moved to New York City without her parents at age fourteen. She knew what she wanted, and she wasn't going to let anyone stop her. She had *temul* in spades.

Given her drive and success, you might expect Jennifer Lawrence would be nailing her negotiations too. When Sony Pictures' email system was hacked in 2014, however, she found out along with the rest of the world that she had earned millions of dollars less for *American Hustle* than her male co-stars, Bradley Cooper and Christian Bale, had. In response, she published an open letter online. She writes that when she heard about the hack and realized what had happened:

I didn't get mad at Sony. I got mad at myself. I failed as a negotiator because I gave up early. I didn't want to keep fighting over millions of dollars that, frankly, due to two franchises, I don't need. . . . At the time, that seemed like a fine idea, until I saw the payroll on the Internet and realized every man I was working with definitely didn't worry about being "difficult" or "spoiled."

There's a lot to unpack here. When I lead workshops about influence skills like sales or public speaking, the topic of gender sometimes comes up. In negotiations workshops, gender *always* comes up. And when I'm teaching negotiations to a group of women, we rarely get through the material because we all have So. Much. To. Say. Rants to rant, questions to ask, advice to offer, successes to celebrate, and struggles to analyze. Pull up a chair.

Few women enjoy negotiating. In my surveys, 40 percent of men say they like or love to negotiate, but only 17 percent of women do. As we've seen, salary negotiation is one of the most stressful types of negotiating, so it's not surprising that women do less of this than men do. Global staffing firm Robert Half found only 46 percent of women had negotiated when they received job offers, compared to 66 percent of men—and we're talking about professionals who are undoubtedly aware that job offers are negotiable. The good news here is that the negotiations gap is shrinking—younger women are negotiating at work far more often than their mothers did. Negotiation experience helps close the pay gap, and negotiation training helps close the education gap.

Women get stressed more easily—it's biological—and we have a greater tendency to "tend and befriend" (rather than

fight or flight) when we feel panicked. Thus, in a stressful negotiation, women are more likely to take care of other people and
keep the peace, whereas men are more likely to shoot for the
moon—and keep on shooting. Women tend to judge risk more
accurately, which is one reason they perform better than men
as Wall Street stock traders. It's also why women are less likely
to enter a political race against an incumbent—we judge the
risk, and the stress, and decide maybe it's just not worth it.*

What I've observed is that, in an attempt to avoid negotiating, women may go straight to their bottom line. From their
perspective, this is a generous thing to do, and it really is—
they're giving all they possibly can. But the complication here
is that the other person doesn't know this number is really the
bottom line; they see it as a starting point and may interpret the
unwillingness to budge from it as stubbornness or even stinginess. They can feel frustrated about the situation and with their
inability to negotiate—perhaps even frustrated enough to walk
away, preventing opportunities for creative, collaborative, even
better solutions. It's not wrong to decide you want to just cut to
the chase and give your real, bottom-line, I-will-walk-unless-
we-can-do-exactly-this offer, but if you do, your communication and style are especially important. Enthusiasm, warmth,
respect, all that.

One reason that even the idea of negotiating can make us
unhappy is the fear of being judged just for asking, or for asking

---

* In races with an incumbent, the incumbent wins 95 percent of the time. In
open primaries—races without an incumbent—women are more likely to run
and more likely to succeed. In 2020, Democratic women were 37 percent of
candidates in primaries and 40 percent in open primaries. When they faced
men in open primaries, they won 73 percent of the time. Republican women
were 20 percent of candidates in primaries and 24 percent in open primaries.
When they faced men in open primaries, they won 50 percent of the time.

too much. It's not crazy; sometimes we do face backlash for our requests. Around the time Jennifer Lawrence was negotiating her contract, Angelina Jolie was being called a brat for her contract demands; we sometimes get called other gender-specific B-words when we seek or use power. No one ever accuses a man of acting bossy. This doesn't mean we can't ask for whatever we want. We should. It just means there are sexist tides to swim through, such as the expectation that women must be warm, and people's tendency to feel slighted when we just say the damn thing without sugarcoating it. This pisses me off. I'm not always warm, and nobody can be unless it's fake. But I can understand that people expect me to be warm, and if I don't show signs of warmth, they might take it personally, or judge me.

Even if my demeanor is warm, this doesn't imply I'm being a pushover. That's what people mean when they say kindness isn't weakness. What I ask for or agree to is completely separate from how I interact with people. Being warm makes people happy, which is something I'm usually aiming for. And being warm makes me happy too. I'm a generally friendly person who asks for whatever I want. I'm clear about my boundaries, and when I say no, I try to do that with warmth and playfulness too: "Are you kidding me?" "I couldn't possibly do that!" "There is absolutely, absolutely, absolutely no way." "I would rather be waterboarded." But that's me. You do you.

When it comes to figuring out what and how much to ask for, and what our boundaries should be, women are at a disadvantage. At least this is true at work, where we don't tend to have as many friends as men do. Herminia Ibarra's research on social networks has found men are more likely to socialize with colleagues from work while women tend to get together with non-work friends. If Jennifer Lawrence had been closer with Bradley Cooper and Christian Bale, she might have felt more comfortable asking, "Hey, what are they offering you?" And men—please do share your salary information with us, like Bradley Cooper and a lot of male actors have now pledged to do for their female co-stars. Okay?

Many women have been taught to work hard, complete our tasks, and go home, expecting that eventually we'll get whatever recognition and rewards we deserve. Executive coach Tara Mohr calls these "good student habits." In *Playing Big,* she writes, "What if girls are doing so well in school because school requires many of the same abilities and behaviors as being a 'good girl': respect for and obedience to authority, careful rule-following, people-pleasing, and succeeding in an externally imposed framework?" She continues, "The idea that good work is enough is strongly reinforced in school, because doing well in school does not require self-promotion. It requires only doing quality work and handing it in to the teacher." But teachers aren't bosses, and school is not the workplace. We need to ask for the raise, the promotion, the assignment to the cool project. We need to figure out how to let people know about the fantastic work we're already doing, and we need strong networks of both men and women supporting each other at work.

When women set their negotiation targets as high as men do, they tend to do just as well as men. This shows that your outcome depends far more on *how much* you ask for than on *how* you ask—important as that is. When economist Nina Roussille analyzed data from thousands of engineers seeking jobs on an online platform, she found that "gender differences in ask salaries explain nearly all of the gap in final offers. I find no evidence of discrimination against women. In fact, conditional on their resume characteristics, women get slightly more bids than men and, conditional on interviewing, women are just as likely as men to get a final offer." In other words, in this case at least, employers are willing to pay women as much as men; but we need to take responsibility for asking for as much as men do, as many times as it takes.

So far we're talking about situations in which a negotiation is already under way, but one of the biggest gender differences in negotiations is that women are far less likely than men are to realize they *can* negotiate. Multiple surveys, field studies, and experiments have found the negotiation gender gap is greatest when the situation is ambiguous. My colleague Barbara Biasi found that when the state of Wisconsin changed its contract with the teachers' union to allow for some discretion in teachers' pay, male teachers started getting paid more than female teachers, with the gender gap widening each year. Once men realized they could negotiate, they did; women, not so much.

When marketing professor Deborah Small and her colleagues brought participants into the lab to play the word-search game Boggle, players were told they would be paid between three dollars and ten dollars. At the end of the game, a researcher tallied up their points, handed them three dollars, and said, "Here's three dollars. Is three dollars okay?" (Everyone who asked for more money got it. They could get up to ten dollars if they kept asking.) Only 3 percent of the women asked for more money. Twenty-three percent of the men did.

Linda Babcock, a co-author of the Boggle experiment who literally wrote the book on gender and negotiations (*Women Don't Ask*), discovered that even she had gender blind spots.

She realized she was handing out the best teaching assignments to her male PhD students. Why? They asked for them.

On behalf of ourselves and those we care about, we can be like Linda Babcock's male PhD students, asking. Regardless of our gender, we have to ask. But when we're in a position of power, we don't have to wait for others to ask. When we're in leadership roles, we can make sure that power and money and prestige aren't just flowing to those who ask loudest and most often. And when we grant a request to one person, we can make the same offer to those who could have asked for it—which is what Linda Babcock did once she understood what was happening. She started assigning teaching more fairly.

You may have heard that when women negotiate on behalf of other people, they do as well as men and sometimes better. This success isn't about selflessness; it's about a difference in approach. When women negotiate for others, we set bigger goals, we're more persistent, we're more confident and warm, and we're less needy. We feel more comfortable (less stressed), and we don't take the situation personally. We're happier, so the negotiator on the other side is happier. But we need to find a way to do this for ourselves, too.

If the idea of negotiating on behalf of others makes you feel more comfortable, try using it as a frame when you're negotiating for yourself. It's true, when you think about it: Every time you negotiate, you're smoothing the way for other women to negotiate successfully in the future. You're serving as a role model. And when you negotiate more money for yourself, this allows you to be more generous with others. When you negotiate more time for yourself, you can be at your best more often, which benefits other people, too.

The year after the Sony Pictures email hack, Jennifer Lawrence went back to the negotiating table, this time for a lead role in the film *Passengers*. I don't know what target salary she asked for, but I do know the twenty million dollars she negotiated made her Hollywood's highest-paid actress, and I know she earned eight million dollars more than her male co-star. I also know she made a two-million-dollar donation to Kosair Children's Hospital in her home state of Kentucky and became a major donor to Louisville's Fund for the Arts.

In the past, Jennifer Lawrence had given up negotiating because she didn't want to keep fighting over two million dollars she didn't need. She still didn't *need* the money when she negotiated the *Passengers* contract, but this time she was clear on what a difference it could make and why it mattered for her to model this behavior for the millions of woman who looked up to her. Her decision to negotiate was a gift to herself and to a heck of a lot of other people.

Who's going to benefit when you decide to negotiate?

CHAPTER EIGHT

Defense Against the Dark Arts

One of the most interesting and dangerous things about a shark is nearly invisible. You have to get close to its face to see the dark pores speckling its snout and cheeks. Those pores lead beneath the skin to narrow, jelly-filled canals that interconnect and empty into cavities called *Ampullae of Lorenzini,* named after the seventeenth-century physician who first described them. But Lorenzini had no idea what they were for. It wasn't until the 1960s that researchers discovered the ampullae serve as a sixth sense. They're attuned to the presence of electricity. All living beings emit an electromagnetic field, and the ampullae allow sharks to locate prey animals even when they're hiding under the sand. Electroreceptors aren't unique to sharks, but sharks have the most sensitive ones in the animal kingdom. A great white shark can sense an electromagnetic charge as subtle as one-millionth of one volt. Sharks are drawn, quite literally, to power.

In this chapter, we'll explore the dark side of influence. As you amplify your power, you'll attract more attention from the shark-like individuals for whom you are both rival and prey. They are cold-blooded, willing to bully, cheat, manipulate, and deceive people to get what they want. Some desire dominance and some seek sex. But mostly they're just hunting for money.

Geneen Roth and her husband, Matt, were looking for a financial adviser. Geneen was a writer and a counselor to women struggling with their relationship to food; Matt was a business speaker. They weren't wealthy, but they had a comfortable life and they were hoping to make it a little more comfortable.

Louis Izarro seemed to be someone who could help them with that. They would meet at his house in wine country. He wore fine, tailored suits and Gucci shoes, and he drove a Mercedes with vanity plates. Geneen's Gator brain picked up on these details, all of which told her, *Here's a man who knows about money.* She and Matt hired him as their tax consultant, despite the fact that he wasn't licensed. He would create deeds of trust for them so they could keep their money safe.

Over the years, Izarro socialized with them at book parties and dinner parties, professional boundaries eventually blurring into something closer to friendship. So when he casually mentioned that he had an exclusive opportunity to invest in a tech stock that hadn't yet gone public—this was only for his most special clients—Geneen felt a tingle. *He sees us as special.*

"I want you to put everything you have into it because this is going to make you billions. If it doesn't do well, I'll give you every cent back that you put into it."

Suddenly Geneen and Matt were being ushered through a secret doorway into a realm where people became billionaires overnight. Although they hadn't been focusing their efforts on accumulating money, this unexpected opportunity triggered feelings of desire. Why shouldn't they be like all the other people who had second houses, third houses, boats, and all those fabulous clothes? Was this too good to be true? Well, wasn't it how the rich get richer, leveraging their money to generate more? Izarro might not have been licensed to invest Geneen and Matt's money, but he was their friend. And he was making a no-risk offer. To play it safe, they gave Izarro only a quarter of their life savings to invest in the tech stock. They didn't need to be billionaires. Multimillionaires was good enough.

A year and a half later, as the stock was about to go public, Geneen and Matt tried to reach Louis Izarro to discuss details of the IPO. But he was nowhere to be found. In a panic, they started looking into all the other, smaller investments he had managed for them over the years, only to discover their money had never gone into those accounts. Louis Izarro had been stealing from them the entire time he was pretending to be their friend.

Wounded by their experience with Izarro and now well into midlife, Geneen and Matt wanted nothing to do with flashy advisers or get-rich-quick schemes. They needed something safe with modest but solid returns, and their wealthy and accomplished friend Richard suggested they join an investment fund his father had discovered years before. It was outperforming the market, and since its inception it had never lost money. It was really open only to friends and family, but Richard wanted them to have access after losing so much to Izarro. And who better to manage their money than the former chairman of the Nasdaq Stock Market, the second-largest stock exchange in the world?

With the exception of five thousand dollars in a checking account and the money they had put down on their house, Geneen and Matt invested everything they had with Bernie Madoff. The stock market would plunge from time to time, and friends investing in mutual funds would groan. Yet volatility never hit Madoff investors. Geneen and Matt received a dot-matrix-printed statement every month showing their investment growing steadily.

Although these quaint-looking statements were reassuring, something about the situation didn't feel quite right. Perhaps it was the bad experience with Izarro, but when a friend asked her advice about investing with Madoff, Geneen told her to diversify instead. It wasn't smart to put all your investments in one place, Geneen said, even though that's what she had done.

Doubts are whispers, not sirens. And hope can obscure clear thinking. Over the years Geneen often asked Richard how Madoff was able to deliver such consistent returns, and every time, he would launch into a long-winded explanation of Madoff's highly sophisticated split/strike conversion strategy. John Oliver has joked, "If you want to do something evil, wrap it in something boring." This strategy was so boring and complicated that Geneen's mind would inevitably begin to wander. "After five minutes of not understanding anything he said, I couldn't wait for him to shut up," she writes in her memoir, Lost and Found. "I filled in the gaps of my understanding with a self-constructed fantasy: Until the day he got arrested, I believed that Bernie Madoff was a close friend of Richard's father's and that together they started a small—very small—investment business that included each of their families and maybe thirty of their closest friends. My fantasy was lovely and utterly wrong."

When FBI agents knocked on the door of Bernie Madoff's New York apartment on December 11, 2008, he knew why they were there.

"We're here to find out if there's an innocent explanation."

"There is no innocent explanation," Madoff answered.

For at least sixteen years and perhaps decades longer, he had been running a Ponzi scheme so large that its assets—had they actually existed—would have dwarfed any Wall Street bank. The FBI investigation would reveal that thirty-seven thousand investors from 136 countries had investments (or so they thought) of sixty-five billion dollars with Bernie Madoff. Yet because the money was all coming in through feeder funds like Richard's (it turned out he was a victim, not an accomplice), investors could be conned into believing they were part of a small group that was lucky to have such a special opportunity. Madoff had cultivated a mystique that helped him avoid answering questions. If you were too inquisitive, he didn't want your money. And if you were one of the fund managers bringing money to Bernie Madoff, you were getting hefty kickbacks, so you didn't dig too deep.

By the time Geneen and Matt gave Madoff their life savings, he had already sucked in hedge funds, charities, and major banks, as well as DreamWorks Animation CEO Jeffrey Katzenberg, Holocaust survivor and Nobel Prize winner Elie Wiesel, the owner of the New York Mets, and actor Kevin Bacon (who really must be connected to everyone). Had Madoff embezzled all the funds at once, he would have been found out. But some investors had withdrawn their money along the way, giving the fund the appearance of legitimacy. Those withdrawals had been covered by new investors like Geneen and Matt—that's how a Ponzi scheme works.

Madoff's investors weren't stupid people. Con artists prey on successful people—those who earn higher salaries, have more education, and even have higher financial literacy—

because they have more money. These are people who think they know what they're doing, or at least that people they trust know what they're doing. But it's precisely this mindset that makes them vulnerable to manipulation.

We are terrible at spotting liars. In experiments with more than fifteen thousand participants, psychologist Paul Ekman has found that people can detect lies with only 5 percent greater accuracy than random chance. Even highly trained lie detection experts do only 10 percent better than chance, although they have a great deal of confidence in their judgments. Polygraphs themselves are so unreliable as to be inadmissible as evidence in court. If you're a parent, you're pretty sure you know when your child is lying, but you're probably wrong about that too. The cues we rely on—signs of discomfort—are misleading. Plenty of people telling the truth are uncomfortable, and plenty of liars are perfectly calm. Particularly the ones who have a lot of practice, which makes them the ones you most need to watch out for. This is why we need to look for other signs.

Every year in the United States, 10 to 15 percent of adults will fall for some kind of scam. But in almost every case, there were red flags that could have alerted them to danger had they known what to look for. Shark detectors.

The Red Flags of Manipulation

Despite their best efforts, manipulators throw off clues, red flags that should make you wary. But that first red flag can be difficult to spot. Manipulative tactics are designed to shift you into Gator mode so you're reacting instead of rationally assessing the situation. (This is why it's so much easier to spot red flags when someone else is the target: You're in Judge mode, and they're stuck in Gator mode.) Skillful manipulators know how to create the kind of turbulence that turns your instinct for self-preservation against you.

So, let's take a closer look at indications that you may have aroused a shark's interest. None of these are necessarily damning on their own, but if you see any one of these signs, keep a keen eye out for more.

Red flag #1: "The Ether"

Falling victim to a shark is so embarrassing. What were you thinking giving your bank information to a stranger? What were you thinking when you went to that "business meeting" in his hotel room at ten P.M.? Or when you gave all your cash to the engineering student who lost his wallet and needed to buy textbooks? We all have stories like this, and the answer to the question "What were you thinking?" may surprise you.

You weren't. At least not the way you usually do. Here's how one con man described his strategy to Doug Shadel, author of *Outsmarting the Scam Artists*. "As a master closer, I made it my first objective to get the victim 'under the ether.' Ether is that fuzzy state when your emotions are stirred up and you're so agitated that you won't know which way is up and which is down. Once I have gotten you into this condition, it doesn't matter how smart or dumb you are. Ether trumps intelligence every time."

This is what happens when the Gator gets overloaded before the Judge gets a chance to intervene. This delusional state explains the frequently bizarre behavior we exhibit in a crisis.

After one police officer accidentally shot himself, he repeatedly dialed 411 before finally asking the operator to transfer him to 911. On September 11, 2001, upon discovering that their tower had been hit by a plane, many people spent a precious half hour collecting their things and calling their families before walking slowly down the stairs.

Con artists and other manipulators intentionally stir up our emotions to ensure we can't think clearly. What makes this worse is the fact that *when you're in the ether, you don't know it.* You're like a drunk reaching confidently for the car keys—in an altered state but unaware of it. Those decisions that are so impossible to explain in hindsight? Ether.

Any massive surge of emotion can put you in this vulnerable state. Late one night I was woken up by a phone call from an unknown number in Mexico, a stranger with a thick accent who was speaking fast and in obvious distress. "Your brother, he has just been in a terrible car accident."

Oh, no! My heart started pounding. My throat went dry.

"He's unconscious, they're taking him to the hospital."

Who had been in a car accident? Did he mean my sister Mika? I thought she was home in Philadelphia, but was she traveling? I was confused, scared, and desperate to help. I said, "I don't have a brother, but tell me what—" The line went dead. Looking back on it, if the scammer had happened to say "your sister," I would have been all in.

Another classic ether generator is greed. As Upton Sinclair once wrote, "It is difficult to get a man to understand something when his salary depends on his not understanding it." Lust is a powerful ether generator. So is anger. "Believe it or not," one con artist bragged, "some of my best sales came from unhappy customers calling me to scream and yell about how they were lied to about the product. I would let them vent until they were blue in the face, then I would close them. Emotion is emotion. Anger is just as good as excitement or fear."

Ether can be induced physically too. Research has recently confirmed what priests, shamans, generals, and cult leaders have known for a long time—that when people engage in synchronized, rhythmic behaviors like drumming, marching, dancing, or chanting, they become more compliant. Because they feel energized and connected to the group, they're more cooperative. And ether becomes even more powerful when rhythmic group activities are combined with mind-scrambling loud music, strobe lights, or sleep deprivation. Excitement, euphoria, anxiety, confusion, connectedness, or spiritual rapture: All of these states make it hard to think clearly. Ether can make any one of us a victim, anytime, no matter how smart we are. Since we probably won't realize we're caught up in the ether, here are some other signs that the sharks are circling. One of the most visible is a close relative to ether: urgency.

Red flag #2: Urgency

Urgency can create an irrational state known in German as *Torschlusspanik,* or "gate-closing panic." The term dates back to the Middle Ages, when, at dusk, peasants would rush back to their homes in the castle's keep, terrified of being shut outside when the gates closed at nightfall.

To place this ancient word in a contemporary context, *Torschlusspanik* is what led to the Great Toilet Paper Panic of 2020. As the COVID pandemic disrupted supply chains, people around the world rushed out to buy all the toilet paper they could get their hands on (in some cases enough to last for years), alarming other people and spreading *Torschlusspanik* until store shelves were bare. Police had to break up toilet paper brawls in Sydney and California. In Hong Kong, armed robbers stole six hundred rolls of toilet paper from a supermarket, leaving the cash registers untouched.

Urgency comes from the fear of not having enough, whether it's time, supply, or opportunity. Fear of missing out (FOMO) can lead us to do things we'd never dream of under ordinary circumstances. Neuroscientists have found that urgency over-stimulates the parts of the brain that help us gauge value (I must have this thing!) while sidelining the parts that help us with planning (Budget? What budget?). We assume sales are exciting because of the deals on offer, but what excites us even more is the sense of urgency they create.

Nearly every transactional sales pitch employs urgency in some form. A salesperson might say something like "At our company we don't negotiate price. However, we do offer same-day incentives. So if you do choose to purchase today, I can offer you some discounts. Does that sound fair?"

It does sound fair, or even better than fair, right? But the same-day incentive is a gambit to get the Gator to make a gut decision before the Judge has time for second thoughts. You can't expect yourself to make smart decisions under time pressure or when you're in the throes of FOMO. I make it a policy to sleep on any big decision, and when I'm asking someone else to make a big decision, I invite them to sleep on it too. This way we can be sure that both the Gator and the Judge are saying yes. When you take this approach, you soon discover that most urgency tactics are bluffs. If they want to sell you something today, do you really think they'll turn you away tomorrow?

In case you might be planning to use urgency in a sharky moment of your own, you should know that it often backfires. In a marketing research experiment involving 310,000 purchase decisions, researchers from Google's UK Market Insights team found that tactics like "today only!" and "only two rooms left" were the least effective of all the behavioral strategies they tested. And the most likely to piss people off. Or, as the researchers politely put it, it tended to "provoke a negative reaction."

Red flag #3: Exclusivity

Exclusivity is related to urgency in that it's about limited availability, but it's a subtler variation on the theme. Depending on your worthiness—or your wealth—you could be granted access to this exclusive opportunity, available only to the special few. Whereas urgency is an appeal to your inner two-year-old (*You can't have this*), exclusivity plays to your inner teenager (*Do you want to be one of the cool kids?*). Exclusivity is the VIP badge, the Ivy League school, the celebrity event, the Diamond/Platinum level, the club or social network that requires a referral from a member. Exclusivity promises status. When some part of your subconscious mind is asking, *Am I worthy?* exclusive opportunities respond, *Yes, if.*

Exclusivity tactics are bolstered by flattery, uncertainty, FOMO, or all of the above. The research on flattery can be easily summed up: It probably works on you, even if you think it doesn't, even if you know there are ulterior motives, and even if your flatterer is only a computer telling you how wonderful you are. Uncertainty about status makes us especially vulnerable to exclusivity. And FOMO throws gasoline on the fire.

At six hundred dollars a pound, *kopi luwak* is the world's most expensive coffee. It comes from the hills of Indonesia, home to the Asian palm civet, or *luwak*. This civet is a tan-colored animal that looks like the offspring of a housecat and a possum. Luwaks are fond of coffee cherries—the fruit with the coffee bean inside. As coffee cherries pass through the luwak's digestive tract, the undigestible beans collect a special combination of enzymes said to leave the beans less acidic when excreted. These beans are cleaned, roasted, brewed, and sipped.

Yes, the world's most expensive coffee is made of cat-possum poop. It may sound gross, but if you were a tourist in the highlands of West Java listening to a sales pitch, part of you would feel that YOU MUST HAVE THE CAT-POSSUM COFFEE AT ANY PRICE! For those who live in the highlands of West Java, though, *kopi luwak* is just another stupid overpriced thing the tourists buy. (Yes, I did buy it. No, it wasn't that special. And I later learned the animals are mistreated and 80 percent of *kopi luwak* is fake anyway.)

Part of the reason Bernie Madoff was so successful at getting people to give him their money was that he wouldn't take on just anyone as a client. You had to have a referral. In cults—personal development cults, business cults, and spiritual cults—exclusivity takes the form of high-priced, limited access to a charismatic leader. A small group retreat might cost tens of thousands of dollars. Annual membership in the VIP circle might run more than a hundred thousand dollars. Many of these organizations use high-pressure sales tactics that encourage devotees to spend money they don't have, maxing out credit cards or cashing out retirement savings. Gurus will say it's a choice freely made, but when they use a mind-bending mix of ether and exclusivity on the vulnerable, I say it isn't.

The pull of exclusivity can diminish a bit when we're given time to think, but it doesn't necessarily go away. *Oh, hello, ego. There you are.* When you feel the tug, check your surroundings for a predator.

Red flag #4: Too Good to Be True

As Maria Konnikova writes in *The Confidence Game*, "Everyone has heard the saying 'If it seems too good to be true, it probably is.' But when it comes to our own selves, we tend to latch on to that 'probably.'"

Claims that are too good to be true are often accompanied by an urgency ploy. If you had more time to consider, you'd start to see the holes. In the UK TV show *Real Hustle,* a hidden camera crew follows a team of actors as they perpetrate famous cons on an unsuspecting public. In one episode, "Black Money," a glib talker sells spray-painted pieces of paper to a crowd of people at a flea market who end up elbowing each other out of the way, waving cash, desperate to buy as much paper as they can.

To you, the observer in Judge mode, this con seems patently ridiculous. The crowd, however, has been told that the national mint overprints money, and because destroying currency is a crime, they paint the surplus bills black to render them unusable. After hijacking a truckload of this currency, its new owners have figured out a way to restore it using a special chemical spray and a roller. The hawker demonstrates the process, transforming a black painted piece of paper into a ten-pound note right before your eyes—and you can buy *ten* of these canceled notes, along with the solution and the roller, *for only £10*. You heard that right: £100 of canceled but easily restorable notes—worth ten times what you'd be paying for them. But you'd better be quick; these men need to unload their black money right away.

A smart person couldn't possibly fall for this story, right? Yet money-washing scams have been carried out successfully all over the world, bilking smart people out of thousands of dollars. Victims of scams rarely report the situation to the police because they're understandably embarrassed, and sometimes, as in this case, because they had participated in a shady deal.

At a safe remove from the ether—the persuasive barker, the excited crowd—it's easy to see that this offer is too good to be true. If the thieves have a truckload of canceled currency and the means to restore it, why on earth would they sell it at a 90 percent discount? And why would they confess their crime so publicly? The scenario doesn't make sense, but it's unfolding so quickly—and the victims see tangible proof: spray-painted bills turning into real ten-pound notes. Not to mention the social proof, too: Lots of other people (maybe in on the scam) are clamoring to buy.

Red flag #5: Half-Truths

Lies are obvious signs of trouble. But bluffing, misleading, misrepresenting, and exaggerating are red flags too. People who treat facts casually will treat you casually, too. A yoga guru once told me he could drive from one side of Los Angeles to the other in ten minutes because "when you're spiritually evolved, standard rules of time don't apply to you." I later learned that multiple women had accused him of being a sexual predator; I guess time's rules weren't the only ones that didn't apply to him.

Marketers bear more than a little responsibility for the idea that truth is optional. In the movie *Elf,* Will Ferrell plays a man raised by elves in the North Pole. Shortly after his arrival in New York City, he notices a sign outside a diner and runs inside, joyfully exclaiming, "You did it! Congratulations! 'World's Best Cup of Coffee.' Great job, everybody, great to meet you!"

His naïveté is funny because we're so used to ignoring claims like this. Everyone knows that a sign touting the world's best cup of coffee doesn't mean anything. But when you think about it, it really does. It means that whoever says this stuff really doesn't care if it's true or not.

Some phrases always perk my ears up: "I promise," "God's honest truth," "This is 100 percent for real," "Honestly," and "I'm going to level with you here." Why does this person feel the need to promise, certify, or declare their honesty? They must expect you to be suspicious. That can't be good. Half-truths or unsolicited promises should put you on alert.

Red flag #6: Magical Thinking About Money

Many personal development coaches and spiritual leaders embrace the idea that our thoughts are responsible for whatever comes into our lives. When we think positively about wealth, for example, and imagine ourselves living in abundance, money is more likely to come our way; wealth will be attracted to us. For Protestant Christians this is the "prosperity gospel"; for spiritual seekers it's the "Law of Attraction."

Anecdotal evidence springs organically from these teach-

202 / Influence Is Your Superpower

ings. Those who do experience abundance are eager to share their stories because their good fortune reflects well on them. They're spiritual, "woke," attuned, loved by God. You'll hear from people who were once completely broke but demonstrated their faith by putting down their credit card, and a higher power came to their aid. On the other hand, those who remain poor or mired in debt aren't inclined to speak up because of what their failure means: They're unworthy, and unloved by the higher power.

Barbara Ehrenreich writes about this kind of magical thinking in her book *Bright-Sided:*

> "When my sister arrived from New York over the holidays, she plopped a hand-tooled leather satchel on my piano bench and said, 'See the beautiful bag I manifested for myself?' The DVD of *The Secret* had encouraged her to believe that she deserved this object, that it was hers for the taking, so she had charged it on her Amex card."

If you're coming across the Law of Attraction in contexts where you're being encouraged to part with large chunks of money, take a pause. Even if you accept the premise, you can see how your belief could make you vulnerable to people who want to benefit themselves.

Like the other red flags we're discussing, this one isn't a smoking gun. But it is an invitation to take a closer look and make sure that what's going on is legit. If exclusivity is involved, and it often is, maybe you don't have to jump right to the Platinum Team. And maybe you could manifest the money *before* swiping your card.

Red flag #7: Ignoring Your Firm No

Did I encourage you earlier to be persistent, a Kindly Brontosaurus? Yes, I did. But a Kindly Brontosaurus hangs out politely or asks permission to follow up again later. If a Kindly Brontosaurus is asked to go away or stop asking, it does. When you respond to someone's request with a firm no, they should leave you alone. If they persist, you'll know they don't care what you want, and this is a huge red flag. If you have equivocated, trying to take care of their feelings, you may wonder if there's been a misunderstanding. You may feel responsible for it. But persistence after a firm no is a big red flag.

Red flag #8: Alternating Hot and Cold

The most psychologically abusive way to treat someone is with a mix of kindness and cruelty. If you've had a close relationship with someone who did this to you—maybe a parent, a partner, or a boss—you're familiar with this toxic cocktail of hope and dread. *Maybe if I do things just right this time, it will all work out.* If the other person was consistently cruel, at least you'd know what to expect. You could prepare yourself. But not knowing means you can never relax, and constant stress can make you compliant: You accept this as the new normal. Many people trapped in abusive relationships fail to recognize them for what they are.

Sometimes the emotional roller coaster comes from a team of two people working together, the good cop, bad cop routine you've seen in so many movies. This is no longer a go-to strategy for police interrogations, if it ever was; by the 1940s it was already seen as antiquated. But it's still common in organized cons and in manipulative sales situations.

Time-share pitches are notorious for using high-pressure tactics, so I was curious to sit through one. While on a beach vacation, my friend and I were promised a free scuba diving adventure if we listened to a pitch for a time-share at an up-scale resort, so why not? Before the spiel, a friendly sales agent named Carlos chitchatted with us over a nice breakfast. After the presentation we toured the beautiful resort, and Carlos invited us to invest. We politely declined. He dropped the price. We declined again. It wasn't so bad, really. We were ready to go scuba diving.

But they weren't ready to give us the passes. When Carlos's manager checked in to see how things were going, Carlos told him we weren't interested. The manager looked at me like a hawk eyeing a chipmunk and took Carlos's seat across the table. He grilled us, accusing us of being greedy and two-faced, of not having ever intended to seriously consider the opportunity, of trying to scam them for free scuba diving.

He had a point, of course, but we argued otherwise, just as he intended. By accusing us, he was putting us in the position of having to defend ourselves. *Of course we were interested in the resort. Yes, it was obviously a wonderful getaway, and a time-share was a great way to enjoy it at a reasonable price.* Not only did this mean we had to enumerate the benefits of the time-share, but it might even make us feel guilty enough to sign on. Still, we said no. He threw his pen across the room and stormed off, furious.

Carlos, who had been standing there looking stricken the whole time, apologized profusely and asked us to please hang on for just one minute. He trotted after his boss. When he returned, he apologized again for his boss, who was having a terrible day. He gave us a woven blanket and a bottle of rum as a peace offering. Then he quoted us a lower price than he had ever been able to offer anyone because his boss felt so bad, and Carlos told us it would really make his day if we took advantage of this amazing deal.

In some situations, the bad cop is a bogeyman who doesn't even exist. The person you're talking to would love to give you what you want, but it's just not up to them. I once worked for a small business owner whose business cards read "Assistant Director." "So, who's the director?" I asked. "There isn't one," he replied. "I just want everyone to see me as the good guy."

Whenever there's a not-so-good guy in the picture, or maybe just outside the frame, the good guy might not be what he seems.

Red flag #9: A Funny Feeling

Gavin de Becker, one of the world's top experts in personal security (and personal violence), insists that nearly all of the hundreds of victims of personal crimes he has interviewed had a funny feeling that could have allowed them to walk away safely. Their Gator was signaling, *Something's not right here,* but then denial kicked in and explained it away. We make excuses because we don't want to think badly of others, and we'll die before we have to be rude. Sometimes literally.

These feelings of unease can be lifesavers, but they're also prone to error and ugly biases. Your subconscious alarm system is designed to keep you and your tribe safe, but it can also be overprotective. We learn to ignore our funny feelings because so often they turn out to be wrong. That creaking stair in the middle of the night? It was just your child getting a glass of water, so the next time you wake up to a sound in the house, you figure it's probably nothing and go back to sleep.

We hear horror stories on both sides of this divide. A funny feeling ignored can have deadly consequences, but an overreaction can lead to tragedy too. It can be hard to sort out whether the instinctual inner alarm is signaling genuine danger or just primal, prejudicial fear. *Not like me! Not one of us!*

A British diplomat who audited my course shared an experience from the aftermath of the 7/7 terrorist attack in London. Bombs in three Underground stations and one double-decker bus had killed fifty-two people and injured seven hundred more. Uncertain if the violence was over, Londoners remained on edge. The diplomat was riding the tube when a well-dressed Middle Eastern–looking man wearing a prayer cap boarded the train with a duffel bag. The stranger sat down, opened a copy of the Koran, and began to pray. The diplomat felt his blood pressure soar. *What's in the duffel bag? Why is he praying? Is he a suicide bomber about to fulfill his mission? Should I alert the conductor? Should I pull the alarm? What if I'm wrong? What if he's just devout?*

The diplomat did not raise the alarm, but he did get off the train before it reached his stop, feeling confused and ashamed. He also recognized the irony in the situation: He himself was a well-dressed Middle Eastern–looking man, holding a bulky briefcase instead of a duffel. *He* might have been giving other people a funny feeling, too.

I don't have any brilliant, one-size-fits-all advice about separating valid hunches from the rest. This is deep, murky, Gator territory. You don't have conscious control over your gut reactions and fears. We are all biased in some ways, and although you can learn to notice some of your biases, it is impossible to control them. What you can control is what you *do* about those hunches. You can distinguish between your reactions to people going about their own lives and those who are trying to interfere with yours.

Whenever you get a funny feeling about someone who's trying to influence you, or if you notice one of the other red flags listed here, be on the lookout for more. Or just say no as firmly as necessary and walk away. And remember that nobody is immune to bad actors all of the time, even people who are highly trained to resist them; when the Gator gets overloaded, the Judge is hard to reach. Don't beat yourself up about it. With a little practice, though, you can become better attuned to the red flags around you and enhance your own sixth sense for any sharks that might be circling.

Angels and Demons

Marie was the coolest person I had ever met. I was sixteen, she was two years older, and both of us had moved to Italy to spend a year without our parents, hosted by local families. I was a fan of French films, and Marie seemed like she was starring in one. She didn't make any effort to be the center of attention, she just was. When she looked at you, you felt naked. And of course she was beautiful. Bright feline eyes with thick, dark lashes. Long, shiny hair she wore loose. Plump lips and a crooked tooth that was somehow perfect. She wasn't skinny and really didn't care what anyone thought about that. Or about her.

Back in the States, my friends and I might feign indifference to the world, but we were keenly attuned to every reaction, by everyone, to everything we did. I hadn't even noticed this obsessive self-monitoring until I met Marie. She was remarkable for being herself. I wanted to be Marie too but I understood the impossibility of being more yourself by trying to be someone else. I did take up smoking for a while because Marie looked so cool tilting her head to blow the smoke away from you without breaking eye contact.

When American Thanksgiving rolled around in November, a group of exchange students met up in Ancona to celebrate the holiday at our American friend's house. Her host family was away, so she and I cooked our first-ever turkey. Just one giant leg that took hours and tasted awful. But our Dutch friend had brought a few bottles of wine, so we had plenty to drink. We performed a drunken pantomime show with our hands through the sleeves of each other's sweaters. We laughed like children because we were.

In the late afternoon Marie and I said *ciao* to our friends and walked a mile to the bus stop, tipsy and shivering. We waited and waited for the bus, long past its scheduled arrival, sucking on Marie's cigarettes for imaginary heat. Just as we were discussing what to do, a dark Mercedes quietly pulled up. The tinted passenger window slid down, revealing a handsome face.

"You look cold." He smiled. "Where are you headed?"

He had a strong accent, not Italian. Wavy black hair, tan skin, and bright white teeth.

"We're waiting for a bus to the train station."

The handsome man said something to his companion, then grinned back at us. "It's right on our way." As he stepped out to open the back door, he bowed chivalrously. "Get in."

Marie and I looked at each other—and shrugged. The men would flirt with us but Marie had fended off advances with just a look. The station was only ten minutes away, the bus might not be coming at all, and it was so damn cold. We got in.

The driver greeted us but didn't seem to understand Italian. He wore sunglasses and focused on the road. The handsome man made small talk, asking where we were from and how long we had been in Italy. Instead of answering when we asked where they were from, he challenged us to guess. Our guesses made him laugh. He told us we were beautiful, and joked, "But maybe not so smart? No, no, you are very smart."

Marie was the first to notice something amiss. "We need to get to the station." The station was in the city center, but the driver had entered the coastal highway.

"This is the way to the station," our handsome friend tried to assure us.

"No," Marie insisted, "it's not. We have a train to catch and we need to get home."

He groaned like a puppy. "Okay, I'm sorry. I confess that I asked my friend to take the scenic route, but we'll get you to the station. You see, we're here on vacation and we've been finding the Italians so unfriendly. But you two, you're so nice. I hope it's not too unpleasant to talk to us, as fellow visitors, for just a few minutes? We're harmless."

I was getting nervous. As Marie explained that our host families were waiting for us, I realized that the handle of Marie's door was missing. So was mine. I pushed the button to roll down the window and yell for help, but the window was locked. I touched Marie's leg and caught her eye. She followed my gaze to her door.

"Where the fuck is the handle?"

Our abductor began to explain the car had just been in the shop, the mechanics hadn't finished—

Marie cut him off. "Stop the fucking car and let us out."

He apologized for the misunderstanding, and he hoped we weren't scared. But I was very scared of whatever they wanted to do to us and how much worse it might be if we made them angry.

Marie, however, flew into a rage. She slammed the front

seat, screaming at the top of her lungs, "STOP THE FUCKING CAR! STOP THE FUCKING CAR! STOP THE FUCKING CAR, YOU MONSTERS!"

Our abductor dropped the charm offensive. "Calm down, you crazy bitch!"

Marie roared and kicked as the driver cursed in his language and turned off the highway. Marie was in a fury, and I was in awe. The driver pulled over and the no longer handsome man got out to open the door for us. "You're a goddamn lunatic, you know that?"

We stepped out and I gulped the cold air like a goldfish.

There's a saying in animal training, "Everything with a mouth bites." You should never assume that just because a creature is small or cute that it can't hurt you. I hadn't realized you could raise your voice to a stranger, let alone to full-grown men. It hadn't occurred to me, even in terror, not to be nice. But Marie was a honey badger, a dragon, a demon. She taught me that I, too, was an animal with a mouth.

When Ripley was ten, we were eating breakfast at an outdoor hotel restaurant. There was no one else in our section. A man walked over with his tray, said hello, and made a comment about the weather. I agreed that it was lovely. He tried to make conversation and I responded with clipped answers, expecting him to pick up on the universal polite signal for "go away."

"Maybe I can join you."

"No, thanks. We want to eat by ourselves."

He started to sit down. "Don't worry, I'm harmless. I just like talking to little girls."

I stood, put my hand out in a stop gesture, and raised my

voice. "You may not sit with us. We didn't invite you and WE DON'T WANT YOU HERE. LEAVE."

He called me a crazy bitch, and he left. Ripley was surprised and impressed. Now she knows she can raise her voice too, and that her life doesn't have to be in danger before she tells a creep to back the bleep off.

Being a nice person doesn't mean you can't defend yourself. And being a guardian doesn't mean looking like an angel.

CHAPTER NINE

Dreaming Bigger and Better

As you progress along the path to becoming a more and more influential person, at some point you may find yourself ready to dream bigger than ever before. You'll scan the world around you and ask, *How could this be even better?* And an idea will come. It might not be banging pots and pans to get your attention, or tsking at you about what you should be doing with your one wild and precious life. It might be silent as a firefly. But you'll feel the magic, and wonder, *Who, me?*

Maybe your bigger, better idea will be creative—the book that only you can write, the next unicorn start-up, the film that will change the world. Maybe your big dream is a foundation, a platform, or a movement. Maybe it's taking the risk to step out of the neat life you have built for yourself and discover what makes you feel alive. Maybe your big dream is tackling a problem big enough to be worthy of you: achieving social justice; solving the climate crisis; making sure everyone has access to clean water, medicine, and education. Maybe it's reaching the stars or the unexplored ocean deep.

When you set off in pursuit of this dream, you'll face worthy adversaries, external and internal. And you'll need every influence tool at your disposal. It will get messy—and it will be beautiful. While the study of influence is a science, the practice of influence is an art.

Let Tunisia Make History Once More

At the end of 2010, on the coast of North Africa, Tunisia was suffering through the twenty-third year of Zine El Abidine Ben Ali's dictatorial rule. Thirty percent of Tunisia's young people were unemployed; they were also in debt, too poor to marry, and burdened with supporting their families. One was a young man named Mohamed Bouazizi, who sold apples without a permit. When his scale was confiscated by the authorities, he was so desperate that he demanded a meeting with the governor but he was turned away. In the street outside the governor's office, before a crowd of horrified onlookers, Bouazizi poured gasoline all over his body and set himself on fire. "How do you expect me to make a living?" he cried out.

This was the torch that lit the Arab Spring.

Five thousand people turned out for Bouazizi's funeral. From there, the protests grew and the uprising spread. Five thousand turned to ten thousand, crowds taking over the streets and spilling out into all the city squares, demanding the resignation of President Ben Ali. On January 14, Ben Ali fled the country, and his successor was chosen in the first true democratic election in the Arab world. The protests in Tunisia would inspire protests and revolts across the region, with the people of Egypt, Libya, and Yemen forcing the removal of their own dictators. People came together to speak out and demand change. The world watched, holding its breath.

One of the people glued to the news coverage was a German Algerian strategist named Belabbes Benkredda. Although his father had been a freedom fighter in the Algerian revolution, Belabbes (pronounced bell-ah-BESS) was born and raised in Germany. Being a rebel there involved growing your hair and singing in a grunge rock band, which he did. Belabbes studied international relations in the UK and landed a cushy job in Dubai, working as a spin doctor for the government. Before the Arab Spring, he had been enjoying the intellectual challenge of his work and the comfort of the expat lifestyle. But as he watched democracy being born, he heard a voice whispering, *What are you doing?* Arab democracy was young, fragile, and needed all the help it could get.

Belabbes quit his job and founded a nonprofit organization called the Munathara Initiative, whose mission was to promote civic engagement through debates—*munathara* means "debate" in Arabic. He tapped his savings, called in every favor, and within thirty days Munathara aired its first show. Over the next few years, the organization expanded across the Arab region. It sponsored debate training workshops for women, youth, and underserved minorities. Its TV shows, pitting winners of online debating contests against celebrities, were watched by millions of viewers.

Success brought ups and downs. Belabbes won a democracy award presented by Madeleine Albright, but his organization was shut down by the government of the United Arab Emirates, which wasn't keen on free speech. He handled that rejection by moving the base of operations, and his work, to Tunisia.

I met Belabbes when he was invited to participate in Yale University's most selective leadership program, the World Fellows. He audited my course, sitting at the back in his blazer and pocket square, listening intently the way highly influential people often do. As we got to know each other outside of class, I learned he was a visionary and a kindred spirit. Despite the pocket square, he turned out to be a goofball who could parody any accent. He was also a great dad. Since we were both divorced, we took our same-age daughters trick-or-treating together. We played table tennis after work. We talked and talked, listened and listened, and fell in love. One of the things I admire most about Belabbes is that he dreams big. This is the story of one dream I got to witness.

In 2019, Tunisia was still the only real democracy in the Arab region, and its second election was imminent. This offered an unprecedented opportunity to set norms for a free and fair electoral process, both in Tunisia and in the wider region. Debates could figure prominently. I had grown up outside Washington, D.C., taking democracy and presidential debates for granted. Of course you voted, and of course you watched debates, even though we had only two parties to choose from. After the revolution in Tunisia, *seventy* political parties had formed—and you didn't even have to be a member of one to run for office. Without debates, how were people going to even hear about all those candidates, let alone be able to compare them? Gators, following the path of least resistance, would vote for a familiar face; without debates, Tunisia's election would be settled by name recognition.

Belabbes wondered, *What would it take to organize a series of televised presidential debates?* He had never done that before—although, to be fair, no one else in the Arab world had either. When the big idea came to him, he also heard a harsher voice whispering, *Who do you think you are?* For a time, he felt paralyzed and unable to take action. But as he gathered his courage, he asked himself, as he always does, *How could it be even better?* Political echo chambers were a problem in the United States, but nothing compared to Tunisia, where thirteen television stations delivered the news, and a family of five might be watching five different news channels, each getting a different spin and a different set of facts. There was no shared political reality, or even a simple split, as we have in the United States. Belabbes wondered, *What would it take to get debates broadcast simultaneously on every station?* It had never happened before, but why not?

Belabbes's big dream had almost zero chance of success. He would be asking people and organizations who had never collaborated on any scale, let alone a grand one, to leave their egos at the door and work together. He would be pitching the importance of debates to political parties, the government, and the media. And before any of that could even begin, the project would require money.

The Federal Foreign Office of Germany had supported Munathara in the past, but that was years ago and Belabbes's contacts had moved on. *Just ask, just ask, just ask.* He picked up the phone and made a cold call, asking the operator for the department that oversaw cultural affairs in the Middle East and North Africa. She transferred the call. Belabbes explained the historic opportunity briefly, but to avoid scaring anyone off, he started with a baby step, pitching a smaller project—televised parliamentary debates. He asked what it would take to get help, and, miraculously, he was invited to send a proposal. He scrambled to pull together a twenty-page document outlining his dream.

To have even a tiny chance of inspiring funders, politicians, government bureaucrats, and broadcasting partners to join together, Belabbes needed a compelling frame. He came up with *"Let Tunisia make history once more."* It was a monumental opportunity: making history with the first televised series of electoral debates in the Arab world. Yet it was manageable. Tunisia had made history once already as the birthplace of the Arab Spring; if you can manage a successful democratic revolution, surely you can manage a debate. And the word "let" added just a touch of mystery and suspense: Could they really do it?

After many rounds of revisions to Belabbes's grant proposal, the German Federal Foreign Office said yes to funding the project. This green light prompted other influential people to step in, too. Fadwa Zidi, a television journalist and producer at Middle East Broadcasting Networks, was so inspired she flew over from Dubai to spend her vacation working long hours to set up production plans. At the end of her two weeks, she and Belabbes had a John Sculley/Steve Jobs moment when she considered the opportunity she would miss if she went back home. He couldn't pay her a salary yet, but she stayed on, believing in the dream, eventually becoming the chief operating officer and executive producer of Munathara and all its debate programs. If the debates were possible, she would make them spectacular.

Belabbes pitched "Let Tunisia make history once more" to the Tunisian election commission, to the national broadcasting agency, and to the leader of the private television syndicate. He pitched the big idea of simultaneous presidential debates to the Swiss Foreign Ministry and to the Open Society Foundations. He was advised by electoral debate organizers in the United States, Chile, and Jamaica. He got the support of a famous political satirist, who offered counsel and teased resistant allies until they came around. Against all odds, a coalition was coming together.

The more excited people got, and the more energy and passion Belabbes invested in the project, the more he stood to win. And to lose. When you dare to dream big, you leave your heart wide open. As his dream began to seem possible, I worried more and more. Every day was a roller coaster. Tunisia's ailing president passed away, which threw the election into uncertainty, then caused it to be moved up two months. This made the timing so tight that Belabbes had to issue press releases before all the agreements had been finalized, a tactic that proved to be both harrowing and effective.

As the dream ballooned from a crazy vision of two debates to a series of seven presidential and parliamentary debates with follow-ups in the spring, the cost soared from $300,000 to $1.4 million. Somehow Belabbes had managed to get funding commitments to cover those expenses, but none of the actual money had come through and contractors needed to be hired and publicity paid for. Belabbes maxed out his credit card and we liquidated our retirement funds to cover expenses temporarily. Then, just when it seemed the various broadcasting partners were aligned, one tried to break away and steal the debate idea for themselves. But as soon as Belabbes found out, he scheduled a press conference to announce the "official" debate plans to the world, and the competitor decided to become an ally again.

As planning for the debates accelerated, the presidential field was taking shape. Twenty-six candidates had stepped up, including two women, a current prime minister, a defense minister, and a former president. Belabbes and his team would have to persuade each one to commit to appearing in an initial round of debates and then, after the first round of voting, a final debate for the two front-runners. The benefit to candidates was clear: name recognition and the chance to share your platform. However, the potential cost was clear too. If you were already well known, you had less to gain—and you stood to lose support if you weren't a skilled debater. So Belabbes planned a Face-Saving Plan B: the empty podium rule: *We'd hate to have an empty podium there with your name on it, and we hope it won't come to that. Come join us.*

The strategy succeeded, and twenty-four of the twenty-six candidates agreed to participate. All except the two who absolutely couldn't. One candidate had fled the country to avoid arrest. And another, the front-runner, had been jailed on suspicions of money laundering and tax evasion. He was a media mogul named Nabil Karoui who was jokingly called Nabil Macaroni, for the bags of groceries he brought to poor families' homes with great fanfare, airing these acts of generosity on his television station.

If Tunisia was truly making history again, then the world needed to know about it. So Belabbes turned his attention to the international press. Press releases led to interviews, which led to more interviews and to headlines echoing his monumental frame. Belabbes was on television every day spreading the word. However, the debates themselves were going to be broadcast only in Tunisian and Arabic, so if you didn't speak those languages, you'd have to wait for the official translations posted the following day. But the moment of truth for news is always when it's breaking. So Belabbes and Fadwa hired the country's best French and English interpreters, and invited diplomats and foreign correspondents to come to watch parties and listen to translated debates in real time. Livestreams would be posted to the Web where anyone could access them, and stories could be filed in the moment of truth as the debates were happening.

When the first presidential debate aired on September 7, 2019, television sets in households, cafés, hookah bars, and hair salons were tuned to the event. Watch parties spilled out into the streets of downtown Tunis as viewers watched candidates take their places at the eight translucent podiums on the shimmering blue and red stage. Louise de Souza, the British ambassador, and Olivier Poivre d'Arvor, the French ambassador, would join Belabbes's watch parties, as would journalists from CNN, the BBC, the Agence France-Presse, and hundreds of others. News channels across the world were covering the historic event. Three million Tunisians—more than half the voting population—and millions more elsewhere in the Arab world, listened as each candidate made their case.

One candidate in particular would capture viewers'

attention—a balding constitutional law professor named Kais Saied. He was an independent candidate running a campaign from his apartment. Saied spoke in stiff, formal, standard Arabic rather than the Tunisian dialect, with such a rigid demeanor that people nicknamed him "Robocop." When the first round of votes were cast, Saied had 18 percent of the vote and Karoui only 16 percent. The two men would face off against each other in the final election.

At this point, the dream that had been so unlikely was not only coming to fruition but going *too well*. Nabil Karoui, still in jail, threatened to contest the election results, claiming that being prevented from participating in the first series of debates had cost him his front-runner status. This was probably true. So Kais Saied agreed to abstain from campaigning while Karoui remained behind bars. With the debates and even the election hanging in the balance, Belabbes published an op-ed advocating for Karoui's release, while Fadwa made contingency plans for broadcasting the debate from the jail.

Karoui was ultimately released on October 9. The final head-to-head debate would take place on October 11, the last night of campaigning before the election just forty-eight hours later. This meant the two-hour debate would play a huge role in determining who would become the next president of the republic.

It was easy to watch the Karoui-Saied debate because it was impossible to watch anything else—it was being broadcast on every single television and radio station. It would be the most-viewed TV event in Tunisian history. Six and a half million out of eleven million citizens tuned in, not including those who followed on the radio and watched livestreams online, or the millions of other viewers watching broadcasts in Egypt, Morocco, Libya, Iraq, and Algeria, along with pan-Arab channels and wire services broadcasting globally. To put it into perspective, no television event in American history has ever reached such a large share of the population—although Neil Armstrong taking his first steps on the moon came close.

From the moment the debate began, it was clear Saied was more prepared and more persuasive. Although he was stiff, his formality conferred authority. Karoui gave rambling, off-the-cuff answers. He stumbled over his words, and his policy statements were vague. Understanding that her husband's poor debate performance could cost him the presidency, Karoui's wife, Salwa Smaoui, burst into the suite where Fadwa and the production team were controlling the live broadcast. Smaoui and her lawyer demanded that the show be ended immediately. The team said no. Smaoui asked if she could pass her husband a note, but they denied her request. The show went on. Karoui's performance did not improve.

Two days later, on October 13, Tunisians elected Kais Saied in a landslide with 73 percent of the vote. Nabil Karoui admitted defeat and sent a statement of congratulations. Tunisia made history—once more. The country's problems weren't miraculously solved, but inspired by these debates, Algeria would soon host its own first televised debates, and voters in other Arab countries would begin asking, *Why not us? Why not here?*

Belabbes Benkredda made his impossible dream come true using many of the ideas and strategies we've been discussing. He embraced rejection, managed resistance, negotiated agreements, identified and handled bullies and sharks, created value, made it easy, leveraged moments of truth, displayed charisma, and offered a compelling frame. But most of the time he wasn't conscious of using any particular influence tools, because through practice they had become second nature. Gator instead of Judge. At many critical junctures he wasn't using any tools at all; he was just dreaming big, asking boldly, and being a Kindly Brontosaurus. Sometimes he didn't even need to ask. He had become a person with an idea that people wanted to say yes to; they reached out to him, asking, "How can I help?" The success of his big dream depended on hard work, plenty of allies, and a good deal of luck, as big dreams always do.

Success also required him to face the question *Am I worthy?* once again. The bigger you dream, and the more successful you become, the more likely it is that internal obstacles will arise to block your way. Success can mess with your head. You worry that you'll never have another great idea again. That your success was just a fluke. This, too, is part of the journey. I feel these doubts every time I attempt something bigger than I've ever done before, and I see some of the smartest, most successful people I know wrestling with those same doubts. I take comfort from novelist Neil Gaiman's anecdote about the fear of greatness. Maybe it will offer you comfort too.

Some years ago, I was lucky enough to be invited to a gathering of great and good people: artists and scientists, writers and discoverers of things. And I felt that at any moment they would realize that I didn't qualify to be there, among these people who had really done things.

On my second or third night there, I was standing at the back of the hall, while a musical entertainment happened, and I started talking to a very nice, polite, elderly gentleman about several things, including our shared first name. And then he pointed to the hall of people, and said words to the effect of, "I just look at all these people, and I think, what the heck am I doing here? They've made amazing things. I just went where I was sent." And I said, "Yes. But you were the first man on the moon. I think that counts for something."

And I felt a bit better. Because if Neil Armstrong felt like an imposter, maybe everyone did. Maybe there weren't any grown-ups, only people who had worked hard and also got lucky and were slightly out of their depth, all of us doing the best job we could, which is all we can really hope for.

As you exercise your influence out in the world, experimenting and taking risks, there are no guarantees of success. You know this already. Too many elements lie beyond your control. But you can choose to be like Neil Gaiman, Neil Armstrong, Belabbes, Davis, Derren, Ethan, Gloria, Jennifer, Jia, Manus, Marie, Natalie, Prince, Shaquille, Stanislav, Sukari, and anyone else you admire. You can give it your best shot. And let your love shine.

You, Me, We

As our paths cross, entwine, diverge, and reconnect, we form a greater whole, a sprawling, living web of influence. You are already part of this collective power. The root of the word "influence" is the Latin *influere*, "to flow in." As a river. A current. Your influence flows from other people, and to other people, and from them to others, and on and on. Sometimes you're aware of those who lifted you up or helped inspire your great ideas, sometimes not. Sometimes you're aware of your own ripple effects, sometimes not. Small nudges here and there, sacrifices by brave and committed individuals, kind acts by not-so-committed individuals, accidents and acts of fate: They all connect us.

Awakening to this web is like embarking on a choose-your-own-adventure book. You can step up to be the hero, play a supporting role as the sidekick, stand your ground as the ally, or sit this one out. You can also change your mind along the way. Not every great idea will be right for you. But when you do choose to step forward, now you can do it bigger and better.

Few of history's turning points can credit just one hero. No one flew down in a cape or swung in on a strand of spider silk to save the world single-handedly. Instead there was an army of angels who spread the word, saying, "Here's what we're going to do." Or they just stepped up and did it. Working together in 1943, the Danish people saved 99 percent of their Jewish neighbors from the Holocaust. In the middle of the night, they ferried them in tiny fishing boats to Sweden and safety. Working together in 2005, the "Cajun Navy" rescued ten thousand of their neighbors from Hurricane Katrina, one of the worst hurricanes in U.S. history. As Rebecca Solnit writes in *Hope in the Dark*, "hundreds of boat-owners rescued people—single moms, toddlers, grandfathers—stranded in attics, on roofs, in flooded housing projects, hospitals, and school buildings. . . . None of these people said, *I can't rescue them all*. All of them said, *I can rescue someone, and that's work so meaningful and important I will risk my life and defy the authorities to do it*. And they did."

Not all battles are yours to fight. But my hope is that when you choose your own, the tools and ideas in this book will help you recruit allies who will improve your chances of succeeding and making the process more enjoyable. Margaret Mead was talking about influence when she famously said, "Never doubt that a small group of thoughtful, committed citizens can change the world; indeed, it's the only thing that ever has."

Together, and with big enough dreams, we can make magic happen. We can reverse the path of climate change. We can eradicate the caste systems that have kept generations of people poor, sick, and humiliated. We can collaborate on technical solutions to cure our worst diseases. We can join together to face the darkness and move beyond our fears.

You don't have to change the *whole* world. Or save it. But each one of us can make a difference for someone. You can help in your community. You can lobby your leaders to get policies passed that will make life easier for the people at work, at your school, or in your town. You can organize the members of your church, mosque, or temple to protect and serve people who need it. You can mediate a conflict within your family. You can be a role model. A mentor. A teacher.

If you've found this book helpful, I hope you'll share what you've learned with other people. Teach a tool. Tell a story. Discuss an idea. And maybe you'll find a minute to let me know how you put your influence into practice. Nothing would give me greater satisfaction than hearing your love stories. Manus and Tom trading up from a paper clip to a car, Stanislav Petrov saying *nyet,* Belabbes making the cold call, Jackie making the Olympic ring doughnuts, Jennifer Lawrence playing bigger and sharing the bounty—all of those were love stories. Strong, vulnerable people saying, *Maybe together, maybe this.* What you do with this book can be a love story too. You and I don't need to be lonely pioneers chopping our own wood, building our own cabins, and mending our own fences. We don't have to go it alone. I can't speak for you, but I wouldn't even want to.

On cold winter days Ripley and I enjoy fires and hot chocolate, but our happiest winter moment came the day a mail truck in our neighborhood got stuck in the snow and we stopped to help. We called a couple of pedestrians over, and soon more stopped to help. The snow was deep and the mail truck's tires kept spinning helplessly. Neighbors from nearby houses brought out shovels and cardboard, ten of us working together. We pushed as hard as we could. Some of us fell into the slush as our boots lost traction, but we got back up. And finally, we got that mail truck back on the road.

The mail carrier thanked us with a wave out the window and drove off to keep delivering the mail. As we all high-fived, our faces were glowing. We didn't work hard together because it's fun to be straining and cold and wet; we worked hard together because choosing to work as a team had made it fun *despite* the cold and wet.

How grown-ups play together is often called "work," although we don't always see it that way. Sometimes we succeed, and sometimes our hearts break open. Sometimes inspiration strikes, our timing is perfect, luck is on our side, and the gates of heaven part for us. And all the time, the seeds of our influence are floating off like the tufts of a dandelion, carried on the wind to places beyond where we can see. Whether we mean to or not, we are planting seeds. We are making history.

Let's Be Friends

It's been a joy to write this book for you. If you've enjoyed reading it, I hope you'll take action on your great ideas! And I'd love to hear how it goes.

If you'd like, there are lots of ways we can connect, starting at zoechance.com. There's a free massive open online course with real-world challenges based on some of the material in this book, a newsletter with influence tips and inspiration from others on the influence path, events across the world, workshops at Yale, and other great ideas and collaborations just getting hatched.

If you'd like to help these ideas spread, I would be so, so, so grateful! You could share on social media how you're making good things happen—even a baby step. Please tag me and #influenceisyoursuperpower so I can celebrate with you. A book review, even a short one, would be amazing! If you'd like to get this book for your organization or your squad, I can hook you up with a discount. Maybe you have other ideas. And if you'd like to make an invitation related to speaking, consulting, media, or research collaboration, come over to zoechance .com. I'm pretty busy, but I'm good at saying no. :-)

And if you'd like to share a personal note about what this book is doing for you, you can reach me at friends@zoechance .com.

Love, Zoe

P.S.: This is Ripley (and her reluctant boyfriend, Gavin).

Index of Tools and Techniques

Discussion Questions

Like so many things in life, this book is more fun when shared with friends. Here are ten questions to get you started discussing some of the ideas.

1. Why is interpersonal influence like a superpower?
2. For you, what's the difference between influence and manipulation?
3. If you've already tried something new from this book, like the 24-Hour "No" Challenge, or the Magic Question, how did that go? What did you learn?
4. What's a strategy from this book that you'd like to try?
5. In what situations do you find it hard to ask or to advocate for yourself? When discussing money? In a romantic relationship? With particular people? In what situations do you find it easy?
6. What does rejection mean to you? How could you reframe it?
7. What's your experience asking for raises or promotions? Is there anything you'd like to do differently in the future?
8. Did you relate to any of the "dark arts" situations in Chap-

ter 8? What happened, and what advice would you give other people?

9. If you could be more influential than you already are, what would you do?

10. Set an implementation intention for practicing one thing you learned from the book or this conversation.

Love Notes

This book was brought to you by a whole team of heroes, each with their own special powers.

Thank you to our writing and editorial team. We committed to doing whatever it took to make this book the best it could be—and we did. When we thought we were nearly done, it wasn't good enough and we started over. We could have gone crazy, but instead we brought out the best in each other. Hilary Redmon, your leadership style embodies the message of this book. You lovingly held us to high standards, opened time warps for us, built enthusiasm at Random House, and scrubbed in like a surgeon on weekends to make careful cuts and tiny stitches all over. You're the editor authors dream of. Ann Marie "Shall I whip up a draft?" Healy, you're the only fearless writer I've ever met. Your unconditional love held our project together as the world fell apart around us. And by "love" I mean not only your sunshine but also your work, through homeschooling and moves and deaths and family vacations. You surpassed "above and beyond" so long ago. Namaste. Peter Guzzardi, Wizard of Ours, you saw order in chaos, found bright spots in the darkness, untangled threads, asked hard questions, and polished our manuscript with a magic cloth. You worked hard and long out of love, and you gifted me the most beautiful thing an author could receive: You taught me how to really write.

Thank you to Alison MacKeen and Celeste Fine, the fairy-godmother agents who collaborated with me for years and got everyone so excited that I came down with impostor syndrome. You figured out before I did what I should really be writing about, helped make the proposal sing, and never stopped helping. (And the voodoo numbers and Ring Pops really did do magic.) You've changed my life.

Thank you to the brilliant research and fact-checking team, Sarah Jeong, Sophie Kaldor, and Ana Victoria Gil. You did the hard and dirty work of digging, uncovering new gems, and sorting the false from the real so we could base this book on solid science. You're already changing the world—Sarah, by including indigenous voices in New Zealand's sustainability policies; Sophie, by breaking new ground in the psychology of extremism; and Ana, by influencing public discourse on Costa Rica's Supreme Court. You're an inspiration to everyone and most certainly to me. I look forward to reading your books.

Thank you, Rodrigo Corral, for the cover. I love your work.

Thank you to the advisers and collaborators who contributed their talents along the way. Thank you, Catherine MacCoun, for the conversations about the "Bad Influence" idea that developed into chapter 8. Thank you, Dedi Felman, for your extensive editorial coaching on the proposal. Thank you, Eamon Dolan, for our brief but meaningful work together and for changing how I think about being "nice." Thank you, Ryan Holiday, for saving me from my great book idea. I started over because of you. Shane Frederick, thank you for vetting the science in chapter 2 and for influencing me to hold high standards for science, both in this book and in life.

Thank you, Angela Duckworth, Art Markman, Ashley Merryman, Charles Duhigg, Mike Norton, and Nick Christakis—I followed your advice as much as I could. Thank you, Joe Kavanagh, my favorite clonkey, for your ideas on how to help this fly. Thank you, Chevon Hicks; I still love the squirt gun concept. Thank you to the fellow authors of BLING for the wisdom, friendship, and forward momentum. Thank you to the brainstorm team—Bun Lai, Emily Gordon, Mason Rabinowitz, Nitya Kanuri, and Slate Ballard—for your great ideas about my ideas.

Thank you to the influence pros who found these ideas worth spreading—and who are doing it. Thank you, Nicole Dewey, Rachel Rokicki, Rachel Parker, and Melanie DeNardo, for using your brilliance and enthusiasm to win publicity for our project. Thank you, Ayelet Gruenspecht, Emani Glee, and Barbara Fillon, for your sage advice and business savvy—and for teaching me about book marketing. Thank you, Random House sales team, for getting these books into readers' hands. Thank you, Tom Perry, for your strategic advice, your blessings, and your role modeling. Thank you to the Fun Team for your enthusiasm in helping spread the word.

Thank you to the international team of special agents bringing this work to so many countries I've lost count. Denise Cronin, Donna Duverglas, Jessica Cashman, Joelle Dieu, Rory Scarfe, and Toby Ernst—you made magic happen. Susanna Abbott and other international publishers: Your diverse and high hopes scared me and motivated me to try my best. To the Yale-Coursera team bringing these ideas to life in our global online course—Belinda Platt, Sara Eppinger, Thom Stylinski, and Rick Leone—wow, what a gift to work with you.

Thank you, Stephanie Dunson, wise and gentle writing coach, for teaching me to "garden." Thank you to the other writing buddies who made writing a pleasure: Amy Dannen-mueller, Ann Marie Healy (again), Ashley Merryman (again), Christa Doran, Christine Chmielewski, David Chance, David Tate, Doina Moulin, John Gonzalez, Kyle Jensen, Margo Steiner, Marianne Pantalon, Natalie Ma, and Teresa Chahine. Thank you, Teri and Tom of Cedarhurst Cafe, for the unofficial co-working space and all the coffee.

Thank you for the extra help, Jaidree Braddix, Tangela Mitchell, and Erin Wynne. Thank you for your painstaking cpoyediting, Muriel Jorgensen and Louise Collazo.

Thank you to the students, TAs, and course assistants of Mastering Influence and Persuasion, for workshopping these ideas with me. I've learned more from you than you did from me. Thank you, Stephen Dionne, ops manager extraordinaire.

Thank you to the giants whose work inspired mine. Without you, there is nothing.

I'm also indebted to those who didn't work directly on this project but have profoundly influenced it.

Thank you to those who took care of my life so the writing could happen. Karen Chance, mom, spiritual teacher, close friend, and co-parent—you made this possible. And our conversations about the book—it's all here. Mandy Keene, coach, cheerleader, teacher, and longtime friend, you're responsible for so much of my happiness and success. The Magic Question was just the beginning. Xiomara Sacaza, thank you for making order out of chaos and showing me what faith looks like.

I'm grateful to everyone who helps me spread ideas beyond the book. Thanks to the Stern Speaking team for believing in me before I did, and thank you to the Yale SOM comms team for being early readers and for sharing my class with the world. Thank you to the mentors who have inspired me to dream big and have fun—Bob Goff, Dan Ariely, Jeff Arch, Kim Benston, Mark Young, Mike Norton (again), and Rob Sherman: I'm paying it forward. Thank you to Katie Orenstein and The OpEd Project: I will be forever grateful for how the Public Voices Fellowship helped me find my voice.

Thank you to Andrew Metrick, Edi Pinker, Gal Zauberman, Jim Baron, Nathan Novemsky, Ravi Dhar, and Ted Snyder, for helping me change my job to a calling so I could write this book and do more of what I love.

Thank you to all the friends and family who teach me how to be both kind and influential. Christy, Jess, Jen, Molly, Taly, Talula, and Teresa (again) for keeping me going, and laughing. Dad, Jaye, Mika, and Shane (again), for your love and support always. Lulu: to the end of the multiverse and back! Amira, I wanted to be your stepmom since we first met. Belabbes, chief adviser, biggest dreamer, true love, I'd marry you again a million times.

Thank you, dear reader, for engaging with these ideas. If they help you become more influential, or help you help others along that path, then our labors of love were well spent.

Image Credits

Stroop Test	Adapted by Mapping Specialists Ltd.
Paperclip to a car	Yale School of Management
Cat, fish, bird, snake	Nobukyuki Kawai
Tink the puppy	Niv Weisenberg
False polarization bias	Data: Moore-Berg et al., *PNAS* 2020 Original art by Beyond Conflict and refinements by Mapping Specialists Ltd. Used by permission of Beyond Conflict.
Debate watch party in Tunis	Zoubeir Souissi/Reuters
Ripley and Gavin	Ashley McNamara
Author photo	Ian Christmann

Endnotes

I've prepared these research notes for you with as much attention to detail and accuracy as possible. I've already omitted from the manuscript many famous experiments because new data have called the original results into question, but no doubt some of the work I have cited will turn out not to replicate. And of course future research will help us understand influence even better. Therefore, from time to time I'll be updating these notes at zoechance.com. Enjoy.

Chapter One: Becoming Someone People Want to Say Yes To

4   **when people are asked about influence strategies and influence tactics, they describe them as "manipulative," "sneaky," and "coercive"** This was from a survey I ran with participants from multiple countries. I asked some of them what words came to mind when they heard the word "influence." Most (73 percent) used positive words like "leader," "powerful," and "helpful." But when I asked instead about "influence strategies" and "influence tactics," most of them (57 percent and 83 percent) used negative descriptors like "manipulative," "sneaky," "coercive," "underhanded," and "aggressive."

4   **Robert Cialdini and Chris Voss encourage us to use "weapons of**

influence" for "beating our opponents" I may not agree with everything in these books, but they're brilliant. Bob is a researcher who has conducted many of the most famous studies of influence. Before writing his book, he went undercover as a car salesman. Chris is a former FBI hostage negotiator. Robert B. Cialdini, *Influence, New and Expanded: The Psychology of Persuasion* (New York: Harper Business, 2021); Chris Voss and Tahl Raz, *Never Split the Difference: Negotiating as If Your Life Depended on It* (New York: Harper Business, 2016).

5   **far less likely to be sued for malpractice regardless of their patients' outcomes** Nalini Ambady, Debi LaPlante, Thai Nguyen, Robert Rosenthal, Nigel Chaumeton, and Wendy Levinson, "Surgeons' Tone of Voice: A Clue to Malpractice History," *Surgery* 132, no. 1 (2002): 5–9, https://doi.org/10.1067/msy.2002.124733.

5   **executives who are trained to communicate get rated as better leaders** John Antonakis, Marika Fenley, and Sue Liechti, "Can Charisma Be Taught? Tests of Two Interventions," *Academy of Management Learning and Education* 10, no. 3 (2011): 374–96, https://doi.org/10.5465/amle.2010.0012.

Chapter One and a Half: Searching for *Temul*

14   **"the look in the eye of a horse that is racing where it wants to go, no matter what the rider wants"** Jack M. Weatherford, *Genghis Khan and the Making of the Modern World* (New York: Crown, 2004).

16   **my most shocking early discovery was that the majority of my hypotheses were wrong** Sadly, the biggest thing PhD students are wrong about is their decision to go to grad school—50 percent of them don't finish, because grad school wasn't what they expected. Robert Sowell, Ting Zhang, and Kenneth Redd, *Ph.D. Completion and Attrition: Analysis of Baseline Program Data from the Ph.D. Completion Project*, Council of Graduate Schools, 2008, https://cgsnet.org/phd-completion-and-attrition-analysis-baseline-program-data-phd-completion-project.

Chapter Two: Influence Doesn't Work the Way You Think

20   **"Operations of [conscious] thought are like cavalry charges in a battle"** Alfred N. Whitehead, *An Introduction to Mathematics* (New York: Henry Holt, 1911).

20   **Nobel Prize winner Daniel Kahneman's book** If there's a bible of behavioral economics, this is it. Daniel Kahneman, *Thinking, Fast and Slow* (New York: Farrar, Straus and Giroux, 2011).

If you'd rather read about Danny Kahneman's work in a journalistic format, this book by the author of *Moneyball* is great too: Michael Lewis, *The Undoing Project: A Friendship That Changed Our Minds* (New York: W. W. Norton, 2017).

And if you'd like to ponder current thinking on System 1 and System 2 more deeply, this article might interest you. Keith Stanovich and Richard West were the original researchers who coined the frames System 1 and System 2 and brought other dual process theories together under this umbrella: Jonathan St. B. T. Evans and Keith E. Stanovich, "Dual-Process Theories of Higher Cognition: Advancing the Debate," *Perspectives on Psychological Science* 8, no. 3 (2013): 223–41, https://doi.org/10.1177%2F1745691612460685.

23   **could read the word "red" faster than they could identify the color** J. Ridley Stroop, "Studies of Interference in Serial Verbal Reactions," *Journal of Experimental Psychology* 18, no. 6 (1935): 643–62, https://doi.org/10.1037/h0054651.

23   **you would soon become an expert at naming colors** Colin M. MacLeod and K. Dunbar, "Training and Stroop-like Interference: Evidence for a Continuum of Automaticity," *Journal of Experimental Psychology: Learning, Memory, and Cognition* 14, no. 1 (1988): 126–35, https://doi.org/10.1037/0278-7393.14.1.126.

24   **"most of daily life is driven by automatic, nonconscious mental processes"** John A. Bargh and Tanya L. Chartrand, "The Unbearable Automaticity of Being," *American Psychologist* 54, no. 7 (1999): 462–79, https://doi.org/10.1037/0003-066X.54.7.46.

25   **In a study of parole decisions in Israeli courts, researchers Shai Danziger, Jonathan Levav, and Liora Avnaim-Pesso noticed a weird pattern** This study has been a topic of discussion and contention among behavioral science researchers. The reported results are

more dramatic than one should expect to see in a replication, but the pattern persisted when the researchers reran their analyses in a rebuttal response. (If you're familiar with behavioral science, you know it's not unusual for published experiments to overstate the general, real-world relationship between two variables. In fact, it's the norm.)

The original paper: Shai Danziger, Jonathan Levav, and Liora Avnaim-Pesso, "Extraneous Factors in Judicial Decisions," *Proceedings of the National Academy of Sciences* 108, no. 17 (2011): 6889–92, https://doi.org/10.1073/pnas.1018033108.

The critiques: Keren Weinshall-Margel and John Shapard, "Overlooked Factors in the Analysis of Parole Decisions," *Proceedings of the National Academy of Sciences* 108, no. 42 (2011): E833, https://doi.org/10.1073/pnas.1110910108.

Andreas Glöckner, "The Irrational Hungry Judge Effect Revisited: Simulations Reveal That the Magnitude of the Effect Is Overestimated," *Judgment and Decision Making* 11, no. 6 (2016): 601–10. (Glöckner rationally questions the magnitude of the effect.) http://journal.sjdm.org/16/16823/jdm16823.pdf.

The authors' response. ("The original results replicate in every analysis; case order and the meal break remain robust predictors of the parole decision.") Shai Danziger, Jonathan Levav, and Liora Avnaim-Pesso, "Reply to Weinshall-Margel and Shapard: Extraneous Factors in Judicial Decisions Persist," *Proceedings of the National Academy of Sciences* 108, no. 17 (2011): E834, https://doi.org/10.1073/pnas.1112190108.

26 **evaluate a professor's competence based on a silent, six-second clip of the professor teaching** Nalini Ambady and Robert Rosenthal, "Half a Minute: Predicting Teacher Evaluations from Thin Slices of Nonverbal Behavior and Physical Attractiveness," *Journal of Personality and Social Psychology* 64, no. 3 (1993): 431–41, https://doi.org/10.1037/0022-3514.64.3.431.

26 **identify the most highly rated salespeople from a sample of regional sales managers using three twenty-second clips of just their voices** Nalini Ambady, Mary Anne Krabbenhoft, and Daniel Hogan, "The 30-Sec Sale: Using Thin-Slice Judgments to Evaluate Sales Effectiveness," *Journal of Consumer Psychology* 16, no. 1 (2006): 4–13, https://doi.org/10.1207/s15327663jcp1601_2.

26   **were able to predict from merely the sound of the surgeons'
**   **voices which ones had been sued for malpractice** Nalini Ambady,
       Debi Laplante, Thai Nguyen, Robert Rosenthal, Nigel Chaumeton,
       and Wendy Levinson, "Surgeons' Tone of Voice: A Clue to Malprac-
       tice History," *Surgery* 132, no. 1 (2002): 5–9, https://doi.org/10.1067
       /msy.2002.124733.

26– **Whether the thin slices were of body language, tone of voice, or
27   faces, they all conveyed valuable information and yielded remark-
**   **able predictive accuracy** Nalini Ambady and Robert Rosenthal,
       "Thin Slices of Expressive Behavior as Predictors of Interpersonal
       Consequences: A Meta-Analysis," *Psychological Bulletin* 111, no. 2
       (1992): 256–74, https://doi.org/10.1037/0033-2909.111.2.256.

27   **predicted with astonishing 70 percent accuracy which candidates
**   **had gone on to win their races** Alexander Todorov, Anesu N. Man-
       disodza, Amir Goren, and Crystal C. Hall, "Inferences of Compe-
       tence from Faces Predict Election Outcomes," *Science* 308, no.
       5728 (2005): 1623–26, https://doi.org/10.1126/science.1110589.

         Even more astonishing, kids' judgments are just as accurate.
       When Swiss children viewed pairs of faces and picked who they'd
       prefer to be the captain of their boat, their choices predicted 71
       percent of results in the French parliamentary runoff election. Ac-
       curacy was unrelated to age. John Antonakis and Olaf Dalgas, "Pre-
       dicting Elections: Child's Play!" *Science* 323, no. 5918 (2009):
       1183, https://doi.org/10.1126/science.1167748.

27   **Gators make snap judgments, and once they have done so, they
**   **don't let go** Gator-focused deciders are happier with their decisions
       and feel they reflect their true self. Sam J. Maglio and Taly Reich,
       "Feeling Certain: Gut Choice, the True Self, and Attitude Certainty,"
       Emotion 19, no. 5 (2019): 876, https://doi.org/10.1037/emo0000490.

         And they're more willing to defend those decisions: Sam J.
       Maglio and Taly Reich, "Choice Protection for Feeling-Focused De-
       cisions," *Journal of Experimental Psychology: General* 149, no. 9
       (2020): 1704–18, https://doi.org/10.1037/xge0000735.

27   **having more time to ponder doesn't improve the accuracy of thin
**   **slice social predictions, and some studies have found that giving
**   **participants more time actually made their predictions *less* accu-
**   **rate** Ambady and Rosenthal, "Thin Slices of Expressive Behavior as
       Predictors of Interpersonal Consequences: A Meta-analysis." Psy-

chological Bulletin 111, no. 2 (1992): 256–274, https://doi.org
/10.1037/0033-2909.111.2.256.

28 **more neural fibers sending messages from the limbic system to the neocortex than there are going in the opposite direction** This is a fascinating book about the neurobiology of risk, stress, and decision-making. John Coates, *The Hour Between Dog and Wolf: How Risk Taking Transforms Us, Body and Mind* (New York: Penguin, 2012).

28 **chocolate shaped like dog doo** Paul Rozin and April E. Fallon, "A Perspective on Disgust," *Psychological Review* 94, no. 1 (1987): 23–41, https://doi.org/10.1037/0033-295X.94.1.23.

29 **"Your eyes can make out fine detail only in a keyhole-sized circle at the very center of your gaze covering one-tenth of one percent of your retina"** This cool book is actually about the neuroscience of sleight-of-hand magic. Stephen Macknik, Susana Martinez-Conde, and Sandra Blakeslee, *Sleights of Mind: What the Neuroscience of Magic Reveals About Our Everyday Deceptions* (New York: Henry Holt, 2010).

30 **caring about ethical issues made them *less* likely to seek out information** Kristine R. Ehrich and Julie R. Irwin, "Willful Ignorance in the Request for Product Attribute Information," *Journal of Marketing Research* 42, no. 3 (2005): 266–77, https://psycnet.apa.org/record/2005-09529-008.

31 **when you give people a reason and an opportunity to fool themselves, they do, for as long as they can** Zoe Chance, Michael I. Norton, Francesca Gino, and Dan Ariely, "Temporal View of the Costs and Benefits of Self-Deception," *Proceedings of the National Academy of Sciences* 108, no. 3 (2011): 15655–59, https://doi.org/10.1073/pnas.1010658108.

Zoe Chance and Michael I. Norton, "The What and Why of Self-deception," Current Opinion in *Psychology* 6 (2015): 104–7, https://doi.org/10.1016/j.copsyc.2015.07.008.

Zoe Chance, Francesca Gino, Michael I. Norton, and Dan Ariely, "The Slow Decay and Quick Revival of Self-deception," *Frontiers in Psychology* 6 (2015): 1075, https://doi.org/10.3389/fpsyg.2015.01075.

32 **Most people award custody to Parent B. And most people deny custody to . . . also Parent B** Eldar Shafir, "Choosing versus Rejecting: Why Some Options Are Both Better and Worse Than Others,"

Memory and Cognition 21, no. 4 (1993): 546–56, https://doi.org
/10.3758/BF03197186.

34 **There's one pixel for every Bengal tiger alive** You can find moving
images of other animals in this powerful campaign too. The original
concept for Population by Pixel was created for the World Wildlife Fund by Yoshiyuki Mikami, Nami Hoshino, and Kazuhiro Mo-
chizuki at Hakuhodo C&D.

37 **"The left hemisphere made up an answer that fit the situation"**
Michael S. Gazzaniga, "Cerebral Specialization and Interhemi-
spheric Communication: Does the Corpus Callosum Enable the
Human Condition?" *Brain* 123, no. 7 (2000): 1293–1326, https://
doi.org/10.1093/brain/123.7.1293.

Chapter Two and a Half: The Path of Least Resistance

39 **The 5 A Day campaign was deemed a huge success. . . . But . . .
[d]espite their dramatically heightened awareness, people did not
change their behavior** For a detailed description of the 5 A Day
fiasco—and the most authoritative science on habits, generally—see
Wendy Wood, *Good Habits, Bad Habits: The Science of Making
Positive Changes That Stick* (New York: Farrar, Straus and Giroux,
2019).

   Or the briefer version here: Wendy Wood and David T. Neal,
"Healthy Through Habit: Interventions for Initiating and Maintaining
Health Behavior Change," *Behavioral Science and Policy* 2, no. 1
(2016): 71–83, https://doi.org/10.1353/bsp.2016.0008.

39– **consumption of fruits and vegetables in the United States actually
40 *declined* by 14 percent. Results in the UK were similarly disappointing** Jenny Hope, "Millions Spent on 5-a-Day Mantra but Now
We're Eating Even LESS Vegetables," *Daily Mail*, April 9, 2010,
https://www.dailymail.co.uk/health/article-1264937/Millions-spent
-5-day-mantra-eating-LESS-vegetables.html.

   Sarah Stark Casagrande, Youfa Wang, Cheryl Anderson, and Tif-
fany L. Gary, "Have Americans Increased Their Fruit and Vegetable
Intake? The Trends Between 1988 and 2002," *American Journal
of Preventive Medicine* 32, no. 4 (2007): 257–63, https://doi.org
/10.1016/j.amepre.2006.12.002.

40 **"53 had no impact at all—and the results of the four good ones**

were so meager it was barely worth mentioning" This book on parenting research is so interesting that I've gifted it to a bunch of friends with small children. Po Bronson and Ashley Merryman, *NurtureShock: New Thinking About Children* (New York: Twelve, 2009).

The original McMaster study: Helen Thomas, "Obesity Prevention Programs for Children and Youth: Why Are Their Results So Modest?" *Health Education Research* 21, no. 6 (2006): 783–95, https://doi.org/10.1093/her/cyl143.

41   **that one question explains one-third of their willingness to buy again, to increase their business with the company, or to rave about it to other people** Matthew Dixon, Nick Toman, and Rick DeLisi, *The Effortless Experience: Conquering the New Battleground for Customer Loyalty* (New York: Portfolio/Penguin, 2013).

For a shorter version, see Matthew Dixon, Karen Freeman, and Nicholas Toman, "Stop Trying to Delight Your Customers," *Harvard Business Review* (July–August 2010), accessed March 13, 2021, https://hbr.org/2010/07/stop-trying-to-delight-your-customers?registration=success.

41   **10 percent of car buyers decide not to be car owners anymore because ride-sharing is easier than owning a car** Peter Henderson, "Some Uber and Lyft Riders Are Giving Up Their Own Cars: Reuters/Ipsos Poll," Reuters, May 25, 2017, https://www.reuters.com/article/us-autos-rideservices-poll/some-uber-and-lyft-riders-are-giving-up-their-own-cars-reuters-ipsos-poll-idUSKBN18L1DA.

43   **Text-message reminders significantly increase show-up rates for doctor's appointments** Frank J. Schwebel and Mary E. Larimer, "Using Text Message Reminders in Health Care Services: A Narrative Literature Review," *Internet Interventions* 13 (2018): 82–104, https://doi.org/10.1016/j.invent.2018.06.002.

43   **speed up loan repayments** *Building Behavioral Design Capacity in Financial Health,* Ideas 42, December 13, 2019, http://www.ideas42.org/blog/project/behavioral-design-project/.

43   **improve medication adherence** Katie A. Kannisto, Marita H. Koivunen, and Maritta A. Välimäki, "Use of Mobile Phone Text Message Reminders in Health Care Services: A Narrative Literature Review," *Journal of Medical Internet Research* 16, no. 10 (2014): E222, https://doi.org/10.2196/jmir.3442.

43   **increase vaccination rates** Elyse O. Kharbanda, Melissa S. Stock-

well, Harrison W. Fox, Raquel Andres, Marcos Lara, and Vaughn I. Rickert, "Text Message Reminders to Promote Human Papillomavirus Vaccination," *Vaccine* 29, no. 14 (2011): 2537–41, https://doi .org/10.1016/j.vaccine.2011.01.065.

43   **and help students turn assignments in on time** William Humphrey Jr., Debbie Laverie, and Alison Shields, "Exploring the Effects of Encouraging Student Performance with Text Assignment Reminders," *Journal of Marketing Education* 43, no. 1 (2021): 91–102, http://dx .doi.org/10.1177/0273475319836271.

43   **For those who did show up, two-thirds of the cases were dismissed, resulting in seventy-eight hundred fewer arrest warrants from just this one experiment** Alissa Fishbane, Aurelie Ouss, and Anuj K. Shah, "Behavioral Nudges Reduce Failure to Appear for Court," *Science* 370, no. 6517 (2020): 1–10, https://doi.org/10.1126 /science.abb6591.

44   **they stocked the gym with cliffhanger audiobooks** Katherine L. Milkman, Julia A. Minson, and Kevin G. M. Volpp, "Holding the *Hunger Games* Hostage at the Gym: An Evaluation of Temptation Bundling," *Management Science* 60, no. 2 (2014): 283–99, https:// doi.org/10.1287/mnsc.2013.1784.

Chapter Three: The No That Saved the World

47   **The word that saved the world was "no." Or more precisely, *nyet*.** This historic incident didn't become publicly known until 1998, when Stanislav Petrov's superior, Colonel General Yuriy Vsyevolodovich Votintsev, published his memoir. According to Petrov, Votintsev "neither rewarded nor reprimanded" him for his behavior, but he retired early the following year. In 2013, he was awarded the Dresden Peace Prize, and in 2017 he passed away. I loved this award-winning documentary about him. Peter Anthony (dir.), *The Man Who Saved the World* (Statement Film, 2014), http:// themanwhosavedtheworldmovie.com.

53   **"I must decline, for secret reasons"** Elwyn Brooks White, *Letters of E. B. White* (New York: Harper & Row, 1976).

53   **Adam Grant's bestselling book *Give and Take*** Adam Grant, *Give and Take: A Revolutionary Approach to Success* (New York: Penguin Books, 2013).

54　"Instead of trying to help all the people all the time with all the requests, successful givers reserve their generosity for givers and matchers" (A. Grant, personal communication, July 5, 2021).

54　Stress and exhaustion even temporarily lower IQ and bias people toward unpleasant memories There is no more compelling book about the societal impacts of stress and depletion than this one. Sendhil Mullainathan and Eldar Shafir, *Scarcity: Why Having Too Little Means So Much* (New York: Henry Holt, 2013).

54　managers who felt most swamped ran teams with the worst performance and lowest profits Robert F. Lusch and Ray R. Serpkenci, "Personal Differences, Job Tension, Job Outcomes, and Store Performance: A Study of Retail Managers," *Journal of Marketing* 54 (1990): 85–101, https://doi.org/10.1177%2F002224299005400106.

56　a slightly mean experiment to see what happens in people's heads when they get left out Naomi I. Eisenberger and Matthew D. Lieberman, "Why Rejection Hurts: A Common Neural Alarm System for Physical and Social Pain," *Trends in Cognitive Sciences* 8, no. 7 (2004): 294–300, https://doi.org/10.1016/j.tics.2004.05.010.

59　Jia walked in and tried to order Olympic symbol doughnuts You can watch the heartwarming video here: Jia Jiang, *Rejection Therapy Day 3—Ask for Olympic Symbol Doughnuts. Jackie at Krispy Kreme Delivers!* (2012), accessed June 13, 2021, https://www.youtube.com/watch?v=7Ax2CsVbrX0.

　　And read more about his rejections here: Jia Jiang, *Rejection Proof: How I Beat Fear and Became Invincible Through 100 Days of Rejection* (New York: Harmony, 2015).

60　We possess a kind of "stress immune system" Check out chapter 8. Coatese also describes resilience research on mice and studies of "toughened individuals." John Coates, *The Hour Between Dog and Wolf: How Risk Taking Transforms Us, Body and Mind* (New York: Penguin, 2012).

61　The most successful salespeople will check back six or seven times after hearing a no This is the number I've heard from multiple sales trainers and sales managers. I've tried and failed to find an academic or reputable consulting source for it—if you have one, please let me know.

62　She had written a book on the power of introversion (*Quiet*)

Susan Cain, *Quiet: The Power of Introverts in a World That Can't Stop Talking* (New York: Random House, 2012).

Chapter Three and a Half: Just Ask

65 **People who ask for what they want get better grades** Jessica Mc-Crory Calarco, *Negotiating Opportunities: How the Middle Class Secures Advantages in School* (New York: Oxford University Press, 2018).

65 **more raises and promotions, bigger job opportunities** Linda Babcock and Sara Laschever, *Women Don't Ask: Negotiation and the Gender Divide* (Princeton, N.J.: Princeton University Press, 2003).

65 **and even more orgasms** David A. Frederick, H. Kate St. John, Justin R. Garcia, and Elisabeth A. Lloyd, "Differences in Orgasm Frequency Among Gay, Lesbian, Bisexual, and Heterosexual Men and Women in a U.S. National Sample," *Archives of Sexual Behavior* 47 (2018): 273–88, https://doi.org/10.1007/s10508-017-0939-z.

The power of "just" asking in fundraising and charitable giving can't be overestimated. For example, when estate attorneys just asked whether their clients wanted to make a charitable bequest, it doubled and sometimes tripled the number of bequests. Michael Sanders and Sarah Smith, "A Warm Glow in the After Life? The Determinants of Charitable Bequests" (working paper no. 14/326, Centre for Market and Public Organisation, University of Bristol, Bristol, UK, June 2014), http://www.bristol.ac.uk/media-library/sites/cmpo/migrated/documents/wp326.pdf.

Hugh Radojev, "Over 80 Per Cent of Public Donate to Charity Because They Are Asked, Says Survey," *Civil Society News*, May 12, 2017.

65 **Managers saw extension requests as a good sign of capability and motivation** Jaewon Yoon, Grant Donnelly, and Ashley Whillans, "It Doesn't Hurt to Ask (for More Time): Employees Often Overestimate the Interpersonal Costs of Extension Requests" (working paper no. 19-064, Harvard Business School, Cambridge, Mass., 2019), https://www.hbs.edu/ris/Publication%20Files/19-064%20(3)_5758eb4a-6e1c-47dc-a4af-c21a958460d7.pdf.

65 **On average, they were two to three times more likely to grant**

favors than participants had expected Francis J. Flynn and Vanessa K. Bohns, "Underestimating One's Influence in Help-Seeking," in Douglas T. Kenrick, Noah J. Goldstein, and Sanford L. Braver, *Six Degrees of Social Influence: Science, Application, and the Psychology of Robert Cialdini* (New York: Oxford University Press, 2012), 14–26, https://doi.org/10.1093/acprof:osobl/9780199743056.003.0002.

Vanessa Bohns has done a lot of other interesting research related to misperceptions related to asking and helping, and on our misperceptions of our own influence. Vanessa K. Bohns, *You Have More Influence Than You Think* (New York: W. W. Norton, 2021).

66   **generosity can stimulate the brain's reward circuitry** Jo Cutler and Daniel Campbell-Meiklejohn, "A Comparative fMRI Meta-Analysis of Altruistic and Strategic Decisions to Give," *Neuroimage* 184 (2019): 227–41, https://doi.org/10.1016/j.neuroimage.2018.09.009.

Lena Rademacher, Martin Schulte-Rüther, Bernd Hanewald, and Sarah Lammertz, "Reward: From Basic Reinforcers to Anticipation of Social Cues," in M. Wöhr and S. Krach, eds., *Social Behavior from Rodents to Humans, Current Topics in Behavioral Neurosciences,* vol. 30 (Cham, Denmark: Springer, 2015), 207–21, https://doi.org/10.1007/7854_2015_429.

66   **volunteers are happier and healthier than non-volunteers** Ricky N. Lawton, Iulian Gramatki, Will Watt, and Daniel Fujiwara, "Does Volunteering Make Us Happier, or Are Happier People More Likely to Volunteer? Addressing the Problem of Reverse Causality When Estimating the Wellbeing Impacts of Volunteering," *Journal of Happiness Studies* 22 (2021): 599–624, https://doi.org/10.1007/s10902-020-00242-8.

Francesca Borgonovi, "Doing Well by Doing Good: The Relationship Between Formal Volunteering and Self-reported Health and Happiness," *Social Science and Medicine* 66, no. 11 (2008): 2321–34, https://doi.org/10.1016/j.socscimed.2008.01.011.

Stephanie L. Brown, Randolph M. Nesse, Amiram D. Vinokur, and Dylan M. Smith, "Providing Social Support May Be More Beneficial Than Receiving It: Results from a Prospective Study of Mortality," *Psychological Science* 14 (2003): 320–27, https://doi.org/10.1111%2F1467-9280.14461.

Stephen G. Post, "Altruism, Happiness, and Health: It's Good to

Be Good," *International Journal of Behavioral Medicine* 12 (2005): 66–77, https://doi.org/10.1207/s15327558ijbm1202_4.

66 **people tend to feel better about spending money on others than on themselves** Elizabeth W. Dunn, Lara B. Aknin, and Michael I. Norton, "Spending Money on Others Promotes Happiness," *Science* 319, no. 5870 (2008): 1687–88, https://doi.org/10.1126/science .1150952.

Lara B. Aknin, Christopher P. Barrington-Leigh, Elizabeth W. Dunn, et al., "Prosocial Spending and Well-being: Cross-cultural Evidence for a Psychological Universal," *Journal of Personality and Social Psychology* 104, no. 4 (2013): 635, https://doi.apa.org/ doi/10.1037/a0031578.

Elizabeth W. Dunn, Claire E. Ashton-James, Margaret D. Hanson, and Lara B. Aknin, "On the Costs of Self-interested Economic Behavior: How Does Stinginess Get Under the Skin?" *Journal of Health Psychology* 15, no. 4 (2010): 627–33, https://doi.org /10.1177%2F1359105309356366.

66 **toddlers . . . [were] most delighted of all to give away their own Goldfish** Lara B. Aknin, J. Kiley Hamlin, and Elizabeth W. Dunn, "Giving Leads to Happiness in Young Children," *PLoS One* 7, no. 6 (2012): E39211, https://doi.org/10.1371/journal.pone.0039211.

67 **outrageous asks can work out in your favor even when the answer is no** Of course you wouldn't make outrageous asks repeatedly to the same person. But you know that already.

67 **the "juvenile delinquents at the zoo" study** Robert B. Cialdini, Joyce E. Vincent, Stephen K. Lewis, Jose Catalan, Diane Wheeler, and Betty Lee Darby, "Reciprocal Concessions Procedure for Inducing Compliance: The Door-in-the-Face Technique," *Journal of Personality and Social Psychology* 31, no. 2 (1975): 206–15, https://doi .org/10.1037/h0076284.

The 2020 replication: Oliver Genschow, Marieka Westfal, Jan Crusius, Leon Bartosch, Kyra Isabel Feikes, Nina Pallasch, and Mirella Wozniak, "Does Social Psychology Persist over Half a Century? A Direct Replication of Cialdini et al.'s (1975) Classic Door-in-the-Face Technique," *Journal of Personality and Social Psychology* 120, no. 2 (1975): E1–E7, https://doi.org/10.1037/pspa000026.

68 **We tend to ask women for favors and help** KerryAnn O'Meara, Alexandra Kuvaeva, Gudrun Nyunt, Chelsea Waugaman, and Rose

Jackson, "Asked More Often: Gender Differences in Faculty Work-load in Research Universities and the Work Interactions That Shape Them," *American Educational Research Journal* 54 (2017): 1154–86, https://doi.org/10.3102/0002831217716767.

Chapter Four: The Curious Qualities of Charisma

71 **tend to use "I" and other first-person pronouns more frequently** James W. Pennebaker, *The Secret Life of Pronouns: What Our Words Say About Us* (New York: Bloomsbury Press, 2011).

If you don't feel like reading an entire book about pronouns, you can find some of Pennebaker's research summarized here: James W. Pennebaker, "The Secret Life of Pronouns," *New Scientist* 211, no. 2828 (2011): 42–45, https://doi.org/10.1016/S0262-4079(11)62167-2.

These power and status effects are highly context-specific. For example, these researchers found that people who had made fewer posts in online message board communities—and thus were and felt lower-status within that community—used "I" more often. Amanda Dino, Stephen Reysen, and Nyla R. Branscombe, "Online Interac-tions Between Group Members Who Differ in Status," *Journal of Language and Social Psychology* 28, no. 1 (2009): 85–93, https://doi.org/10.1177%2F0261927X08325916.

First-person pronouns aren't the only linguistic "tell" for low status—jargon use is another. Zachariah C. Brown, Eric M. Anicich, and Adam D. Galinsky, "Compensatory Conspicuous Communica-tion: Low Status Increases Jargon Use," *Organizational Behavior and Human Decision Processes* 161 (2020): 274–90, http://dx.doi.org/10.1016/j.obhdp.2020.07.001.

And among academics, using "Dr." or "PhD" in an email signa-ture is too. Cindy Harmon-Jones, Brandon J. Schmeichel, and Eddie Harmon-Jones, "Symbolic Self-Completion in Academia: Evidence from Department Web Pages and Email Signature Files," *European Journal of Social Psychology* 39, no. 2 (2009): 311–16, https://doi.org/10.1002/ejsp.541.

71 **actors used first-person pronouns more frequently than directors did** David M. Markowitz, "Academy Awards Speeches Reflect So-

cial Status, Cinematic Roles, and Winning Expectations," *Journal of Language and Social Psychology* 37, no. 3 (2018): 376–87, https://doi.org/10.1177%2F0261927X17751012.

72 **letters written in Arabic by lower-ranking Iraqi officers to their more senior colleagues** Ewa Kacewicz, James W. Pennebaker, Matthew Davis, Moongee Jeon, and Arthur C. Graesser, "Pronoun Use Reflects Standings in Social Hierarchies," *Journal of Language and Social Psychology* 33, no. 2 (2014): 125–43, https://doi.org/10.1177%2F0261927X13502654.

72 **analyzed pronoun choices in essays written by depressed college students** Stephanie Rude, Eva-Maria Gortner, and James Pennebaker, "Language Use of Depressed and Depression-vulnerable College Students," *Cognition and Emotion* 18, no. 8 (2004): 1121–33. https://www.tandfonline.com/doi/abs/10.1080/02699930441000030.

77 **Manson made him feel as though he were the only other person in the room** Eric Lofholm, *The System: The Proven 3-Step Formula Anyone Can Learn to Get More Leads, Book More Appointments, and Make More Sales* (Rocklin, CA: Eric Lofholm International, 2013), 59.

77 **talking about ourselves activates the same areas of the brain as money, sex, and chocolate** Diana I. Tamir and Jason P. Mitchell, "Disclosing Information About the Self Is Intrinsically Rewarding," *Proceedings of the National Academy of Sciences* 109, no. 21 (2012): 8038–43, https://doi.org/10.1073/pnas.1202129109.

78 **when people are getting to know each other, those who ask more questions are better liked** Karen Huang, Michael Yeomans, Alison Wood Brooks, Julia Minson, and Francesca Gino, "It Doesn't Hurt to Ask: Question-Asking Increases Liking," *Journal of Personality and Social Psychology* 113, no. 3 (2017): 430–52, https://psycnet.apa.org/doi/10.1037/pspi0000097.

78 **slowly progressed to more personal questions, like "When was the last time you cried?"** Arthur Aron, Edward Melinat, Elaine N. Aron, Robert Darrin Vallone, and Renee J. Bator, "The Experimental Generation of Interpersonal Closeness: A Procedure and Some Preliminary Findings," *Personality and Social Psychology Bulletin* 23, no. 4 (1997): 363–77, https://doi.org/10.1177%2F0146167297234003.

79 **your name has a unique signature that activates self-referential**

parts of your brain Dennis P. Carmody and Michael Lewis, "Brain Activation When Hearing One's Own and Others' Names," *Brain Research* 1116, no. 1 (2006): 153–58, https://doi.org/10.1016/j .brainres.2006.07.121.

Your brain has a unique reaction to your name even when you're sleeping: Fabien Perrin, Luis García-Larrea, François Mauguière, and Hélène Bastuji, "A Differential Brain Response to the Subject's Own Name Persists During Sleep," *Clinical Neurophysiology* 110, no. 12 (1999): 2153–64, https://doi.org/10.1016/S1388 -2457(99)00177-7.

80 **listeners judge people with lower-pitched voices as stronger** Casey A. Klofstad, Rindy C. Anderson, and Stephen Nowicki, "Perceptions of Competence, Strength, and Age Influence Voters to Select Leaders with Lower-pitched Voices," *PloS One* 10, no. 8 (2015): E0133779, https://doi.org/10.1371/journal.pone.0133779.

80 **more competent, more attractive** Cara C. Tigue, Diana Borak, Jillian O'Connor, Charles Schandl, and David Feinberg, "Voice Pitch Influences Voting Behavior," *Evolution and Human Behavior* 33 (2012): 210–16, https://doi.org/10.1016/j.evolhumbehav.2011.09.004.

80 **more dominant, and more likely to be good leaders** Casey Klofstad, Rindy Anderson, and Susan Peters, "Sounds like a Winner: Voice Pitch Influences Perception of Leadership Capacity in Men and Women," *Proceedings of the Royal Society B: Biological Sciences* 279, no. 1738 (2012): 2698–704, http://dx.doi.org/10.1098/ rspb.2012.0311.

83 **Charisma isn't something you *are*. It's something you *do*** Journalist Robert Stein writes about meeting the "two Marilyns": the quiet, shy, not even beautiful behind-the-scenes Marilyn Monroe and the public bombshell. "Up close, her face was pale and fragile, with no Technicolor glow, and her eyes had none of the confidence that radiated from the screen." On the subway, no one recognized her, but back on the street, she "took off the coat, fluffed up her hair, and arched her back in a pose. In an instant she was engulfed, and it took several shoving, scary minutes to rewrap her and push clear of the growing crowd." Robert Stein, "Do You Want to See Her?" *American Heritage* 56, no. 6 (November/December 2005), https:// www.americanheritage.com/do-you-want-see-her.

Olivia Fox Cabane shares that story and other great ones. Olivia Fox Cabane, *The Charisma Myth: How Anyone Can Master the Art and Science of Personal Magnetism* (New York: Portfolio/Penguin, 2013).

83 **public speaking, which is scary for most of us** There's a widely cited "fact" that people fear public speaking more than they fear death—of course that's not true. Some studies asking people to check their fears off on a list have found more people checking off "public speaking" than anything else. But we don't usually fear things unless we're facing them (hence public speaking comes up more often than death, sharks, etc.). And lists like these neglect our real, deepest fears, like not being worthy or not being loved. While it's true that most people have some discomfort or anxiety about public speaking, the "fact" about fearing it more than death is just an artifact of a bad survey design.

In a survey of successful professional actors including Broadway stars and Tony nominees, 84 percent reported getting stage fright. I'm a professional speaker and former actor, and I get stage fright too. Gordon Goodman and James C. Kaufman, "Gremlins in My Head: Predicting Stage Fright in Elite Actors," *Empirical Studies of the Arts* 32, no. 2 (2014): 133–48, https://doi.org/10.2190%2FEM.32.2.b.

86 **In class, we spend a lot of time practicing . . . pauses** I knew pauses were important, but I didn't know *how* important until Jeremey Donovan visited our class as a guest speaker/presentation coach. I had written him a fan letter after reading his book, and he came to coach students on, mostly, pauses. It was transformational. Jeremey Donovan, *How to Deliver a TED Talk: Secrets of the World's Most Inspiring Presentations* (New York: McGraw-Hill Education, 2013).

88 **this technique—connecting with many by connecting with one—is shining** Joey Asher, *15 Minutes Including Q and A: A Plan to Save the World from Lousy Presentations* (Atlanta: Persuasive Speaker Press, 2010).

Chapter Four and a Half: Moments of Truth

93 *Moments of truth are situations in which someone is particularly likely to be open to your influence* Proctor and Gamble is usually

credited with the "moments of truth" concept, but it was actually Jan
Carlzon, the former CEO of SAS (Scandinavian Airlines), who coined
the phrase in the influence context. Jan Carlzon, *Moments of Truth*
(New York: Harper Perennial, 1989).

93   **saw Cebu Pacific's message appear beneath their feet as if by
magic** This genius and award-winning "Rain Codes" campaign was
masterminded by Kenny Blumenschein, Paul Ho, Sean Chen, and
Paul Sin at Geometry Global.

94   **inspired by the pharaohs to bury his five-hundred-thousand-
dollar Bentley** This genius and award-winning campaign was masterminded by Marcelo Reis, Guilherme Jahara, Rodrigo Jatene,
Marcelo Rizério, and Christian Fontana at Leo Burnett Tailor Made.
The campaign reached 172 million people on social media with
only six Facebook posts and generated twenty-two million dollars in
earned media. The total cost of six thousand dollars made it one of
the best advertising investments in world history. (Thank you, Shane,
for sharing it with me.)

The biggest factor in determining whether people become organ
donors is still ease. Nearly all the difference in organ donation rates
by country can be explained by ease: opt-in versus opt-out policies.
It's easy to check a box to opt in or opt out—just not as easy as not
checking a box. Eric J. Johnson and Daniel Goldstein, "Do Defaults
Save Lives?" *Science* 302, no. 5649 (2003): 1338–39, https://doi
.org/10.1126/science.1091721.

95   **Decisions about the near term tend to be based on concrete con-
siderations like process and feasibility** Nira Liberman and Yaacov
Trope, "The Role of Feasibility and Desirability Considerations in
Near and Distant Future Decisions: A Test of Temporal Construal
Theory," *Journal of Personality and Social Psychology* 75, no. 1
(1998): 5–18, https://doi.org/10.1037/0022-3514.75.1.5.

Yaacov Trope and Nira Liberman, "Temporal Construal," *Psychological Review* 110, no. 3 (2003): 403–21, https://doi.org/10.1037
/0033-295x.110.3.403.

96   **asked if they were planning to vote, and then asked what, specifically, were their plans** David W. Nickerson and Todd Rogers, "Do
You Have a Voting Plan?: Implementation Intentions, Voter Turnout,
and Organic Plan Making," *Psychological Science* 21, no. 2 (2010):
194–99, https://doi.org/10.1177/0956797609359326.

97   *"To all those who use our competitors' products: Happy Father's Day."* This cheeky campaign was masterminded by Matthew Bull, Roger Paulse, Myles Lord, and Jason Kempen at Lowe Bull in South Africa.

Chapter Five: The Life-Changing Magic of a Simple Frame

98   **Derren Brown is a psychological illusionist who knows more about influence than pretty much anyone** Seriously. Besides being an award-winning performer, Derren Brown is a bestselling author of funny, smart books on psychology, magic, and happiness. In class, we learn about fake mind reading in *Tricks of the Mind,* and we watch *The Push* to learn about the dark arts of influence. If you're a psychology nerd, you'll enjoy his Milgram experiment replication on *The Heist.* (My favorite show so far, though, is *Apocalypse.* He told me it's his favorite too.) Derren Brown, *Tricks of the Mind* (London: Transworld, 2006).

99   **the invisible gorilla experiment** You can find the video online and experiment on your friends. You'll blow their minds. Daniel J. Simons and Christopher F. Chabris, "Gorillas in Our Midst: Sustained Inattentional Blindness for Dynamic Events," *Perception* 28, no. 9 (1999): 1059–74, https://doi.org/10.1068/p281059.

100   **once you have milk and snow at the center of your attention, it's a lot harder to come up with other white things like clouds and coconut flakes** Sendhil Mullainathan and Eldar Shafir, *Scarcity: Why Having Too Little Means So Much* (New York: Henry Holt, 2013).

109   **Luntz tested an alternative frame, the "death tax"** If you don't already know about Frank Luntz, you'll be amazed at the impact he has had on U.S. politics, on a broad variety of issues. While I was writing this book, he was collaborating with former CDC director Tom Frieden to find a frame that would motivate vaccine-hesitant Trump voters to get a COVID vaccine. (Their most effective message was "More than 90% of the doctors who have been offered this vaccine have chosen to get it.") Frank Luntz, *Words That Work: It's Not What You Say, It's What People Hear* (New York: Hachette Books, 2008).

110   **give people the choice to pay off credit card expenses by category**

Grant E. Donnelly, Cait Lamberton, Stephen Bush, Zoe Chance, and Michael I. Norton, " 'Repayment-by-Purchase' Helps Consumers to Reduce Credit Card Debt" (working paper no. 21-060, Harvard Business School, Cambridge, Mass., 2020), http://dx.doi.org/10.2139 /ssrn.3728254.

110 **Achieving small, immediate goals creates a sense of momentum and persistence** David Gal and Blakeley B. McShane, "Can Small Victories Help Win the War? Evidence from Consumer Debt Management," *Journal of Marketing Research* 49, no. 3 (2012): 487–501, https://doi.org/10.1509%2Fjmr.11.0272.

Ran Kivetz, Oleg Urminsky, and Yuhuang Zheng, "The Goal-Gradient Hypothesis Resurrected: Purchase Acceleration, Illusionary Goal Progress, and Customer Retention," *Journal of Marketing Research* 43, no. 1 (2006): 39–58, https://doi.org/10.1509%2Fjmkr .43.1.39.

Yan Zhang and Leilei Gao, "Wanting Ever More: Acquisition Procedure Motivates Continued Reward Acquisition," *Journal of Consumer Research* 43, no. 2 (2016): 230–45, https://doi.org/10.1093 /jcr/ucw017.

113 **test alternative frames to find the one that would have the best chance of motivating people to take action on global warming** Researchers at Spark Neuro tested "climate crisis," "environmental destruction" (this had higher emotional responses among Republicans than "climate crisis"), "environmental collapse," and "weather destabilization." You can read about it here: Kate Yoder, "Why Your Brain Doesn't Register the Words 'Climate Change,' " *Grist,* April 29, 2019, https://grist.org/article/why-your-brain-doesnt-register -the-words-climate-change/.

114 **Impressed by their server's flawless memory . . . they decided to test it** Bob Cialdini shares this story in his follow-up to *Influence.* It's a great book. Robert Cialdini, *Pre-Suasion: A Revolutionary Way to Influence and Persuade* (New York: Simon and Schuster, 2016).

115 **able to recall more details of incomplete tasks than completed ones** Bluma Zeigarnik, "On Finished and Unfinished Tasks," in W. D. Ellis, ed., *A Source Book of Gestalt Psychology* (London: Routledge and Kegan, 1938), 300–314.

116 **All three frames in just six words** Marie Kondo, *The Life-Changing*

Magic of Tidying Up: The Japanese Art of Decluttering and Organizing (Berkeley, Calif.: Ten Speed Press, 2014).

Chapter Six: Inner Two-Year-Olds

123 **When a snake or a spider image whizzed by, viewers began to sweat** Arne Öhman, Anders Flykt, and Francisco Esteves, "Emotion Drives Attention: Detecting the Snake in the Grass," *Journal of Experimental Psychology: General* 130, no. 3 (2001): 466–78, https://doi.org/10.1037/0096-3445.130.3.466.

124 **75 percent could tell that B was a snake** Nobuyuki Kawai and Hongshen He, "Breaking Snake Camouflage: Humans Detect Snakes More Accurately Than Other Animals Under Less Discernible Visual Conditions," *PLoS One* 11, no. 10 (2016): E0164342, https://doi.org/10.1371/journal.pone.0164342.

124 **people tend to value losses about twice as heavily as similarly sized gains** The original, elegant prospect theory paper: Daniel Kahneman and Amos Tversky, "Prospect Theory: An Analysis of Decision Under Risk," *Econometrica* 47, no. 2 (1979): 263–92, https://doi.org/10.1142/9789814417358_0006.

Aggregating measurements in six hundred studies in 150 papers across multiple disciplines, these authors found the mean loss aversion coefficient to be between 1.8 and 2.1. Alexander L. Brown, Taisuke Imai, Ferdinand Vieider, and Colin F. Camerer, "Meta-analysis of Empirical Estimates of Loss-Aversion" (CESifo working paper no. 8848, 2021), https://ssrn.com/abstract=3772089.

At the time of writing, there was also some controversy over the real-world prevalence of loss-aversion. David Gal and David D. Rucker, "The Loss of Loss Aversion: Will It Loom Larger Than Its Gain?" *Journal of Consumer Psychology* 28, no. 3 (2018): 497–516, https://doi.org/10.1002/jcpy.1047.

125 **classic reactance experiment with actual two-year-olds** In this study, the reactance effect showed up only for the boys. Some studies find gender differences and others do not. Age differences play a role, too, and some people are just more reactant than others. Sharon S. Brehm and Marsha Weinraub, "Physical Barriers and Psychological Reactance: 2-yr-olds' Responses to Threats to Freedom,"

Journal of Personality and Social Psychology 35, no. 11 (1977): 830–36, https://psycnet.apa.org/doi/10.1037/0022-3514.35.11.830.

This article summarizes a lot of the work on reactance theory. Anca M. Miron and Jack W. Brehm, "Reactance Theory—40 Years Later," *Zeitschrift für Sozialpsychologie* 37, no. 1 (2006): 9–18, https://doi.org/10.1024/0044-3514.37.1.9.

People who are "hard to get" can be more attractive too (as you know). Erin R. Whitchurch, Timothy D. Wilson, and Daniel T. Gilbert, "'He Loves Me, He Loves Me Not . . . ': Uncertainty Can Increase Romantic Attraction," *Psychological Science* 22, no. 2 (2011): 172–75, https://doi.org/10.1177%2F0956797610393745.

Also, forbidden objects are remembered better and recognized more quickly. Grace Truong, David J. Turk, and Todd C. Handy, "An Unforgettable Apple: Memory and Attention for Forbidden Objects," *Cognitive, Affective, and Behavioral Neuroscience* 13, no. 4 (2013): 803–13, https://link.springer.com/article/10.3758/s13415-013-0174-6.

126 **people don't mind giving money to the government in the form of lottery tickets** B. F. Skinner, *About Behaviorism* (New York: Knopf, 1974).

127 **dig in deeper just to spite you** Sometimes people who feel strongly about a particular issue respond to conflicting information by adopting an even more extreme point of view—the *backfire effect*. When this was first documented, it got a lot of media attention and people assumed it was common; now we know it's not. Zak L. Tormala and Richard E. Petty, "What Doesn't Kill Me Makes Me Stronger: The Effects of Resisting Persuasion on Attitude Certainty," *Journal of Personality and Social Psychology* 83, no. 6 (2002): 1298, https://psycnet.apa.org/doi/10.1037/0022-3514.83.6.1298.

Brendan Nyhan and Jason Reifler, "When Corrections Fail: The Persistence of Political Misperceptions," *Political Behavior* 32, no. 2 (2010): 303–30, https://doi.org/10.1007/s11109-010-9112-2.

Todd Wood and Ethan Porter, "The Elusive Backfire Effect: Mass Attitudes' Steadfast Factual Adherence," *Political Behavior* 41, no. 1 (2019): 135–63, https://doi.org/10.1007/s11109-018-9443-y.

Brendan Nyhan, "Why the Backfire Effect Does Not Explain the Durability of Political Misperceptions," *Proceedings of the National*

Academy of Sciences 118, no. 15 (2021): e1912440117, https://doi
.org/10.1073/pnas.1912440117.

128 **when food is framed as healthy, some people translate that to
     mean it tastes bad** Raj Raghunathan, Rebecca W. Naylor, and
     Wayne D. Hoyer, "The Unhealthy = Tasty Intuition and Its Effects
     on Taste Inferences, Enjoyment, and Choice of Food Products,"
     Journal of Marketing 70, no. 4 (2006): 170–84, https://doi.org
     /10.1509%2Fjmkg.70.4.170.

129 **meat eaters (like everyone else) don't like to hear that their
     choices make them bad people** Julia A. Minson and Benoît Monin,
     "Do-gooder Derogation: Disparaging Morally Motivated Minori-
     ties to Defuse Anticipated Reproach," *Social Psychological and
     Personality Science* 3, no. 2 (2012): 200–207, https://doi.org/
     10.1177%2F1948550611415695.

132 **invite the other person to open up by reflecting back their state-
     ment as a question** I learned this from former FBI hostage negotiator
     Chris Voss. He has also influenced me to ask "why" less and "how"
     and "what" more often. In class we crack ourselves up practicing the
     late-night FM DJ voice. Chris Voss and Tahl Raz, *Never Split the
     Difference* (New York: Harper Business, 2016).

133 **after complying with a gentle nudge to lie, for instance, people
     become more receptive to believing the lie** Leon Festinger and
     James M. Carlsmith, "Cognitive Consequences of Forced Compli-
     ance," *Journal of Abnormal and Social Psychology* 58 (1959): 203–10,
     https://doi.org/10.1037/h0041593.

133 **a free money sign made people walk on by or cross the street to
     avoid the researchers giving away fifty-dollar bills** This study was
     conducted by Ayelet Gneezy, Stephen Spiller, and Dan Ariely, and
     reported in *Predictably Irrational*. My students have run similar ex-
     periments trying to give away $5 bills, finding that about half the
     people they approach refuse to take the money. Dan Ariely, *Predict-
     ably Irrational: The Hidden Forces That Shape Our Decisions* (New
     York: Harper Collins, 2009).

134 **affirm their freedom of choice by actually stating that they're free
     to choose** This simple idea is a game-changer. I learned it from
     Mike Pantalon, a psychologist who was working in the ER at Yale
     and had only a few minutes to try to influence people to do really

hard things like kick addictions. His book is wonderful. Michael Pantalon, *Instant Influence: How to Get Anyone to Do Anything— Fast* (New York: Little, Brown, 2011).

Mike's work builds on research in motivational interviewing— persuading people to make changes in their lives by asking them questions. William R. Miller and Stephen Rollnick, *Motivational Interviewing: Helping People Change* (New York: Guilford Press, 2012).

137 **Journalist and author Jessica Winter describes how the Kindly Brontosaurus secures a seat** Her article is the only place I've come across the "Kindly Brontosaurus." I love this frame for gentle persistence, and so do my students. Jessica Winter, "The Kindly Brontosaurus," *Slate,* August 14, 2013, https://slate.com/human-interest /2013/08/the-kindly-brontosaurus-the-amazing-prehistoric-posture -that-will-get-you-whatever-you-want.html.

Chapter Six and a Half: Deep Listening

144 *false polarization bias* The false polarization bias results from a Gator shortcut: Once we've organized the stuff in our head into categories, we magnify their differences. As these authors point out, even sorting various shades of purple into "red" and "blue" makes them appear more different than they actually are. Jacob Westfall, Leaf Van Boven, John R. Chambers, and Charles M. Judd, "Perceiving Political Polarization in the United States: Party Identity Strength and Attitude Extremity Exacerbate the Perceived Partisan Divide," *Perspectives on Psychological Science* 10, no. 2 (2015): 145–58, https://doi.org/10.1177/1745691615569849.

The image is from this paper: Samantha L. Moore-Berg, Lee-Or Ankori-Karlinsky, Boaz Hameiri, and Emile Bruneau, "Exaggerated Meta-Perceptions Predict Intergroup Hostility Between American Political Partisans," *Proceedings of the National Academy of Sciences* 117, no. 26 (2020): 14864–72, https://doi.org/10.1073 /pnas.2001263117.

There is also a false consensus bias: We imagine people like us, or people we like, to agree with us more than they actually do. Sharad Goel, Winter Mason, and Duncan J. Watts, "Real and Perceived Attitude Agreement in Social Networks," *Journal of Personality and*

Social Psychology 99, no. 4 (2010): 611, https://psycnet.apa.org /doi/10.1037/a0020697.

144 **People miscalculate how much members of the opposing side disagree with them on many hot-button issues like gun control, racism, and religion** See Yudkin, Hawkins, and Dixon, "The Perception Gap: How False Impressions Are Pulling Americans Apart." (More in Common white paper, June 2019), https://psyarxiv.com /r3h5q/download?format=pdf.

Also on the climate: Adina T. Abeles, Lauren C. Howe, Jon A. Krosnick, and Bo MacInnis, "Perception of Public Opinion on Global Warming and the Role of Opinion Deviance," *Journal of Environmental Psychology* 63 (2019): 118–29, https://doi.org /10.1016/j.jenvp.2019.04.001.

Media coverage contributes to the problem: Matthew Levendusky and Neil Malhotra, "Does Media Coverage of Partisan Polarization Affect Political Attitudes?" *Political Communication* 33, no. 2 (2016): 283–301, https://doi.org/10.1080/10584609.2015.1038455.

And social media contributes to the problem too, because messages with moral-emotional content like outrage and disgust capture more Gator brain attention and drive higher engagement. William J. Brady, Julian A. Wills, John T. Jost, Joshua A. Tucker, and Jay J. Van Bavel, "Emotion Shapes the Diffusion of Moralized Content in Social Networks," *Proceedings of the National Academy of Sciences* 114, no. 28 (2017): 7313–18, https://doi.org/10.1073/pnas.1618923114.

144 **the more vehement our own views are, the more extreme we imagine views on the other side to be** Daniel Yudkin, Stephen Hawkins, and Tim Dixon, "The Perception Gap."

You can test your own perception gap at this link (June 2021): https://perceptiongap.us.

145 **we can't discount their opinion as easily while hearing their voice** Juliana Schroeder, Michael Kardas, and Nicholas Epley, "The Humanizing Voice: Speech Reveals, and Text Conceals, a More Thoughtful Mind in the Midst of Disagreement," *Psychological Science* 28, no. 12 (2017): 1745–62, https://doi.org/10.1177%2F09567976177 13798.

145 **Putting someone else's feelings into words has a stress-relieving effect on your own brain** Matthew D. Lieberman, Naomi I. Eisenberger, Molly J. Crockett, Sabrina M. Tom, Jennifer H. Pfeifer, and

Baldwin M. Way, "Putting Feelings into Words," *Psychological Science* 18, no. 5 (2007): 421–28, https://doi.org/10.1111%2Fj.1467 -9280.2007.01916.x.

146 **You can usually find a whisper of those same values in yourself, which helps you develop empathy** Being reminded of something you have in common with someone—even something arbitrary— also makes you feel closer to them. Jay J. Van Bavel, Dominic J. Packer, and William A. Cunningham, "Modulation of the Fusiform Face Area Following Minimal Exposure to Motivationally Relevant Faces: Evidence of In-Group Enhancement (Not Out-Group Disregard)," *Journal of Cognitive Neuroscience* 23, no. 11 (2011): 3343– 54, https://doi.org/10.1162/jocn_a_00016.

146 **Putting someone's feelings into words . . . calms down activation in their amygdala, where the brain processes fear and stress** Lisa J. Burklund, J. David Creswell, Michael R. Irwin, and Matthew D. Lieberman, "The Common and Distinct Neural Bases of Affect Labeling and Reappraisal in Healthy Adults," *Frontiers in Psychology* 5 (2014): 221, https://doi.org/10.3389/fpsyg.2014.00221.

Chapter Seven: Creative Negotiations

152 **Ginger Graham, one of the company's senior leaders** Ginger Graham, "If You Want Honesty, Break Some Rules," *Harvard Business Review* 80, no. 4 (2002): 42–47, 124, https://hbr.org/2002/04/if-you -want-honesty-break-some-rules.

152 **Negotiating a raise or a promotion is so stressful that most people never do it** *"Salary and Compensation Statistics on the Impact of COVID-19,"* Randstad, 2020, https://rlc.randstadusa.com/for-business /learning-center/future-workplace-trends/randstad-2020-compensation -insights.

158 **Kids from middle-class families negotiated with their teachers seven times as often** Jessica McCrory Calarco, *Negotiating Opportunities: How the Middle Class Secures Advantages in School* (New York: Oxford University Press, 2018).

158 **the biggest dissatisfactions with work centered on low pay and lack of opportunity—yet the majority of those executives had never tried to negotiate a raise or a promotion** *Reinvent Opportunity: Looking Through a New Lens,* Accenture, 2011, https://www

.accenture.com/t20160127T035320Z__w__/us-en/_acnmedia
/Accenture/Conversion-Assets/DotCom/Documents/About-Accenture
/PDF/1/Accenture-IWD-Research-Embargoed-Until-March-4-2011
.pdf.

More detail about the Accenture survey: Twenty-five percent of
people said they got more money than they were expecting, an additional 38 percent said they got the raise they were expecting, 17
percent got more money but not as much as they were hoping for,
and 5 percent did not get a raise but did get some other type of incentive.

Only 15 percent got nothing. Kimberly Weisul, "Easiest Way to
Get a Raise and Promotion," CBS News, March 9, 2011, https://
www.cbsnews.com/news/easiest-way-to-get-a-raise-and-promotion/.

163 **Experienced negotiators ask twice as many questions and spend
twice as much time listening** Neil Rackham, "The Behavioral Approach to Differences Among Negotiators," in Roy J. Lewicki, David
M. Saunders, and John W. Minton, eds., *Negotiation: Readings, Exercises, and Cases* (Boston: Irwin/McGraw-Hill, 1999), 387–389.

163 **generosity inspires trust and reciprocation** Generous first offers inspire reciprocal generosity. Martha Jeong, Julia A. Minson, and Francesca Gino, "In Generous Offers I Trust: The Effect of First-Offer Value
on Economically Vulnerable Behaviors," *Psychological Science* 31,
no.6(2020):644–53, https://doi.org/10.1177%2F0956797620916705.

Nice people got better outcomes in interdepartmental negotiations. Aukje Nauta, Carsten K. De Dreu, and Taco Van Der Vaart,
"Social Value Orientation, Organizational Goal Concerns and
Interdepartmental Problem-solving Behavior," *Journal of Organizational Behavior* 23, no. 2 (2002): 199–213, https://doi.org/10.1002
/job.136.

People negotiating with computer agents were more satisfied,
more willing to recommend to friends, and more willing to renegoti-
ate when the computer agent was warm. Pooja Prajod, Mohammed
Al Owayyed, Tim Rietveld, Jaap-Jan van der Steeg, and Joost Broek-
ens, "The Effect of Virtual Agent Warmth on Human-Agent Negotiation," *Proceedings of the 18th International Conference on
Autonomous Agents and MultiAgent Systems* (2019): 71–76, http://
ii.tudelft.nl/~joostb/files/AAMAS2019.pdf.

But nice doesn't always win. Here's a counterexample. In this study, though, being "nice" is demonstrated with self-focus, diminishers, and uncertainty while being "tough" is demonstrated with urgency. So the real story is more complicated. Martha Jeong, Julia Minson, Michael Yeomans, and Francesca Gino, "Communicating with Warmth in Distributive Negotiations Is Surprisingly Counterproductive," *Management Science* 65, no. 12 (2019): 5813–37, https://doi.org/10.1287/mnsc.2018.3199.

170 **when he offered only one option, up to 97 percent of people chose to wait rather than deciding on a purchase** Daniel Mochon, "Single-Option Aversion," *Journal of Consumer Research* 40, no. 3 (2013): 555–66, https://doi.org/10.1086/671343.

170 **multiple equivalent simultaneous offers, or *MESOs*** Geoffrey J. Leonardelli, Jun Gu, Geordie McRuer, Victoria H. Medvec, and Adam D. Galinsky, "Multiple Equivalent Simultaneous Offers (MESOs) Reduce the Negotiator Dilemma: How a Choice of First Offers Increases Economic and Relational Outcomes," *Organizational Behavior and Human Decision Processes* 152 (2019): 64–83, https://doi.org/10.1016/j.obhdp.2019.01.007.

170 **people tend to favor middle options** Itamar Simonson, "Choice Based on Reasons: The Case of Attraction and Compromise Effects," *Journal of Consumer Research* 16, no. 2 (1989): 158–74, https://doi.org/10.1086/209205.

171 **Average-sized people chose ponchos labeled "medium" regardless of the actual size** Drazen Prelec, Birger Wernerfelt, and Florian Zettelmeyer, "The Role of Inference in Context Effects: Inferring What You Want from What Is Available," *Journal of Consumer Research* 24, no. 1 (1997): 118–25, https://doi.org/10.1086/209498.

171 ***Goldilocks strategy*** Carl Shapiro and Hal R. Varian, *Information Rules: A Strategic Guide to the Network Economy* (Boston: Harvard Business School Press, 1998).

Chapter Seven and a Half: Negotiating While Female

178 **she published an open letter online** Jennifer Lawrence, "Why Do I Make Less Than My Male Co-Stars?" *Lenny*, October 13, 2015, https://us11.campaign-archive.com/?u=a5b04a26aae05a24bc4efb63e&id=64e6f35176&e=1ba99d671e#wage.

179 **only 46 percent of women had negotiated when they received job**

offers, compared to 66 percent of men Diane Domeyer, *"How Women Can Negotiate Salary,"* Robert Half Blog, March 2, 2020, https://www.roberthalf.com/blog/salaries-and-skills/how-women-can -negotiate-salary-with-confidence.

179 **younger women are negotiating at work far more often than their mothers did** Benjamin Artz, Amanda H. Goodall, and Andrew J. Oswald, "Do Women Ask?" *Industrial Relations* 57, no. 4 (2018): 611–36, https://doi.org/10.1111/irel.12214.

179 **negotiation training helps close the education gap** A meta-analysis of 51 studies found that much of the gender gap comes down to practice. Jens Mazei, Joachim Hüffmeier, Philipp Alexander Freund, Alice F. Stuhlmacher, Lena Bilke, and Guido Hertel, "A Meta- Analysis on Gender Differences in Negotiation Outcomes and Their Moderators," *Psychological Bulletin* 141, no. 1 (2015): 85–104, https://doi.org/10.1037/a0038184.

A negotiation training intervention with middle-school girls in Zambia increased their school attendance by helping them negoti- ate with their parents. The informational and the girls' empower- ment interventions had no effect. Nava Ashraf, Natalie Bau, Corrine Low, and Kathleen McGinn, "Negotiating a Better Future: How Interpersonal Skills Facilitate Intergenerational Investment," *Quar- terly Journal of Economics* 135, no. 2 (2020): 1095–151, https:// doi.org/10.1093/qje/qjz039.

180– **Women get stressed more easily . . . have a greater tendency to**
181 **"tend and befriend" . . . when we feel panicked . . . tend to judge risk more accurately . . . perform better than men as Wall Street stock traders . . . are less likely to enter a political race against an incumbent** I was fascinated by Po Bronson and Ashley Merryman's discussion of the biology of stress and gender differences in stress and competition; see chapters 4 and 5. Po Bronson and Ashley Mer- ryman, *Top Dog* (New York: Hachette Books, 2014).

181 **men are more likely to socialize with colleagues from work while women tend to get together with non-work friends** The original paper documenting the differences was this one. Herminia Ibarra, "Homophily and Differential Returns: Sex Differences in Network Structure and Access in an Advertising Firm," *Administrative Sci- ence Quarterly* 37, no. 3 (1992): 422–47, https://doi.org/10.2307 /2393451.

182 **"good student habits"** See chapter 5 for this discussion (but I learned something helpful in every chapter). Tara Mohr, *Playing Big: Find Your Voice, Your Mission, Your Message* (New York: Avery, 2015).

182 **When women set their negotiation targets as high as men do, they tend to do just as well** Linda C. Babcock, *Women Don't Ask* (Princeton, N.J.: Princeton University Press, 2003).

    Edward W. Miles, "Gender Differences in Distributive Negotiation: When in the Negotiation Process Do the Differences Occur?" *European Journal of Social Psychology* 40, no. 7 (2010): 1200–1211, https://doi.org/10.1002/ejsp.714.

182 **"gender differences in ask salaries explain nearly all of the gap in final offers"** Nina Roussille, "The Central Role of the Ask Gap in Gender Inequality" (University of California at Berkeley working paper, January 2021), https://ninaroussille.github.io/files/Roussille_askgap.pdf.

183 **Once men realized they could negotiate, they did; women, not so much** Barbara Biasi and Heather Sarsons, "Information, Confidence, and the Gender Gap in Bargaining," *AEA Papers and Proceedings* 111 (2021): 174–78, https://doi.org/10.1257/pandp.20211019.

183 **Only 3 percent of the women asked for more money. Twenty-three percent of the men did.** Deborah A. Small, Michele Gelfand, Linda Babcock, and Hilary Gettman, "Who Goes to the Bargaining Table? The Influence of Gender and Framing on the Initiation of Negotiation," *Journal of Personality and Social Psychology* 93 (2007): 600–613, https://doi.org/10.1037/0022-3514.93.4.600.

183 **who literally wrote the book on gender and negotiations** Because of Linda Babcock's work, more women have started negotiating, and negotiating for more. The gap has narrowed but it persists. Babcock, *Women Don't Ask*.

184 **when women negotiate on behalf of other people, they do as well as men and sometimes better** Emily T. Amanatullah and Michael W. Morris, "Negotiating Gender Roles: Gender Differences in Assertive Negotiating Are Mediated by Women's Fear of Backlash and Attenuated When Negotiating on Behalf of Others," *Journal of Personality and Social Psychology* 98, no. 2 (2010): 256–67, https://doi.org/10.1037/a0017094.

Chapter Eight: Defense Against the Dark Arts

187 **Geneen Roth** Geneen Roth's book is about the spiritual lessons she learned from these experiences. I can't imagine what it takes to find gratitude on the other side. Geneen Roth, *Lost and Found: Unexpected Revelations About Food and Money* (New York: Viking, 2011).

190 **Con artists prey on successful people—who earn higher salaries** If you want to read more about cons and con artists, check out Maria Konnikova's meticulously researched and wickedly fun book. Maria Konnikova, *The Confidence Game: Why We Fall for It . . . Every Time* (New York: Penguin, 2016).

191 **have more education** David Tennant, "Why Do People Risk Exposure to Ponzi Schemes? Econometric Evidence from Jamaica," *Journal of International Financial Markets, Institutions, and Money* 21, no. 3 (2011): 328–46, https://doi.org/10.1016/j.intfin.2010.11.003.

191 **higher financial literacy** A con artist puts it bluntly: "Stupid people don't have fifty thousand dollars lying around to give me." Doug Shadel, *Outsmarting the Scam Artists: How to Protect Yourself from the Most Clever Cons* (Hoboken, N.J.: Wiley, 2012).

   Karla Pak and Doug Shadel, *AARP Foundation National Fraud Victim Study* (Washington, D.C.: AARP, 2011), https://assets.aarp.org/rgcenter/econ/fraud-victims-11.pdf.

191 **experts do only 10 percent better than chance, although they have a great deal of confidence** Paul Ekman writes about collected research on lie detection in this book. Paul Ekman, *Telling Lies: Clues to Deceit in the Marketplace, Politics, and Marriage* (New York: W. W. Norton, 2009).

   Police perform worse than college students because they think almost everyone lies. Saul M. Kassin, Christian A. Meissner, and Rebecca J. Norwick, "'I'd Know a False Confession if I Saw One': A Comparative Study of College Students and Police Investigators," *Law and Human Behavior* 29, no. 2 (2005): 211, https://doi.org/10.1007/s10979-005-2416-9.

196 **tactics like "today only!" and "only two rooms left" were the least effective** Alistair Rennie, Jonny Protheroe, Claire Charron, and Gerald Breatnach, *Decoding Decisions: Making Sense of the Messy Middle* (Think with Google white paper, 2020), https://www

.thinkwithgoogle.com/_qs/documents/9998/Decoding_Decisions _The_Messy_Middle_of_Purchase_Behavior.pdf.

Researchers found that in situations of scarce resources, activation increased in a brain region linked to subjective value (the orbitofrontal cortex) and decreased in a region linked to higher-order goals and planning (the dorsolateral prefrontal cortex). As a result of these brain-based biases—overvaluing the current opportunity while doing less forward thinking—participants were willing to pay more for consumer products. Inge Huijsmans, Ili Ma, Leticia Micheli, Claudia Civai, Mirre Stallen, and Alan G. Sanfey, "A Scarcity Mindset Alters Neural Processing Underlying Consumer Decision Making," *Proceedings of the National Academy of Sciences* 116, no. 24 (2019): 11699–704, https://doi.org/10.1073/pnas.1818572116.

197 **the world's most expensive coffee is made of cat-possum poop** Okay, technically the world's most expensive coffee is Black Ivory. Can you guess what it's made of? Right, elephant poop. But the global market is only four hundred pounds per year.

198 **"we tend to latch on to that 'probably'"** Konnikova, *The Confidence Game*.

201 **"See the beautiful bag I manifested for myself?"** There's more malevolence and greed in the "positive thinking" industry than you realize. (The story about the satchel isn't about Ehrenreich's sister; she's quoting someone else.) Barbara Ehrenreich, *Bright-Sided: How the Relentless Promotion of Positive Thinking Has Undermined America* (New York: Metropolitan Books, 2009).

204 **victims of personal crimes . . . had a funny feeling** This book will change your behavior. We role-play the kidnapping in chapter 4 in class. Gavin De Becker, *Protecting the Gift: Keeping Children and Teenagers Safe (and Parents Sane)* (New York: Dell, 2013).

Chapter Nine and Three-Quarters: You, Me, We

226 **"And they did."** Rebecca Solnit, *Hope in the Dark: Untold Histories, Wild Possibilities,* 3rd ed. (Chicago: Haymarket Books, 2016).

226 **"a small group of thoughtful, committed citizens can change the world"** Nancy C. Lutkehaus, *Margaret Mead: The Making of an American Icon* (Princeton, N.J.: Princeton University Press, 2018).

Index

Page numbers of illustrations appear in italics.

PHOTO: © IAN CHRISTMANN

ZOE CHANCE is an award-winning teacher and researcher at Yale School of Management, where she teaches the blockbuster course that birthed this book. She earned her doctorate from Harvard, publishes in top academic journals, and speaks about good influence on television and around the world. Her framework for behavioral change is the foundation for Google's global food policy. Before joining academia, Chance managed a two-hundred-million-dollar segment of the Barbie brand, helped out with political campaigns, and worked in less glamorous influence jobs like door-to-door sales and telemarketing. She lives with her family in New Haven, Connecticut, and is donating half her profit from this book to fight the climate crisis.

zoechance.com

About the Type

This book was set in Optima, a sans serif typeface with a neo-classical flavor. It was designed in 1952–55 by Hermann Zapf (b. 1918) and issued by both Stempel and Linotype in 1958.